teach yourself...
C

CHARLES SIEGEL

MIS: PRESS

MANAGEMENT INFORMATION SOURCE, INC.

COPYRIGHT

DEDICATION

This book is dedicated to my mother, Ethel Navasky Siegel, with all my love.

ACKNOWLEDGMENTS

Special thanks for technical criticism and advice to Joe Walton, an excellent programmer and an even better friend.

TABLE OF CONTENTS

INTRODUCTION

Over the past few years, C has become the most popular computer programming language. C's speed and power have always made it a favorite language for operating systems and engineering applications. Now, it has also become the most popular language for software development and everyday business applications. At the same time, it has also become much more accessible to the general public because two excellent, low-cost compilers for the IBM-PC are now available: Borland's Turbo C and Microsoft's QuickC.

Beginning programmers often want to start by learning C, but teachers and friends usually tell them that C cannot be learned as a first language because it is too obscure and complex. So many people spend six months or more learning BASIC or Pascal because they believe that it is necessary to master a simpler language before they can start working with C—the language they really want to learn.

The fault is not with the C language; it is with the approach most books take to discussing C. It is possible to introduce C in a simple way—simple enough that it can be studied by beginners. You can learn to program in C and write many useful programs without bothering with the features that make C unsuitable as a first programming language. In fact, in some ways, C is ideal as an introduction to programming because it shows you the way that computers really work.

This book is aimed at beginners: all it requires is that you know how to type at the computer keyboard and that you own (or are willing to buy) a C compiler. The appendices will introduce the two most popular C compilers for the IBM-PC—Turbo C and QuickC—to readers who have never used them before, though this book uses a general form of the C language that should work with most computers and C compilers. This book is intended to introduce beginners to programming concepts while teaching the C language.

C has many advanced features that the beginning programmer should not be concerned with. For example, you can manipulate individual bits in C as you often do in Assembly Language programming. Even books that claim to make C easy generally start out by teaching all the advanced features of the language before getting down to actual programming. The first chapter usually contains a long list of "operators," including not only "logical operators" and "arithmetic operators" but also "bitwise operators." The chapters that follow include equally detailed discussions of the language's other features and equally long lists to memorize.

Beginning programmers must learn what operators are and examine examples of their use. Beginners must also learn the essential facts about what programming languages do — such as defining variables, looping, and getting input from the user — rather than memorize long lists of operators. Beginners should be able to concentrate on the basics without bothering with advanced features of a language, such as its ability to manipulate individual bits.

The obscure abbreviations sometimes used by C pose additional obstacles to beginning programmers. These abbreviations save you time if you are already familiar with programming, but learning them is too much of a burden when you are beginning. These abbreviations will be introduced in the last chapters of this book; by then, you will probably welcome them because they save you the trouble of a few extra keystrokes. The use of abbreviations is most damaging when controls over program flow are abbreviated, as they are in the **for** loop in C. A beginner must see the logic of the programming language as clearly as possible to see what the language does one step at a time rather than have all the steps condensed in a single convenient — but obscure — statement.

Instead of introducing all of the language's features before allowing you to do any real programming, this book does the opposite. You will be writing and compiling small but useful programs in Chapter 1. By Chapter 8, you will develop rather complex programs such as an address book. This book covers all these steps, using a clear, easy-to-understand version of the language.

This method is much like learning a foreign language. You are not expected to learn all of the language's grammatical rules before you do any reading. Before you learn the past tense, you are given stories to read that use only the present tense.

Likewise, this book will have you using your C compiler to write programs before you learn the whole language, and it will introduce you to the basics of programming — things like structured (or modular) programming, defining variables, controlling program flow through loops and if-else statements, handling strings, using arrays — all the things you would normally learn in a book that is an introduction to programming through BASIC or Pascal.

Approached in this spirit, C is actually a much better introduction to programming than BASIC. C gives the new programmer more insight into the way the computer actually works than BASIC does, and C programs are written with a structure that makes them much easier to follow than BASIC programs.

C is sometimes called a "low-level high-level language" because it is closer to the way that computers actually work than languages such as BASIC. In computer jargon, **low-level** refers to languages, such as Assembly Language, that go through every step of what the computer hardware does. This type of language is very powerful but difficult to learn and use. **High-level** languages are farther from how the computer actually works; they are designed to fit in with the way people think rather than with the way computers operate. C has some of the advantages of both; it is low-level in the sense that it works more like the computer than most high-level languages do, and it is high-level in the sense that its program structure is easy to follow.

Now, beginning programmers usually read books or take introductory courses to learn how computers actually work, but they learn high-level languages that do not illustrate the principles covered in introductory courses. For example, most beginning programmers are puzzled that words or other forms of text are referred to as **strings** in BASIC and other languages. In introductory courses, they learn that computers use bytes to represent individual characters, and it follows logically that text must be treated as a type of list or string of bytes. The way BASIC handles strings, however, is so far from the way computers actually handle text that beginning programmers never really get a practical grasp of how computers handle strings. In C, on the other hand, it is very apparent that for the computer, text is simply a string of characters.

Likewise, beginning programmers learn in introductory courses that computer memory consists entirely of binary digits and that the computer can look at those digits either as numbers or as characters; BASIC, however, separates the two types of data so completely that this fact never becomes apparent to beginning programmers. In C, on the other hand, it is very clear that the computer looks at the same bits of data in different ways; it is so easy to understand that you will use it as one of your first examples of programming in this book. In background classes, begginers also learn that a computer has an **address** for each of its bytes, but BASIC does not allow you to use these addresses; again, C makes it clear how the computer works. The list could go on and on.

Despite their "closeness" to the hardware, however, C programs can be easier to understand than most BASIC programs. To see why this is true, consider a short history of computer programming, which will be a useful background for what you learn in the first few chapters of this book.

Computers work with ones and zeros. They must do three different things with this form of data. There must be a cheap way to store the data for long periods of time; this is called **secondary storage**. There must be a fast way to store and retrieve the data for immediate use when the computer is running; this is called **primary storage, main memory,** or **random access memory** (**RAM**). Also, there must be a way to manipulate and change the data; this is called the **central processing unit** or **CPU**.

Historically, several different forms of hardware have been invented to perform each of these tasks. Computers once used punch cards for long-term storage; now they use magnetic disks or tape. Computers once used magnetic cores wired by hand for main memory; now they use microchips. CPUs were once built of vacuum tubes that blinked on and off as the data changed; now they consist of tiny microprocessors.

All of these forms of hardware handle only binary data. Data can be represented by locations on a floppy disk that are magnetized or not magnetized, by vacuum tubes that are on or off, or by locations on a card that are punched out or not. In any case, each bit of data has just two possible values — a 1 or a 0. The exact form of the hardware used is not really important; it is simply a convenient way of representing ones and zeros. This most basic unit of data — which can be either 1 or 0, on or off — is called a "binary digit" or, for short, a **bit**.

Because they store data in the form of bits, computers naturally use binary arithmetic. Though you do not need to learn binary arithmetic, it is good to have a general knowledge of the system. The binary system is not hard to understand. Just remember that in the decimal system (the ordinary arithmetic system), 10 represents 10^1, 100 represents 10^2, 1000 represents 10^3, and so on. Likewise, in the binary system, 10 represents 2^1, 100 represents 2^2, 1000 represents 2^3, and so on. In the binary system, then, 1 is 1, 10 is 2, 11 is 3, 100 is 4, 101 is 5, 110 is 6, 111 is 7, 1000 is 8, 1001 is 9, and so on.

Letters and other characters on the keyboard are also represented by patterns of ones and zeros. It is the same idea as Morse Code, which was also invented because a technology (the telegraph) could only represent two values — dots and dashes. The code that has become the overwhelming favorite for representing characters on computer systems is referred to as **ASCII**, which stands for **American Standard Code for Information Interchange**. Apart from the normal 26 alphabetic characters, in both uppercase and lowercase, there are codes for special characters, such as the question mark and exclamation point, and control characters, such as carriage return, tab, and form-feed. Computer designers adopted the convention of using 8 bits to represent these characters, which allows for 2^8 (256) characters. Standard ASCII includes 128 characters, but the IBM-PC uses an extended form of ASCII with 256 characters to allow for foreign characters and some basic graphics characters used for drawing boxes and other items.

The group of eight bits used to represent one character is really the basic unit of information that the computer handles — the **byte**. If a computer is working with text, it simply works with a list of bytes, each a binary number representing a character.

Like data, instructions — statements that tell the computer to add two numbers or to manipulate data in any other way — are also represented by ones and zeros. Each brand of CPU has its own **instruction set**: the pattern of ones and zeros that it recognizes as instructing it to manipulate its data. Every CPU has **registers**, which are temporary holding places for data that it is working on, an **Arithmetic Logic Unit**, which is wired to perform the operations in its instruction set on the data in the registers, and a **control unit**, which tells the Arithmetic Logic Unit what to do next. To add two numbers, for example, you must first put in the control unit the binary numbers that make the system move each of the binary numbers to be added from RAM to the registers used for addition. Then, you must put in the control unit the binary number that makes the system add the numbers in those registers and store the answer in another register. Finally, you must put in the control unit the binary number that makes the system move the answer from the register to a given location in RAM.

At first, people actually wrote entire programs that were lists of these instructions, each written as a pattern of ones and zeros. Because long lists of ones and zeros can rapidly cause strain to your eyes (and your brain), programmers soon invented **symbolic** languages. They made an English-like word, such as ADD or SUB, represent each binary control code in a computer's instruction set, and they wrote a program to read these words and replace each one with the proper binary number. This sort of symbolic language is still used when programmers must be in close touch with the hardware: it is referred to as **Assembly Language**, and the program that translates the words to binary numbers is referred to as an **assembler**.

Though it is a great improvement over writing lists of binary codes, programming in Assembly Language is difficult and requires considerable technical knowledge. You must go through all the steps the computer goes through, and you must know which registers are used for addition (and for the computer's other operations) and which register the answer ends up in. In the late 1950's and the 1960's, big businesses began to use computers for massive amounts of data processing, and there was no chance of finding enough programmers with the technical training needed to write in Assembly Language.

Instead, computer scientists invented what they named high-level languages, such as BASIC (Beginner's All-purpose Symbolic Instruction Code) and COBOL (COmmon Business Oriented Language). You can think of these new high-level languages as being far above the level of the actual machine code. By contrast, Assembly Language is a low-level language that is closer to the level of the machine and more difficult to use. An old programmer's saying is "the lower the level of the language, the higher the level of pay."

Originally, some inventors of COBOL claimed that it was so easy to use that companies would not need computer programmers any longer; managers would just write the code themselves (in their spare time, no doubt). This prediction was too optimistic, of course, but COBOL was simple enough that, during the 1960's, companies could hire people who had never programmed before, put them through a four-week training course, and then put them to work writing business programs. Computer scientists had written programs that would take very simple commands and translate them into Assembly language. The new programmer could simply write ADD AMOUNT-A TO AMOUNT-B GIVING AMOUNT-C. The COBOL compiler would automatically generate the assembly language code needed to put the numbers stored as AMOUNT-A and AMOUNT-B into the registers used for addition, perform the addition, and take the amount in the register that holds the result and store it as AMOUNT-C.

Two types of programs allow you to use this sort of simple command: **compilers**, which permanently translate the source code into machine language and give you a complete stand-alone program, and **interpreters**, which translate the source code one line at a time each time the program is run. Needless to say, compiled programs run much more quickly than those that must be interpreted as they are run (usually about ten times as fast). Interpreters require less memory than compilers, which is why BASIC, an interpreted language, became popular on microcomputers in the days when most computers had small memories. Compiled languages, such as COBOL, were always more popular on mainframe computers, and, now that RAM is cheap and abundant, compilers are popular on microcomputers; there are even BASIC compilers now. Of course, you must have a C compiler, such as the QuickC or Turbo C compiler for the IBM-PC, to run the programs in this book.

The original versions of BASIC and COBOL suffered from the typical problem of early high-level languages: they were unstructured. Most computer programs perform relatively complex tasks and must do many things. For example, a program might read a list of employees' names, select employees who have been working less than a year, sort these names in alphabetical order, produce a report that lists these employees alphabetically, sort the names in chronological order, and produce a report that lists these employees in the order in which they were hired. Each of these functions is also complex in itself. For example, to produce a report, you must count how many lines have been printed; when the count reaches the number of lines that one page can hold, you must print a few blank lines for the lower margin of the page and the upper margin of the next page, add one to the current page number, print a header for the new page that includes the name of the report and the new page number, skip a line, and go back to printing lines of the report again. Of course, you do not want to write this part of the program twice if you are producing two reports. Instead, each time the file is sorted and ready to be printed, you direct the program to the section that prints and formats reports. You control the program's flow.

In Assembly Language, program flow is controlled using the instruction JMP (short for JUMP), BR (short for BRANCH), or some similar instruction that directs the flow to continue at another point in the program. BASIC adopted this instruction in the form of the GOTO command. If the report-printing feature is in line 10300 of a BASIC program, for example, you can use the command GOTO 10300 when it is time for the program to print. Suppose that a year later, a new programmer is hired to modify that program. When he is reading the program and trying to understand how it works, a command such as GOTO 10300 is not much more helpful than the old string of binary digits. The programmer must flip through the pages, looking for that line number, keeping one finger at the starting point, as a reminder of what happened last. A few dozen lines after line 10300, there will probably be another GOTO and another search through the program.

Programmers refer to this type of code as **spaghetti code** because it gets so tangled up. This type of program was not too hard to understand when you were writing it; it became more difficult when you were going through it again to debug it, and it was impossible when someone new had to figure it out to make changes in it a few years later.

Problems with this type of code led to a new technique called **structured**, or **modular, programming**. The idea is to break up the code into smaller parts named **modules**. The program is written in something similar to outline form. It begins with a series of instructions that includes a list of procedures. The report-writing program previously described might begin with commands listed as follows (written in a programming language that resembles a later, structured version of COBOL):

```
PERFORM PROCEDURE READ-EMPLOYEES.
PERFORM PROCEDURE SELECT-FOR-WORKING-LESS-THAN-ONE-YEAR.
PERFORM PROCEDURE SORT-ON-NAME.
PERFORM PROCEDURE PRINT-REPORT.
PERFORM PROCEDURE SORT-ON-DATE.
PERFORM PROCEDURE PRINT-REPORT.
```

Each of these PERFORM PROCEDURE commands would, as you might expect, make the program execute a **procedure** — a group of instructions detailed later in the program. For example, looking a few pages farther down in the program, you might see something similar to the following:

```
PROCEDURE PRINT-REPORT.
PERFORM PROCEDURE PRINT-LINE.
ADD 1 TO LINE-COUNTER.
IF LINE-COUNTER > 65
     THEN PERFORM PROCEDURE PRINT-HEADER.
```

Likewise, farther down in the code, there would be a procedure called PRINT-LINE and PRINT-HEADER.

Even if you have never programmed, you can imagine how hard it is to figure out a program that starts off with several pages of code that includes all the details about how to read the file and select the names according to the date they were hired and then directs you to the location, several pages farther down, of the code that prints the report. You can imagine how much easier it is to figure out a structured program that begins with this sort of "outline" of the major functions it performs.

It is also much easier to debug structured programs because you can test the modules one at a time and make sure each one does what you expect it to. Obviously, you can pinpoint your error much more quickly if you know what module it is in rather than know only that something is wrong in your 20-page program. It is also much easier to modify structured programs because they are easier to understand and because you can add extra modules to them to perform new tasks rather than modifying the entire program.

Structured programming is so obviously superior that new versions of BASIC have incorporated these techniques, as COBOL tried to do (with mixed success) years ago. Microsoft's QuickBASIC, for example, adds new features to that language that allow you to do structured programming. Most beginners, though, still start by learning the version of BASIC that comes with their computer. They learn bad programming style, and they are forced to figure out programs that are often extremely difficult to follow.

Even structured versions of BASIC and COBOL are makeshift and, in some ways, not truly structured. C, like Pascal, was designed with structured programming in mind, and the form of the language itself strongly encourages you to do structured programming. This is the great advantage of these languages for new users; they start you off with good programming style — not to mention how much easier it is for beginners to follow the programs.

C has two other great advantages that Pascal lacks. As you have seen, C is "close" to the hardware, so it can be the ideal introduction to how computers actually work. More importantly, it is now the language that people ultimately want to use in practical applications. If C is handled correctly, by using a version that avoids advanced features and unnecessary abbreviations, it is the ideal introduction to computer programming.

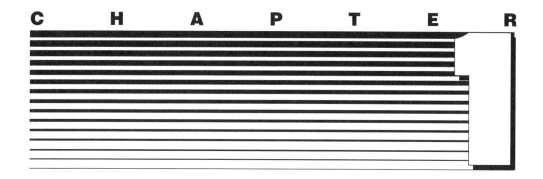

C H A P T E R

1

TALKING WITH THE USER:
printf() and scanf()

YOUR FIRST PROGRAM: PRINTING TO THE SCREEN

As stated in the introduction, the early chapters of this book use programs written in a format that is specially designed to be easy to understand. By the end of this book, you will be working with more conventional — and more obscure — C code. The "educational" style of code that you begin with, however, will let you write and understand useful C programs quickly.

You will begin with a traditional program used to introduce C, which is very easy to understand. All the program does is print the words "Hello, world" on the computer screen. It is important as an introduction to the basic form of the C language.

The program reads as follows, though this initial version is not quite complete:

```
main()                    /* your first program*/
{
printf("Hello, world.\n");
}
```

The first point to notice is the title at the top of this function — **main**(). C uses such functions as the building blocks of its programs, and every C program must have a function entitled **main**(), which is the first section to be executed when the program runs. If the function listed above were used as one module of a larger program, you would give it a descriptive title — you might call it **greet**() because it greets the world — and other functions would call it simply by using the statement **greet**();. You will soon examine a program with more than one function.

Second, notice that the body of the function is surrounded by curly brackets, or braces: { and }. C is a free-form language, which gives the programmer a great deal of flexibility when deciding whether items should be written with extra spaces or new lines. It is possible to write this program as follows,

```
main(){
printf("Hello,world.\n");
}
```

with the opening bracket on the same line as the module name. In more complex programs, however, things look clearer if each curly bracket is on a separate line, and this book will adopt that convention. It is much easier to see that brackets are paired up properly if they line up one above another. In later chapters, you will see how this convention can clarify longer programs.

Third, notice the words **/* your first program */**. Text surrounded by **/*** and ***/** is a **comment**, which is ignored by the C compiler and included purely for the benefit of future programmers who must read through and try to understand your program. Even if you return a year later to a program you wrote, you may find that it is often impossible to remember what you were doing. Good programming style includes many comments.

The compiler ignores new lines for comments also, and comments often are long enough to require many lines. The previous program could be written as follows:

```
main()                          /* your
                                first
                                program */
{
printf("Hello, world.\n");
}
```

Or you could even write it as follows:

```
main()
{/*your
        first
                        program*/
printf("Hello, world.\n");}
```

You can see how jumbled things can become in a free-form language such as C if you do not voluntarily adopt good style.

In this book, all comments will be fully marked as follows for the sake of greater clarity, even though all the slashes and asterisks might not be required:

```
/* your */
/* first */
/* program */
```

Fourth, notice the instruction **printf()**, the first function of the C language that you will learn. Note the most obvious point about it first; it ends with a semicolon (;) as do most C statements.

The name of the function **printf()** stands for PRINT with Formatting. Soon, you will examine some of the ways that this instruction can format variables. In this case, you just see it doing its basic job of printing text to the screen. The text to be printed is placed in quotation marks within the parentheses of **printf()**, and, as you can see, a control character is also placed in the quotation marks. **\n** within the **printf()** statement stands for "new line." When the backslash character (\) appears within the quotation marks of **printf()**, the character following it is called an **escape character** and is not read like the other characters in quotation marks. Usually, the **escape** character instructs the computer what to do rather than functioning as a character of text that is printed to the screen. Because C is a rather low-level language, it does not do much for you; you must explicitly put the new line into the instruction.

Notice that **printf()** has the same basic form as the statement **main()** — a word followed by parentheses. This is the form of all C functions, and C is made up largely of functions. The parentheses can be empty, as **main()** is, or they can contain something that the function does something to, as **printf()** does in this program. The item in the parentheses is usually called an **argument** by C programmers. An argument is much like the object of a verb in ordinary English; you can say "Print," or you can say "Print a word," using the verb with or without an object. Likewise, you can use functions with or without arguments in C. Either way, though, you must include the parentheses at the end of a function word to let the compiler know it is a function.

You can invent functions like this at will, which is why C is so well-suited to structured programming. Suppose, for example, that you wanted a program that printed both "Hello, world" and "Goodbye, world" on the screen. You could write the program as follows:

```
main()                    /* your second program */
{
printf("Hello, world.\n");
printf("Goodbye, world.\n");
}
```

Or you could write a program that does the same thing as follows:

```
main()                  /* third sample program */
{
greet();                /* use function to print hello */
farewell();             /* use function to print goodbye */
}


greet()                 /* function to print hello */
{
printf("Hello, world.\n");
}


farewell()              /* function to print goodbye */
{
printf("Goodbye, world.\n");
}
```

You can actually create functions out of blocks of existing commands, and then you can use those newly created functions just as if they were a part of the language. This feature of C not only makes it well-suited for structured programming, it also makes it indefinitely extensible. You can buy packages at the computer store that contain specialized libraries of C functions that will give the language the capacity for easy database management, for easy creation of windows and other fancy screen displays, or for just about any other purpose you have in mind. You can use the new functions in these libraries just as if they were part of the language.

There is still one missing element in the first sample program at the beginning of this chapter, which you saw was not quite complete. The full program must contain the statement **#include <stdio.h>** as follows:

```
/* CHAPTER 1, EXAMPLE 1 */

#include <stdio.h>              /*your first program */
main()
{
printf("Hello, world.\n");
}
```

The # sign indicates that this statement is an instruction for the precompiler. Your compiler actually goes through your program several times as it compiles the program. The first time through, before it attempts to translate any code, it will simply look for # signs and make any substitutions in the program that are required by the statements that follow.

Notice that the precompiler instruction does not end with a semicolon as ordinary commands do. Also notice the new comment added at the top — /* **CHAPTER 1, EXAMPLE 1** */. This book will use this type of heading at the beginning of any program that is complete and ready to compile — but not for fragments that are used for illustration.

< stdio.h> is short for "standard input-output header." When the compiler sees the statement **#include <stdio.h>**, it will read this header into the program. When the compiler begins translating source code, the header will be present, just as if you had typed it in. You probably will notice that, when they are compiling, Turbo C and QuickC tell you what line they are currently on, and even if you typed in a small six-line program, they will tell you that they are working on lines with numbers in the hundreds because all of the lines in **stdio.h** have been added to the six lines that you entered.

One item included in this header is a declaration of the function **printf()**, which is in a library of functions called the **standard input-output package**. When they are finished compiling the program, Turbo C or QuickC will read any needed functions from this library and link them with the program you wrote. The word "compiling," in its strict sense, only refers to the process of producing a file with an OBJ extension; linking is necessary to produce an executable file with an EXE extension. Turbo C and QuickC will perform this linking automatically after they are done compiling; if you are using an older compiler, you must link the functions with the programs yourself with a linker program. Declaration of any library functions you use must be present, or the compiler will give you an error message telling you that a function it needs is missing. The declaration is a reassurance that the compiler will find this function when it arrives at the linking stage.

The cryptic statement **#include <stdio.h>** must be added, then, because **printf()**, although it is one of the most commonly used statements in C, is technically not part of the language; it belongs to a special library. C's original designers preferred simplicity and elegance over features. They were designing a language for systems programming (and using it to implement the Unix operating system), so they considered speed, efficiency, and power all-important, and they ignored many more mundane features — even features as basic as input/output. You could almost say that they wrote a language with grammar but with no vocabulary. The vocabulary was added by later developers who wrote libraries of functions. Developers of compilers have written extensive libraries of I/O functions, but this book will use only those that have become standard and are included in **stdio.h** in every C compiler.

Now that you have the entire program laid out, you can compile and run it. Enter the program into a file named **greet.c**. The appendices in this book will help you enter and compile the program, using QuickC or Turbo C. If you are using an operating system other than DOS, such as Unix, or if you are using another compiler on the IBM PC, you should refer to your operating manual for instructions on compiling programs. If you are already able to use your QuickC or Turbo C compiler without any hesitation, go ahead and compile the "Hello world" program as it is listed. The appendices are for people who want an introduction to compiling. Compiling really isn't difficult, but, like your first program, your first compile is your most important.

If the compiler produces error messages, make sure your program is identical to the listing. Keep one point in mind when you are correcting errors, particularly later in the book when you are writing longer programs: if the compiler's error message does not make sense to you, it is probably caused by a mistake you made earlier in the program, which the compiler does not consider an error. For example, if the error message tells you that a statement is not terminated by a semicolon, you might actually have left off the semicolon by mistake, so you can just make the correction the compiler indicates. On the other hand, your compiler will probably give you the same message if you leave off the final curly bracket of one of the functions in a program. For example, if you make this error in the sample program you just examined,

```
main()              /* third sample program */
{
greet();            /* use function to print hello */
farewell();         /* use function to print goodbye */


greet()             /* function to print hello */
{
printf("Hello, world.\n");
}
```

the compiler will also say that you have a statement that is not terminated with a semicolon. Because the final curly bracket is missing in the **main**() function, the compiler thinks that the second use of **greet**() is another statement in **main**() rather than the name of a new function. When you receive this sort of irrelevant error message, look above the error that the compiler indicates to find the actual error you made, and also remember that the compiler ignores indentation and spacing. As you will see when you write longer programs, a single minor error, such as leaving out a curly bracket, can make the compiler misinterpret most of the statements that follow and produce a long list of error messages. After you correct such an error, recompile the program rather than taking the time to go through all the mistaken error messages.

After you have successfully compiled the source code in the file **greet.c**, you will have created a new command that you can enter at the DOS prompt, much like the commands that are part of DOS or any other software. Simply type in **greet** at the DOS prompt, and your computer will print "Hello, world."

ASSIGNING VALUES TO VARIABLES

So far, you have learned to make the program "talk" to the user by printing output to the screen. Before you are able to make a program "listen" to the user by receiving input from the keyboard, you must learn about **variables**. Anything the user types in must be stored in a variable so the rest of the program can use it.

Variables are a basic feature of any programming language and are easy enough to understand that an example should make the idea clear without any special explanation. The following statement,

```
x = 10;
```

assigns the value 10 to the variable **x**. This instruction actually makes the computer place the value 10 (in binary form) in the area of memory that has been set aside to hold the variable **x**. Whenever **x** is mentioned later in the program, the program will think of it as representing the number 10. Of course, a later statement can change the value. You can use **x** to represent 10 for part of the program and then use the following statement,

```
x = 20;
```

so that **x** will represent 20 for the rest of the program. Note that, like most statements in C, these assignment statements end with a semicolon.

It is important to emphasize that the symbol = is used for assignment. The statement in C that you just examined is not at all the same as the statement $x = 20$ in algebra, which tells you that **x** equals 20 In C, as in most computer programming languages, $x = 20$ assigns **x** the value of 20, no matter what **x** equals to begin with. It is probably best to read $x = 20$ as "let x equal 20" or "make x equal 20."

Another note on programming style is desperately needed here, since you have just seen a blatant example of bad style. As a general rule, it is not a good idea to give variables names like **x** or **y,** which do not explain what they represent. It is much kinder to users who must later figure out the program — and also kinder to yourself as a programmer — to give variables meaningful names. For example, if **x** in the previous examples is intended to stand for the number of workers, then the statements should be something like **numWrkrs = 10;** and **numWrkrs = 20;.** Likewise, if it stands for the amount paid, use names like **amtPaid = 10** and **amtPaid = 20;.**

Variable names cannot include spaces, or the compiler will read them as more than one word. They also cannot include hyphens, or the compiler will try to sub-tract one variable from another. If it saw **amt-paid,** for example, it would want to subtract the variable **paid** from the variable **amt**. It used to be most common to use the underscore character (_) to make names easier to read by showing divisions between words, such as **num_wkrs** and **amt_paid**. A more recent con-vention, which this book uses, is to use an uppercase letter at the beginning of each new word within the variable. Remember also that the compiler distin-guishes between lowercase and uppercase letters in variable names. If you receive error messages that seem particularly unreasonable to you, such as those telling you that a variable does not exist when you know that it does, check the capitaliza-tion of the variable's name.

Before assigning a value to a variable within a program, you must define the variable's **data type**. Though there are more data types in C, all that are needed for most purposes are these four: **character, integer, long integer,** and **floating decimal point number**, which C names **char, int, long,** and **float,** respectively. A **char** is a single ASCII character; these characters generally represent the charac-ters on your keyboard — letters of the alphabet, numbers, or special characters such as $ and @ — but they also can represent ASCII characters that make the computer beep or instruct the printer to eject a sheet of paper. An **int** is a whole number such as 1, 2, or 25,000. A **long** is a large whole number, such as 1,000,000. A **float** is a number with a decimal point, such as 1.5 or 2.0.

You might already have a few questions. Why is it that the numbers on the keyboard are characters and also integers? Why is the number 2.0 different from the number 2?

The answer lies in the way the computer works. Remember, computer memory represents information as a long string of ones and zeros, which is divided into bytes, each of which is comprised of eight bits. The computer finds individual bytes by giving each byte an address. Bytes are numbered from one up to the number of total bytes in memory. When you assign a value to a variable, the program reserves a portion of memory for that variable. Then, whenever you mention the name **amtPaid** or **numWrkrs** or **x** or **y**, the program examines the portion of memory reserved for that variable and determines what value it contains.

This situation leaves the computer with two problems:

- deciding how much memory to reserve for the variable and what form to store it in when it is creating the variable

- deciding how to interpret the ones and zeros it finds there when it is reading the value of the variable

Different variables require different amounts of storage. A **char** requires just one byte. ASCII code (as you have seen) was designed so each character could be represented by a binary number that is no more than one byte long. When you assign a character value to a variable, ones and zeros that make up the binary form of the ASCII number of that character are stored in the one-byte-long memory location reserved for that variable.

The amount of space that C reserves for an **int** depends on the machine in use. On the IBM-PC and compatibles, C reserves two bytes (a total of 16 bits). A little binary arithmetic will tell you the maximum value of the integer that can be held in this space. Start with two and begin doubling; soon, you will see numbers that are familiar to anyone who has read about computers: 2^6 is 64, 2^7 is 128, and 2^8 is 256. You have probably heard about computers with 64K or 256K of memory. The addresses of memory locations are kept using binary numbers (like everything else in a computer).

Continue doubling: 2^9 is 512, and 2^{10} is 1024. The fact that 2^{10} is just over 1,000 is very convenient for humans, who are accustomed to thinking in terms of decimal numbers. That is why programmers refer to 1024 bytes as 1K. 1K does not mean 1,000, though it is used loosely to mean approximately 1,000. Continue doubling: 2^{11} is 2K, 2^{12} is 4K, and finally (you can fill in the intermediate steps yourself), 2^{16} is 64K — the number that can be stored in a 16-bit integer. Because integers can be positive or negative, the maximum value for an integer in C is 32K (more than 32,000), and the minimum value for an integer is negative 32K (less than -32,000).

The **long** (or long integer) variable will reserve 32 bits to represent an integer, allowing a range of over 1,000,000,000 values. If a variable is an integer that might receive a value larger than 32,000 or so, you must declare it as a **long**. On some computers, C will reserve 32 bits for ordinary **int**s, and you must declare a number as a **short** (another C data type) for a 16-bit integer.

The fourth major data type that you must learn is the **float** — a number that can take non-integer values — which gets its name from the floating decimal point that divides the integer and the fractional part of this number. The number of bytes that C reserves for a **float** varies with the system and is usually four. In any case, a **float** is actually stored in the form of a number called a **mantissa**, plus an **exponent** that tells you what power of ten the **mantissa** is multiplied by. It commonly has a range of more than 10^{38} — large enough that you usually do not have to think about it.

You do not need to worry about memorizing all these details about variable storage and length. Just remember that the data types are **char**, **int**, **long**, and **float**, and remember the basic facts about them: you must use a **long** rather than an **int** for large numbers, and you must use **float**s for calculations that might give you results containing fractions.

Next, you will see how much trouble you can get yourself into when you begin using the **printf()** function to print variables of different data types. Consider first a simple program that prints an integer variable:

```
/* CHAPTER 1, EXAMPLE 2 */
#include <stdio.h>

main()                         /* sample program: */
{                              /* printf with int */
int smplNum;

smplNum = 9;
printf("The sample number is %d.\n",smplNum);
}
```

The only difference between this program and the previous program is that a variable is included in this program as part of the **printf()** function, but this addition requires a few more steps. First, the statement **int smplNum;** is needed to instruct the compiler to reserve a memory location long enough for an integer and to give the contents of this location the name **smplNum**. This is called **declaring** the variable. In this book, for the sake of easier reading, programs always include a blank line after all the variables are declared. You must declare the variable before you do anything with it.

Then, you can assign a value to that variable with the statement **smplNum = 9;**, which puts the binary number 9 in the 16-bit memory location reserved for **smplNum;**. That memory location then looks like the following:

```
0000000000001001
```

Finally, in the **printf()** statement itself, you use another special character, **%d**, in place of the variable within the quotation marks, and then you insert a comma and the name of the variable whose value you want in that position after the quotation marks. When you run the program, it replaces the special character **%d** with an integer interpretation of the variable following the comma.

Compile and run this program so you will become accustomed to working with variables. You might name your source code file **SAMPLNUM.C**. After it is compiled, enter the command **SAMPLNUM** at the DOS prompt. As you might expect, it will print the following on the screen:

```
The sample number is 9.
```

Note that there are two different types of special characters used by **printf()**. One, which you have examined before, is the escape sequence that begins with a backslash, as **\n** does. The new type of special character is the formatting code that begins with a percent sign as **%d** does; it represents a variable and instructs the compiler to print the variable in a certain format.

You will use several of these special formatting characters in this book. As you have already seen, **%d** tells **printf()** that the variable should be printed as an integer. The letter **d** stands for integer because **printf()** can format integers as hexadecimal (base 16) or octal (base 8) numbers as well as ordinary decimal (base 10) numbers. Remember, what **printf()** actually must work with is a binary number. **%d** stands for "decimal," and it will format either an **int** or a **long** as a decimal number.

printf() also uses the obvious special characters **%f** for **floats** and **%c** for characters.

The principle is not difficult to understand, so consider a few examples:

```
/* CHAPTER 1, EXAMPLE 3 */
#include <stdio.h>

main()                  /* sample program */
                        /* printf with char */
{
char smplLtr;

smplLtr = 'a';
printf("The sample letter is %c.\n",smplLtr);
}
```

This program will print the following:

```
The sample letter is a.
```

Note that you use the word **char** plus the name of the variable to declare a character variable, and note also that when you assign a value to a character variable, you must place that value in single quotation marks.

You can also use **printf**() to print more than one variable, as in the following program:

```
/* CHAPTER 1, EXAMPLE 4 */

#include <stdio.h>
main()          /* sample program */
{               /* printf char and int */
char smplLtr;
int smplNum;

smplLtr = 'a';
smplNum = 9;
printf("The samples are %c and %d.\n",smplLtr,smplNum);
}
```

This program will print the following:

```
    The samples are a and 9.
```

You simply place the names of the variables after the final quotation mark of the **printf**() statement with commas between them, and **printf**() will put values in place of the special % formatting characters in the order in which they appear. Consider the following program:

```
/* CHAPTER 1, EXAMPLE 5 */
#include <stdio.h>

main()                          /* sample program */
{                               /* printf two chars */
char smplLtr, othrLtr;

smplLtr = 'a';
othrLtr = 'b';
printf("The samples are %c and %c.\n",smplLtr,othrLtr);
}
```

By now, it should be obvious that this program will print the following:

```
    The samples are a and b.
```

The new point to note here is that you can declare more than one variable in one statement. Just list the variables after the word **char** (or **int** or **float**) with commas between them and a semicolon at the end of the entire statement, and they will all be defined as members of that data type.

Finally, examine **printf()** with a **float** (to prove that programming is not always as simple as it seems):

```
/* CHAPTER 1, EXAMPLE 6 */
#include <stdio.h>

main()                     /* sample program */
{                          /* printf with float */
float smplNum;

smplNum = 9;
printf("The sample number is %f.\n",smplNum);
}
```

This program will not print what you expect; it will print the following:

```
The sample number is 9.000000.
```

The default display for floats includes six decimal places. Methods for controlling this display more precisely are summarized in Chapter 8 because they involve more details than you should bother with at this point. The discussion of **printf**() and variables in this chapter will end with a cautionary note and an indication of C's power.

Be careful not to think of a **char** as being identical to a letter and an **int** as being identical to a number. Consider the following program, for example:

```
/* CHAPTER 1, EXAMPLE 7 */
#include <stdio.h>

main()                      /* sample program */
{                           /* printf with number */
char smplNum;

smplNum = '9';
printf("The sample number is %c.\n",smplNum);
}
```

This program will print exactly the same thing as the first of the formatted **printf**() programs you looked at:

```
The sample number is 9.
```

There is, however, a difference in the way the computer handles the two programs. In the earlier program, where you defined **smplNum** as an integer, the program assigned the value of 9 to it by putting the binary number for nine, 0000000000001001, in its two-byte memory location, as you have already seen. When **printf()** sees the %d, it interprets this number in decimal format as 9. In the later program, on the other hand, where you defined **smplNum** as a character, the program assigned the value 9 to it by writing the ASCII code for the character 9 in its one-byte memory location. 9 is ASCII character number 57, so the program places 00111001 (57 in binary) in that location. Then, when **printf()** sees the %c format for this variable, it moves to its location, retrieves the value, and interprets it as ASCII character 57, which is 9.

You can take advantage of this feature of **printf()** with programs such as the following:

```
/* CHAPTER 1, EXAMPLE 8 */
#include <stdio.h>

main()                  /* print ASCII value of char */
{
char smplChr;

smplChr = '9';
printf("The ASCII value of  %c  is  %d.\n",smplChr,smplChr);
}
```

Both of the special formatting characters in the **printf()** statement read the variable **smplChr**. First, the %c reads the variable as a character; then, the %d goes to the same place in memory and reads the same value as a decimal integer, so the program prints the following:

```
The ASCII value of the character  9  is  57.
```

You almost have a useful program here. It could be very handy to have a small utility that will allow you to type in a character and then give you the ASCII value of that character. You have not yet learned how to get a character from the keyboard and assign it to a variable, but before the end of this chapter, you will write such a program.

The flexibility of **printf()** — the fact that it will display a variable in any format — is one reason for the power and speed of C; it allows you to do things like this ASCII conversion. It can also lead to problems. Other computer languages will give you error messages and refuse to run if you mix up data types. If you use a character as if it were an integer, for example, you must use a special function to explicitly convert the character to its ASCII value before using it that way. C, on the other hand, is sometimes called a "robust" language; it assumes that you know what you are doing and will run the program you have written even if there is an error.

You can imagine what sort of confusion it could cause if you mix data types in the middle of a prolonged mathematical calculation. It is important to watch your data types. If your program produces unexpected results, look through it to see if the data types are what they should be.

GETTING INPUT FROM THE USER

The function **scanf()** is used by C to receive input from the user. The function works very much like **printf()** in reverse and should be easy for you to learn. Consider the following program:

```
/* CHAPTER 1, EXAMPLE 9 */
#include <stdio.h>

main()                      /* sample program */
{                           /* using scanf and printf */
int smplNum;

printf("What sample number do you want to display? ");
scanf("%d",&smplNum);
printf("\nThe number you typed is %d.\n",smplNum);
}
```

First, this program will print the following:

```
What sample number do you want to display?
```

Note that this **printf()** function includes an extra space after the question mark and does not include a **\n** to create a new line after this message because you want the cursor to remain on the same line, with one space between it and the question mark, waiting for the user's input. The program will stop at this point and wait for the user to press one or more keys followed by the Enter key (also known as the Return key). Then, it will assign the value of the keys you pressed to the variable named in **scanf()** in the format given in **scanf()**.

One important point to notice is that the variable named in **scanf()** must have an **&** before it. In C, **&** followed by a variable name refers to the address of that variable in memory; e.g., **&smplNum** is the address of the variable **smplNum**. (As you have learned, all bytes in a computer's memory are numbered sequentially, and the number of a cell is called its address.) You will learn why the ampersand is needed when you look at addresses in C in more detail in Chapter 6; at this point, it is simply necessary to remember that **scanf()** must use the **&** before the name of the variables to which it assigns values.

The **scanf("%d",&samplNum)** statement in this program, then, reads the keyboard input as a decimal number and assigns that value to the variable **smplNum**. For example, if you typed

```
9
```

and then pressed the Enter key, **smplNum** would contain the value 9, and the final **printf()** statement would display the following:

```
The sample number you typed is 9.
```

You could also type

```
123
```

and press the Enter key; **scanf()** will take numbers more than one character long. After all, when you declared the variable as an **int**, the program set aside enough memory for numbers as large as 32K.

Likewise, if **smplNum** had been declared as a **float**, you could enter **float**s of almost any length. Consider the following program:

```
/* CHAPTER 1, EXAMPLE 10 */
#include <stdio.h>

main()                      /* sample 2 of */
{                           /* scanf and printf */
float smplNum;

printf("What sample number do you want to display? ");
scanf("%f",&smplNum);
printf("The number you typed is %f.\n",smplNum);
}
```

If you typed

```
123.456789
```

and pressed Enter, the final **printf()** statement would display the following:

```
The sample number you typed in is 123.456789.
```

On the other hand, if you declared the variable as a **char**, the program would only accept one character from the keyboard. For example, consider the following program:

```
/* CHAPTER 1, EXAMPLE 11 */
#include <stdio.h>

main()                      /* sample program 3 */
{                           /* scanf and printf */
char smplChr;

printf("What character do you want to display? ");
scanf("%c",&smplChr);
printf("The sample you typed is %c.\n",smplChr);
}
```

If you typed

```
ABCD
```

and pressed the Enter key, the program would display the following:

```
    The sample character you typed is A.
```

Only the first character typed would be assigned to the variable **smplChr** because a **char** is defined as a single character. The other characters would be lost.

It is also possible to use **%s** with **scanf()** to get an entire string of characters, such as ABCD, from the user in the same way that you get a **char**, **int**, or **float**. It is more difficult to declare strings in C, however, so they will be covered in Chapter 5.

One other point about **scanf()** will come in handy. The way **scanf()** handles control strings is also the reverse of **printf()**. For example, the statement **printf("%c\n",smplLtr)** will print the variable **smplLet** plus a carriage return. The statement **scanf("\n%c,smplLtr)** will read any character into the variable **smplLtr** except a carriage return. The same is true of any other characters used in the control string; **scanf()** will simply ignore those characters if they are entered by the user. This feature can be useful when you are getting characters or strings from the user and want to filter out certain characters.

AN ASCII CHART PROGRAM

Now, you have learned enough to write your first really useful program, a small utility to give you the ASCII value of any character. This program is very similar to the program you wrote earlier to print out the ASCII value of a variable, but, now that you have learned **scanf()** also, you can ask the user what character he or she wants to look up as follows:

```
/* CHAPTER 1, EXAMPLE 12 */
#include <stdio.h>

main()                    /* print ASCII value of */
{                         /* char asked by user */
char smplChr;

printf("\nWhat character do you want the ASCII value of > ");
scanf("%c",&smplChr);
printf("The ASCII value of  %c  is  %d \n", smplChr,smplChr);
}
```

This program should be quite easy for you to understand. The only question is what command you would like to enter at the DOS prompt to look up ASCII values — something such as ASCCHRT. Just enter this program into the file ASCCHRT.C, and compile it. Now, you have a small stand-alone utility that you can use any time you want to look up the ASCII value of a character. Just enter ASCCHRT at the DOS prompt, and you will be able to look up the value of one character.

SUMMARY

C programs have the following general form:


```
#include <stdio.h>
main()               /* generalized sample */
{
statemt1;
statemt2();
statemt3();
}

statemt2()           /* generalized subroutine */
{
statemt4;
statemt5();
}
```


Functions are the modular building blocks of the program. Each function consists of its name plus one or more statements enclosed in curly brackets. There must be one function named **main**(), and it can execute instructions that are built into the language, included as functions in libraries, or written as functions by the programmer. In this case, the function **statemt2**() is written by the programmer and used within **main**() just like any other statement.

The name of a function must end with parentheses, which may be empty or may include arguments. All statements are terminated by semicolons. Comments, which are surrounded by **/*** and ***/**, are ignored by the compiler and included for the benefit of the programmer. **#include <stdio.h>** is a precompiler instruction that reads in the standard input/output header.

Card promotion snafu

Q Sunday, Aug. 5, the Mercury News Sports section had a column referring to free sports cards being offered by the Upper Deck Co. Proceeds from the 900 phone call were to go to NFL Charities. I called the next day, which is confirmed by my September phone bill, to get cards for my son. I never received them.
— *Terri Quadro, Mountain View*

A The Upper Deck Co. had a large demand for the offer, but some names and addresses left on the voice mail were difficult to understand and many letters were returned as undeliverable, says Karen Solomon, a customer-service representative. Solomon sent us two packs of promotional cards, which we're forwarding to you. Others who didn't receive their cards should send a copy of their phone bill showing the 900 number charge to the Upper Deck Co., 5909 Sea Otter Place, Carlsbad 92008-1989.

acter), **int** (integer), **long** (long integer), and al point). The data type of a variable must be he following,

ents in the program. A value can be assigned n as the following:

The **printf**() command prints output to the screen with formatting of variables; its general form is as follows:

```
printf("\nThe variable is %c",SmplVar);
```

Ordinary characters within the quotation marks will be printed on the screen. Special characters may follow a backslash; for example, **\n** prints a new line. Special characters that refer to variables follow a percent sign and format the variables named after the comma following the final quotation mark. In this case, **%c** means that **SmplVar** should be interpreted as a character. **%d** formats a variable as a decimal integer, **%f** formats it as a float, and **%s** formats it as a string.

The **scanf**() command receives input from the keyboard; its general form is as follows:

```
scanf(%c,&SmplVar);
```

The characters used following the percent sign are the same as in **printf**(). The name of the variable to which they are assigned must be preceded by the ampersand, **&**, which is used to refer to an address.

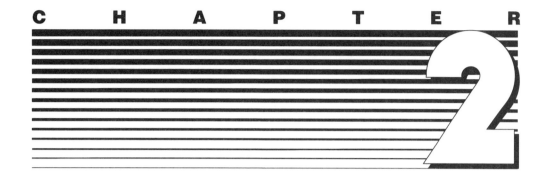

CONTROLLING PROGRAM FLOW

THE WHILE LOOP

The small ASCCHRT utility you wrote in the last chapter is useful by itself, but most actual application programs do not just do one thing for you and then dump you back in the operating system as ASCCHRT does. Most programs start off by displaying a menu with several options. Then, after you have selected one option and are finished working with it, the program brings you back to the main menu and allows you to make another choice. You leave the program only when you choose Quit from the menu.

This type of menu system illustrates, in an understandable way, the three basic ways of controlling the flow of the program. In the Introduction, you saw how confusing programs were when they used GOTO to direct program flow; structured (or modular) programming was introduced to make programs easier to understand. The theoretical foundation for structured programming was a theorem, first proven in 1964 by two mathematicians named Bohm and Jacopini, that GOTO's are not needed for programming. Everything can be done using the three other methods of control flow: sequence, selection, and iteration. In this chapter, you will rewrite the ASCCHRT program as a menu-driven system that uses all three methods of controlling program flow.

You have already used one of these methods — sequence — in the ASCCHRT program. **Sequence** simply means that the program executes one instruction after another in the order in which the instructions appear.

Selection means choosing among two or more possible courses of action; it is generally done using an **if-else** statement (which you will soon examine). A typical menu-driven program, for example, first presents the menu of choices to the user and then uses a prolonged **if-else** statement to direct the flow of the program to one of the several routines that perform the program's different functions.

Finally, after the chosen routine is performed, the program brings you back to the menu you started with; this is **iteration**. Iteration simply means repeating — or reiterating — the same sequence of commands. It is more commonly referred to as "looping."

It is easy to use iteration in C by using the **while** loop, which takes the following form:

```
while(condition)
    {
    statement;
    statement;
    statement;
    }
```

The program will perform that series of statements over and over again, as long as the condition is true. Of course, one of the statements must do something that eventually makes the condition false; otherwise, the program will be stuck in the loop forever. This type of "infinite loop" is a bug that often comes up when you are developing programs; the program will do the same thing over and over again, or it will simply seem to "die" and do nothing if the loop is doing something that is not displayed on the screen. Sometimes, you must turn the computer off to get out of the loop.

All of this should become clear when you rewrite the ASCCHRT program so that it repeats using a **while** loop. To compile this program, you can simply copy the earlier ASCCHRT.C program into a new file called ASCCHRT2.C. Working from the DOS prompt, enter the the following command:

```
COPY ASCCHRT.C ASCCHRT2.C
```

Then, use your editor to make the following changes needed to convert the original into the new version. To introduce basic concepts in a thorough way, the early chapters of this book will include a number of programs, such as the following one, that are similar to each other but with new features added. You can compile all of these programs if you would like the extra experience, or you can simply read some of the programs and compile only the crucial ones. It is not difficult to compile all the programs if you simply copy and modify the previous one each time, and you might find that watching all the programs run makes it easier to understand the concepts they illustrate.

```
/* CHAPTER 2, EXAMPLE 1 */

#include <stdio.h>
main()                          /* print ASCII value of char */
{                               /* with option to repeat */
char smplChr, again;

again = 'A';
while(again == 'A')
    {
    printf("\nWhat char do you want the ASCII value of > ");
    scanf("\n%c",&smplChr);
    printf("\nThe ASCII value of %c is %d\n",smplChr,smplChr);

    printf("\n\nEnter  A  to look up another ");
    printf("\nor any letter to quit ");
    scanf("\n%c",&again);
    }
}
```

The ASCCHRT program from the last chapter is now placed within a **while** loop. Note that the condition following the word **while** is placed in parentheses and that there is no semicolon following it (because it is not a statement in itself—just an introduction to the statements in the brackets that follow).

When the program first encounters this **while**, it checks to see if the condition is true. Because the condition is true, all statements within the loop are executed. Then, when the program reaches the final } of the **while** loop, the program goes back to the **while**. If the condition is still true, the program performs the statements in the **while** loop again; if the condition is untrue, the program skips the statements in the loop and executes the statement following the closing } of the **while** loop.

Because there is no other statement at this point, the program simply ends when the condition of the while loop becomes untrue, and control returns to the operating system. Instead, you could require the user to press another key before continuing by defining an extra variable and adding a few extra lines between the end of the **while** loop and the end of the program:

```
/* CHAPTER 2, EXAMPLE 2 */

#include <stdio.h>
main()                      /* print ASCII value of char */
{                           /* with option to repeat: ver 2 */
char smplChr, again, dummy;

again = 'A';
while(again == 'A')
     {
     printf("\nWhat char do you want the ASCII value of > ");
     scanf("\n%c",&smplChr);
     printf("\nThe ASCII value of %c is %d\n",smplChr,smplChr);
     printf("\n\nEnter  A  to look up another ");
     printf("\nor any letter to quit ");
     scanf("\n%c",&again);
     }
printf("\nEnter any letter to continue . . . ");
scanf("\n%c",&dummy);
}
```

If you do not enter an 'A' when the program asks you whether you want to look up another value, the program will return to the top of the loop and find that the condition is false. Then, it will skip all the statements within the **while** loop and execute the next statement, asking you to press the Enter key and then waiting for the variable that the program calls **dummy** because that variable is never actually used for anything.

There are a few important new points in these programs. First, note that you now use **scanf(\n%c)** rather than just **scanf(%c)**. **scanf()** used with **%s** (for strings), **%f** (for floats), or **%i** (for ints) will read everything entered up to the carriage return and will discard the carriage return. **%c** is more precise; it will read any single character — including the carriage return. In the examples in Chapter 1, in which there was no looping, reading everything up to the carriage return did not cause any problem; the carriage return was simply lost after the program ended. In this case, however, the carriage return would be read by **scanf()** the second time through the loop and assigned to the variable **smplChr** if the **\n** were not there to head it off. You might want to try an example program without the **\n** and see that the second time through the loop it will not wait for input from the user but will give you the ASCII number for the character carriage return — with a carriage return printed right in the middle of the statement. You are seeing what is called the **keyboard buffer** — a small amount of memory the computer reserves to save any keystrokes that you type so they can be passed to the program when the program is ready for them. The buffer can be very handy, for example, if you are a fast typist and tend to get ahead of your programs.

Using **scanf("%c")** with **\n** is not the ideal way to handle the keyboard buffer, however. If the user enters a long word instead of just one character, for example, **scanf()** will read every character in the word, and the program will loop dozens of times until it is done reading each of those characters. If you enter just a carriage return when the program asks for input, the program will ignore the carriage return and keep waiting for input. If this happens, enter a letter to make the program continue. After you learn about strings in Chapter 5, you will be able to handle this type of problem more gracefully, and the experience of handling a stream of characters at a very low level is valuable.

Second, note that statements within the **while** loop are indented, and the brackets of the main program and of the **while** loop are lined up one above the other. Athough this format is not required by the compiler, it is stylistically useful to help the programmer keep track of the logic.

Third, note the double equal sign (= =) in the statement **while(again** = = **'A')**. This symbol should not be confused with the single equal sign (=), which assigns a new value to a variable. The double equal sign tests the current value of the variable. This sign is one of the famous **logical operators**, which means that, when C sees the = =, it evaluates the statement to see if the statement is true or false.

The opposite of the sign $==$ (which means "is equal to") is the sign $!=$ (which means "is not equal to"). Statements that include these signs can be used in combination with each other if you use the sign **&&** (which means "and") or the sign **||** (which means "or") between them. For example, it would be useful to change the condition in the program you have just looked at to the following:

```
while(again == 'A' || again == 'a')
```

When you put the "or" sign, **||**, in the conditional statement, the entire condition is true if the condition on either side of the **||** is true. This can be read as "while **again** equals uppercase A *or* **again** equals lowercase a." In cases where the conditions are more complicated, however, it often clarifies things if you add "it is true" to each statement when you read it in your own mind; you could read the above statement as "while it is true that **again** equals uppercase A *or* it is true that **again** equals lowercase a." Stating it this way makes it obvious that the condition is satisfied if either half is true.

What if you used **&&** instead and wrote the condition as **while(again $==$ 'A' && again $==$ 'a')**? You can read this in your own mind as "while it is true that **again** equals uppercase A *and* it is true that **again** equals lowercase a." When you use **&&**, the condition is satisfied only if both halves are true. In this case, the condition can never be satisfied because **again** cannot be both uppercase A and lowercase a simultaneously.

You can make this condition fancier and, in the process, gain more experience with looping and with logical operators. It is obviously not ideal to have the user type in one letter or one character to perform a task again or any other key to quit. It is fairly common practice to make the user enter either a "Y" if he or she wants to perform a task again or an "N" if he or she wants to quit. If you have formatted disks on an IBM-PC, for example, you know that, when the system is done with one disk, it will ask you, "Do you want to format another (Y/N)?" If you enter any other letter, it will repeat the same question again until it gets a Y or N for an answer.

You can make your program do the same thing by modifying it as follows:

```
/* CHAPTER 2, EXAMPLE 3 */

#include <stdio.h>
main()                    /* print ASCII value of char */
{                         /* with option to repeat: ver 3 */
char smplChr, again;

again = 'Y';
while(again == 'Y' || again == 'y')
    {
    printf("\nWhat char do you want the ASCII value of > ");
    scanf("\n%c",&smplChr);
    printf("\nThe ASCII value of %c is %d\n",smplChr,smplChr);
    again = "x";
    while(again != 'Y' && again != 'y'
                            && again != 'N' && again !='n')
        {
        printf("\nDo you want to look up another (Y/N) > ");
        scanf("\n%c",&again);
        }
    }
}
```

Instead of asking whether the user wants to perform a task again and getting the **again** variable from the keyboard within the normal sequence of the program, you put the question and answer within a **while** loop of its own, which is inside the **while** loop you already have. This technique is known as **nesting** one loop within the other. You keep asking this question "while it is true that **again** does not equal uppercase Y *and* it is true that **again** does not equal lowercase y *and* it is true that **again** does not equal uppercase N *and* it is true that **again** does not equal lowercase n." Because you are using **&&**, all of these conditions must be true for the loop to execute; if **again** equals any of these four characters, the loop will not execute and the program will continue.

Before entering the loop, you make **again** equal 'x'. If you had not done this, **again** would still be equal to uppercase Y, (which you made it equal to at the beginning of the program), and the loop would not execute. Because you have made it 'x', however, the condition is true, and the statements in this inner loop are executed. The program asks "Would you like to look up another (Y/N?)" and gets the **again** variable from the user. Then, it goes back to the top of this inner loop and checks the condition again. If the user entered a Y or an N, either uppercase or lowercase, the condition is not satisfied and the inner loop does not execute a second time. If the user entered any other letter, however, the condition is satisfied: "it is true that **again** does not equal uppercase Y *and* it is true that **again** does not equal lowercase y *and* it is true that **again** does not equal uppercase N *and* it is true that **again** does not equal lowercase n." The inner loop is executed; it asks the same question a second time and will continue asking it until it gets a Y or N answer.

Once the user inputs a Y or N and gets out of the inner loop, the program will reach the final } of the outer loop. This will make it return to the top of the outer loop and test the condition there again to see if "it is true that **again** equals uppercase Y *or* it is true that **again** equals lowercase y." If so, the program will execute that outer loop again and give the ASCII value of another character. If not, it will skip the outer loop and reach the end of the program.

All of this might seem obvious to some readers and obscure to others. In either case, it is valuable to actually follow the flow of the program carefully, step by step, when you are first learning about looping. You should look at the example once more, starting at the first line and following the way that the program flows line by line as the user makes different choices. Be sure you understand just how the flow of logic works.

There is one other thing that you can do to make this program a bit fancier and learn another very common way of using the **while** loop. Most programs clear the screen before executing. C compilers generally have a built-in function to clear the screen, but you can write a simple one of your own as follows:

```
clrscrn()                    /* clear the screen */
{
int counter;

counter = 0;
while(counter != 25)
    {
    printf("\n");
    counter = counter + 1;
    }
}
```

This function simply prints a new line 25 times, and (because the computer screen displays 25 lines) it scrolls anything that is being displayed off the top of the screen.

The function **clrscrn**() illustrates a very common programming practice — the use of a loop with a counter to make the program perform some task a given number of times. The counter starts at zero. The **while** loop that performs the task you want repeats "while it is true that **counter** is not equal to 25" (or to whatever number happens to be the number of times that you want something done). The counter is incremented each time through the loop, so that after 25 times through, the condition will no longer be true and the loop will not be executed again. Incrementing the loop involves a statement that sometimes shocks new students of computer programming:

```
counter = counter + 1;
```

This statement goes against everything you ever learned in algebra, where the equation x = x + 1 would be an absurdity. It is another reminder that the = sign in C stands for assignment — not for equality — and the statement should be read as "make the value of **counter** equal the (current) value of **counter** plus 1."

The function **clrscrn**() also illustrates the fact that C is an extensible language. It is possible to write new functions of your own and use them like any other functions of the language. Even if you have not been compiling all of the earlier versions of this program, you should compile this final version, which uses the new **clrscrn**() function within the **main**() function as follows:

```
/* CHAPTER 2, EXAMPLE 4 */

#include <stdio.h>
main()                        /* print ASCII value of char */
{                             /* with option to repeat: ver 4 */
char smplChr, again;

again = 'Y';
while(again == 'Y' || again == 'y')
    {
    clrscrn();
    printf("\nWhat char do you want the ASCII value of > ");
    scanf("\n%c",&smplChr);
    printf("\nThe ASCII value of %c is %d\n",smplChr,smplChr);
    again = 'x';
    while(again != 'Y' && again != 'y'
                        && again != 'N' && again !='n')
        {
        printf("\n\nDo you want to look up another (Y/N)> ");
        scanf("\n%c",&again);
        }
    }
clrscrn();
}



clrscrn()                            /* clear the screen */
{
int counter;

counter = 0;
while(counter != 25)
    {
    printf("\n");
    counter = counter + 1;
    }
}
```

Note that **clrscrn()** can be used just like any other function of the language (**printf()** or **scanf()**, for example). When the **main()** module reaches **clrscrn()**, it transfers control to the **clrscrn()** function; after **clrscrn()** is done, control returns to the place where it left the main function, and the program continues with the next statement after **clrscrn()** in **main()**. By writing **clrscrn()** as a separate function, you save yourself work because you type in the steps needed to clear the screen only once, although the program uses the steps twice. Also, you actually make the **main()** module easier to read by writing **clrscrn()** in it instead of putting in all of the steps each time they are used and forcing someone who is trying to read the program to figure out each time that all you are doing is clearing the screen.

SELECTION: if-else

Now that you have looked at sequence and iteration, selection is the only other major type of program control that you must learn about. Selection in C usually takes the following form:

```
if(condition)
     {
     statement;
     statement;
     }
else
     {
     statement;
     statement;
     }
```

There can be any number of statements in the brackets following the **if** and the **else**. If the condition is true, the statements following the **if** are executed; otherwise, the statements following the **else** are executed. The **else** and the statements that follow it are optional. You can just have an **if** clause; the statements that follow it will be executed if the condition is true, and nothing will be done if the condition is false.

You can use **if-else** to expand the ASCCHRT program. Instead of just letting the user input a character to find out what its ASCII number is, you can also let the user input the ASCII number and find out what the corresponding character is. To do this, you will write a new **main**() module that provides a small menu screen that allows the user to choose whether he or she wants to look up the ASCII number of a character, look up the character for a number, or quit the program. Then, depending on the choice, the program will branch to a module that is like the ASCCHRT program you have already looked at or to a module that does the same thing in reverse. There are more elegant ways to do the same thing, but this way gives you good practice in building a program out of modules and illustrates the sort of menu system that is common in many applications.

To write this program, use the DOS COPY command to copy the final ASCCHRT program you wrote in the last section to a new file. Then use your editor to edit the file. Copy the old **main**() function so it appears twice. Type over the title **main**() and replace it with **asctoint**() in one case and with **inttoasc**() in the other. The function **asctoint**() does the same thing that the former program did; it gives you the ASCII integer value of the character you enter. You need only modify a few commands in the **inttoasc**() version to make it give you the character of the ASCII integer you enter; it is easy to understand the changes if you look carefully at the next listing.

Now you just need to figure out what the new **main**() module that holds these programs together will look like. It must be some sort of a menu. As a first try, you might just list the three choices, require the user to input one of the choices you have provided (by using a **while** loop, as you did previously), and then use a series of **if** statements to execute whatever choice the user makes. The entire program follows:

```
/* CHAPTER 2, EXAMPLE 5 */
main()                    /* menu for ASCII chart program */
{
char menuOpt;

clrscrn();
printf("MENU - ASCII CHART PROGRAM");
printf("\n--------------------------");
printf("\n\n\n1 - Look up the character for an ASCII number");
printf("\n\n2 - Look up the ASCII number of a character");
printf("\n\n3 - Quit");
```

   continued...

...from previous page

```
menuOpt = ' ';
while(menuOpt != '1' && menuOpt != '2' && menuOpt != '3')
    {
    printf("\n\n\nWHAT IS YOUR CHOICE > ");
    scanf("\n%c",&menuOpt);
    }
if(menuOpt == '1')
    {
    inttoasc();
    }
if(menuOpt == '2')
    {
    asctoint();
    }
clrscrn();
}



asctoint()              /* print ASCII number for */
{                       /* a given character */
char smplChr, again;

again = 'Y';
while(again == 'Y' || again == 'y')
    {
    clrscrn();
    printf("\nWhat char do you want the ASCII value of > ");
    scanf("\n%c",&smplChr);
    printf("\nThe ASCII value of %c is %d\n",smplChr,smplChr);
    again = 'x';
    while(again != 'Y' && again != 'y'
                        && again != 'N' && again !='n')
        {
        printf("\nDo you want to look up another (Y/N) > ");
        scanf("\n%c",&again);
        }
    }
}
```

continued...

...from previous page

```
inttoasc()              /* print character for a */
{                       /* given ASCII number */
int smplInt;
char again;

again = 'Y';
while(again == 'Y' || again == 'y')
     {
     clrscrn();
     printf("\nWhat number do you want the ASCII char of > ");
     scanf("%d",&smplInt);
     printf("\nThe ASCII char for %d is %c\n",smplInt,smplInt);
     again = 'x';
     while(again != 'Y' && again != 'y'
                         && again != 'N' && again !='n')
         {
         printf("\n\nDo you want to look up another (Y/N)> ");
         scanf("\n%c",&again);
         }
     }
}



clrscrn()               /* clear the screen */
{
int counter;
counter = 0;
while(counter != 25)
     {
     printf("\n");
     counter = counter + 1;
     }
}
```

Take a while to examine the logic of this entire program before compiling and running it. With a program this long, it is often best to print the program file so you can follow it. After you are finished editing it, you might want to print out the file so you can line up the entire listing, one page above another. Either use your editor to print it, or save the file, leave the editor, and, at the DOS prompt, enter **PRINT ASCCHRT6.C** (or whatever name you gave the file). Then, examine the listing you printed and follow the program's logic.

The menu prints a title and three choices and forces you to enter a 1, 2, or 3. (Note that these numbers are treated as characters and always placed in single quotes.) If you enter a 1, the program executes **inttoasc()**, which takes an integer, gives you the ASCII character for it, and gives you the opportunity to do the same thing again. When you finally choose not to do it again, you return to the location in which you left off in the **main()** module — i.e., after the **if** statement that made the program execute **inttoasc()**. Rather than having the statement **clrscrn()** at the end of both **inttoasc()** and **asctoint()**, as in the earlier version of the program, this version uses a single **clrscrn()** at the end of **main()**, which is executed after the program returns from either of the other two functions. Because the condition of the second **if** statement is false, the program skips it, clears the screen, and control returns to the operating system. The same type of thing happens if you choose Option 2. Option 3 is there in case the user changes his mind; after seeing the menu, the user might decide this is not the program he thought it was and therefore does not want to look up anything. The program will accept the user's input of 3 and exit from the **while** loop, but then it will not execute either of the following **if** statements; it will simply fall through to the end of the program, clear the screen, and return to the operating system.

Now, compile the program and run it. Test the three menu options and make sure the program flow is what it should be. This program flow is probably quite adequate for an ASCII chart program. People want to look up the ASCII values of characters or the characters for ASCII numbers but generally do not want to do both at once.

In most menu systems, however, you return to the main menu after executing one of the choices and must explicitly choose Quit after executing one of the options. It makes sense to modify this program to make it more like a conventional menu system, both for illustrative purposes and just in case someone wants to look up both characters and values. You could also eliminate the "press any key to continue . . . " message from the **asctoint()** and **inttoasc()** modules; instead, the user would return to the main menu and press 3 to quit the program.

To write a conventional menu system, you will use what is sometimes called an **if-else-if** ladder, which resembles the following:

```
if(condition)
     {
     statement;
     statement;
     }
else if(condition)
     {
     statement;
     statement;
     }
else if(condition)
     {
     statement;
     statement;
     }
else
     {
     statement;
     statement;
     }
```

It is obvious what this listing does; if any of the conditions is true, the program executes the statements under that **if** or **else if**. If none of the conditions is true, the
program executes the statements under the final **else**. (The final **else** is optional;
if it is left out, the **if-else-if** ladder will do nothing if none of the conditions is true.)

This final **else** is very handy for giving error messages; if the user does not choose
any of the correct options, the final **else** is executed automatically. This simplest
way of indicating an error, one that is very common in professional programs, is
to have the computer beep and give the user the list of options again. The beep
is actually an ASCII character itself, ASCII character number 7. The statement
printf("%c",7) will "print" 7 in ASCII "character" form: that is, it will make the
computer beep.

In addition, you can make the menu look better by using the special character **\t**
in the **printf()** statements. **\t** represents tab, as **\n** represents newline, and it can
be used to indent a line. For example, the statement **printf("\t\t\tMENU - ASCII
CHART PROGRAM")** will approximately center the heading of the menu, and
adding a few tabs before each choice will make the menu look more attractive.

To modify the program, then, copy the previous version to a new file, and edit the **main**() module as follows. The menu is placed within a **while** loop — so it repeats until option 3 is entered — the **if/else** ladder is used, and a beep is added. The entire program now looks like the following:

```
/* CHAPTER 2, EXAMPLE 6 */
#include <stdio.h>

main()                  /* menu for ASCII chart program */
{
char menuOpt;

menuOpt = 'x';
while(menuOpt != '3')
     {
     clrscrn();
     printf("\t\t\tMENU - ASCII CHART PROGRAM");
     printf("\n\t\t\t-------------------------");
     printf("\n\n\n\n\n\n\n\n\t\t");
     printf("1 - Look up the character for an ASCII number");
     printf("\n\n\n");
     printf("\t\t2 - Look up the ASCII number of a character");
     printf("\n\n\n\t\t3 - Quit");
     printf("\n\n\n\n\n\n\n\t\t\tWHAT IS YOUR CHOICE > ");
     scanf("\n%c",&menuOpt);
     if(menuOpt == '1')
          {
          inttoasc();
          }
     else if(menuOpt == '2')
          {
          asctoint();
          }
     else if(menuOpt == '3')
          {
          clrscrn();
          }
```

continued...

...from previous page

```
     else
          {
          printf("%c",7);
          }
     }
clrscrn();
}


asctoint()          /* print ASCII number for */
{                   /* a given character*/
char smplChr, again;

again = 'Y';
while(again == 'Y' || again == 'y')
     {
     clrscrn();
     printf("\nWhat char do you want the ASCII value of > ");
     scanf("\n%c",&smplChr);
     printf("\nThe ASCII value of %c is %d\n",smplChr,smplChr);
     again = 'x';
     while(again != 'Y' && again != 'y'
                              && again != 'N' && again !='n')
          {
          printf("\nDo you want to look up another (Y/N)> ");
          scanf("\n%c",&again);
          }
     }
}


inttoasc()          /* print character for a */
{                   /* given ASCII number */
int smplInt;
char again;
```

continued...

45

...from previous page

```
again = 'Y';
while(again == 'Y' || again == 'y')
     {
     clrscrn();
     printf("\nWhat number do you want the ASCII char of > ");
     scanf("%d",&smplInt);
     printf("\nASCII char  %d  is  %c\n",smplInt,smplInt);
     again = 'x';
     while(again != 'Y' && again != 'y'
                          && again != 'N' && again !='n')
          {
          printf("\n\nDo you want to look up another (Y/N)> ");
          scanf("\n%c",&again);
          }
     }
}



clrscrn()              /* clear the screen */
{
int counter;

counter = 0;
while(counter != 25)
     {
     printf("\n");
     counter = counter + 1;
     }
}
```

Compile and run this program. You will notice that it handles errors in a much more professional-looking way than the last version did. Instead of just asking you "WHAT IS YOUR CHOICE >" over and over again if you do not enter 1, 2, or 3, — and scrolling up the screen each time so that the menu eventually disappears entirely — the program beeps to call your attention to the fact that you have made an error, and it rewrites the entire screen so that the menu looks just as it did before. You can play around with the **\n** and **\t** special characters in the **printf**() statements until the screen looks just the way you want it to look.

This program is actually emulating full-screen control by rewriting the entire screen whenever a change is needed. Notice that it rewrites the screen rather slowly and that the **scanf**() that receives user input must be at the bottom of the screen. In this program, that location is a good place for user input; in later programs in this book, user input will look a bit clumsy in that location.

The standard input-output package that comes with C includes relatively primitive I/O capabilities. The way the computer naturally works is by printing one line of text to the screen and then scrolling the whole screen up when it prints another line. In the bad old days before computers used the cathode ray tube — the television-like display that you have on your computer — they used a teletype to interact with the user, and it would type out instructions or error messages one line at a time and would require a carriage return and line feed after each line, like a typewriter. Except for DOS 4.0's new Shell feature, MS-DOS still communicates with you in this native mode; when you are in the operating system, the computer will read your commands and print out error messages, directory listings, or whatever, one line at a time, scrolling the screen up after each line.

Once you enter most programs, however, you usually see an entire screen. A menu, a spreadsheet, a record from a database, or a page from a word-processing document is arranged attractively on the screen — often with some of the text brighter than the rest or outlined to make it clear what you must do, and the user can move the cursor all over the screen to select options or make changes. Of course, this usually provides a great advantage because there are few things more tedious than using an old-fashioned line editor (such as EDLIN, which is built into MS-DOS) and being required to select one line at a time to edit rather than having the full-screen editing capacity that is now standard for text editors and word processors. On the Macintosh, even the operating system uses the entire screen rather than scrolling one line at a time, and users also seem to find this display easier. Once OS/2 or some other Macintosh-like operating system takes over in the IBM-PC world, the average user will no longer have any experience with the computer's traditional mode of printing to the screen one line at a time.

Some computer languages have a built-in capacity to work with the full screen. BASIC, for example, includes the LOCATE command. The statements

```
LOCATE 10,5
PRINT "*"
```

will move the cursor down 10 lines from the top of the screen and five lines in from the left and then will print an asterisk in this location. This feature allows you to receive input from the user anywhere on the center of the screen.

Because C is a low-level high-level language, its standard I/O package uses the computer's native mode of writing to the screen one line at a time, scrolling the screen up as it goes along. Controlling the screen at a low level with C requires some rather detailed and technical commands. There are many developers, however, who have taken advantage of the fact that C is an extensible language and have written libraries of routines for screen control, sometimes called "programmer's toolboxes." You can buy packages that give you capacity not just for the simple cursor control provided by BASIC but also for creating enhanced text, blinking text, windows, multiple windows, moving bar menus, and virtually anything else anyone would ever want to do in terms of screen control. Several low-cost shareware packages are available.

This book, though, will use only the standard input-output package for I/O, and, in fact, will only use some of the functions in that package. It is generally not a good idea for beginners to spend much time learning C functions. When you are working on a project, you can find the functions you need in some library and will learn them instantly, but when you are first studying C, learning one function after another is just a distraction from learning the concepts of the language. In any event, there is no way of predicting what library of screen-control functions you will finally decide to use. Thus, the programs in this book just scroll up the screen one line at a time so that you can control the full screen only by clearing it and rewriting it entirely, and whenever you pause for user input, the cursor will be positioned on the last line. Just remember that you have the potential for incomparably greater control of the screen when you start using additional libraries that extend the language.

A FEW EXTRA TRICKS

Writing this menu system has taken you a long way toward being a competent programmer. There are many professional programmers who spend much of their time writing menu systems that work pretty much like the one you have just written — in COBOL, dBASE, Pascal, and PL-1, as well as in C. The basic ideas about controlling program flow apply to almost any programming language: once you have learned concepts such as these, it becomes easy to learn new languages.

After a program is developed, it usually goes through a long period of testing. Ideally, programs should not be tested by the programmers who write them. The programmers already have a fixed idea of how the program logic works and what cases it should cover, and they tend to test for those cases; if other people perform the testing, they will be much more likely to look at possibilities that the original programmers ignored. In practice, however, particularly in the world of microcomputers, custom programs are often written by consultants who work on their own and must do their own testing.

When you are testing, it is good to imagine that you are an inexperienced user who might want to do unexpected things. Run the program and try to make every conceivable choice that a user might make. Be sure to test the most extreme possibilities. If you are working with text, for example, enter a very long string and see what the program does with that string, and enter a string that has no letters in it at all (just press Enter) and see what the program does with that information. If you are working with numbers, enter a very large number, enter zero, and enter a negative number, and see what the program does with each of them. These extreme cases will most likely turn up the bugs in your program.

Try testing each of the menu options in your ASCII chart program. You should not have any major difficulties entering a character and getting its ASCII number. There will be minor errors if you enter more than one character or a carriage return without a character, which you will learn to deal with after you have learned about strings.

On the other hand, when you try entering numbers and getting ASCII characters for them, you will find the program works perfectly well for medium range numbers but gives you bizarre results if you enter a letter or if you enter small, large, or negative numbers. To correct the first problem by screening out letters and accepting only numbers from the user, you would need to make the program read the number as a string and then check that string and use it only if all digits were entered. Though it is not difficult, you cannot perform this type of error checking until you have learned to work with strings; for that reason, such error checking will be omitted from the sample programs in this book but will be covered in more detail in Chapter 8.

It is easier to correct the other problems, which occur because there are only 128 standard ASCII characters, as you have seen, and 256 characters (numbered from 0 to 255) in the extended ASCII character set used by the IBM-PC. Telling the computer to print the ASCII character for any number larger than this limit is telling it to do something impossible. In addition, the ASCII characters numbered 00 through 31 are control characters. If you enter some of these characters, the program will complete the statement you are printing to the screen with a symbol that stands for a control character, such as a smiling face. In other cases, the program will perform the action that the character represents. For example, if you enter a 7, it will complete the statement by beeping. In some cases, it will just end the statement with a blank. In addition, ASCII character 32 is a space, and having the chart print it would only confuse the reader. Character 255 is unprintable.

To protect users of your program from being confused by this sort of screen display, you must write what are called **error-trapping routines** — parts of the program that anticipate any errors people might make and give them relatively user-friendly messages telling them, in essence, that they are not allowed to do what they are attempting. To trap errors in this program, you must bypass the **inttoasc()** function when the user enters a number that is less than 33 or greater than 254 (on the IBM-PC).

This routine requires new logical operators, representing "less than" and "greater than," that will probably look familiar to you. All of the logical operators are summarized in the following small chart, with the new operators at the end:

Symbol	Meaning
&&	and
||	or
!	not
==	is equal to
!=	is not equal to
>	is greater than
<	is less than
>=	is greater than or equal to
<=	is less than or equal to

Sometimes, only the first three of these symbols are called logical operators and the rest are called relational operators. On the other hand, sometimes the first three are called "Boolean," and "logical operators" is often used as a general term that includes them all.

The four new operators in this chart are identical to the symbols used in algebra and should be easy to understand. The condition **if(counter > 10)** is true if the variable named **counter** has a value that is greater than 10 and false if that variable has a value that is less than or equal to 10.

Using these new operators, you can easily screen out the errors in the **inttoasc**() module. You receive the number from the user as always, but you must take the part of the module that prints the character for that number and make sure it executes only if the number is within the right range. To do this, you must place this part of the module within an **if-else** statement in the following form:

```
if(smplInt < 33 || smplInt > 254)
     {
     PRINT SOME ERROR MESSAGE
     }
else
     {
     PRINT THE ASCII CHARACTER FOR smplInt
     }
```

Note that the condition uses || (or). You want to print the error message if either of the conditions is true (if the number entered is less than 33 *or* the number entered is greater than 254). If you are working on a computer other than an IBM-PC, you have only 128 ASCII characters, numbered from 0 to 127, and you should modify this program accordingly. For you, the condition is as follows:

```
if(smplInt < 33 || smplInt > 126).
```

With this error-trapping added, the **inttoasc**() module reads as follows:

```
/* CHAPTER 2, EXAMPLE 7 */
/* use as replacement of inttoasc() in EXAMPLE 6 */

inttoasc()                  /* print character for a */
{                           /* given ASCII number */
int smplInt;                /* with error trapping*/
char again;

again = 'Y';
while(again == 'Y' || again == 'y')
    {
    clrscrn();
    printf("\nWhat number do you want the ASCII char of > ");
    scanf("%d",&smplInt);
    if(smplInt < 33 || smplInt > 254)
        {
        printf("\nThe number must be between 33 and 254");
        }
    else
        {
        printf("\nASCII char %d is %c\n",smplInt,smplInt);
        }
```

continued...

...from previous page

```
    again = 'x';
    while(again != 'Y' && again != 'y'
                        && again != 'N' && again !='n')
        {
        printf("\n\nDo you want to look up another (Y/N)> ");
        scanf("\n%c",&again);
        }
    }
}
```

This is another example of nesting one form of program control inside another. In this case, the **if-then** is nested within a **while** loop. Nesting appears complicated when described in this way, but it is very easy to understand if you have developed it logically one step at a time and if you indent properly, as in the example. Often, programs nest five or six loops and conditions within each other, and the logic is still not hard to understand.

There is one other modification to the program that you can make now that you know these new operators. In the **clrscrn**() function, you used the condition **while(counter != 25)** to make the loop stop executing after it had printed a new line 24 times. This program is so simple that nothing can go wrong when you use this condition, but as a general matter of programming style, it is much better to use < (less than) or > (greater than) to control loops. It is always possible that, for some reason you did not foresee, the counter will not exactly equal that number before becoming greater than it. The danger is particularly great if you have a condition that involves floating decimal point numbers because of the possibility of what are referred to as **rounding errors**. Remember that the computer uses binary numbers, and its fractions only approximately represent the decimal numbers that you use, so it may round off a fraction into decimal form in a way that the programmer did not anticipate, and the counter will never exactly equal the condition the programmer set up to end the loop. It is best to not even need to think about this sort of problem; thus, you should modify **clrscrn**() by changing the condition from **while(counter != 25)** to **while(counter < 25)**.

There are a few other points of style concerning controlling program flow. These points are sometimes necessary and often are useful to make the flow of logic clearer to the programmer, and they are easy enough to understand.

The statement **break;** will, as the name implies, simply break you out of a loop. The program will continue executing with the next statement after the end of the loop. Notice that **break;** does not end with parentheses; it is one of the relatively few commands in C that is actually part of the language—not a function in a library.

The statement **break;** is often used as a clearer way of writing menus. Instead of placing the condition for quitting the menu up at the top as part of the **while()** statement, you can put the condition for quitting within the loop, where it is obviously parallel with the other choices. This strategy will become very clear if you examine the menu in the last version of the ASCII chart program, which has the following general form:

```
menuOpt = 'x'
while(menuOpt != '3')
      {
      .  .  .  .  .  .  .  .  .  .
      DISPLAY MENU AND GET OPTION 1, 2 OR 3
      .  .  .  .  .  .  .  .  .  .
      if(menuOpt == '1')
            {
            inttoasc();
            }
      else if(menuOpt == '2')
            {
            asctoint();
            }
      else if(menuOpt == '3')
            {
            clrscrn();
            }
      else
            {
            printf("%c",7);
            }
      }
clrscrn();
}
```

Reading through the **if-else** ladder, you will not immediately see why the screen is simply cleared if the choice is 3; you must return to the **while()** function to see that you are not only clearing the screen but also exiting from the program, which can make longer menus more difficult to understand, modify, or debug. Many programmers would prefer to rewrite this menu as something like the following:

```
while(1==1)
    {
    .  .  .  .  .  .  .  .  .  .  .
    DISPLAY MENU AND GET OPTION 1, 2 OR 3
    .  .  .  .  .  .  .  .  .  .  .
    if(menuOpt == '1')
        {
        inttoasc();
        }
    else if(menuOpt == '2')
        {
        asctoint();
        }
    else if(menuOpt == '3')
        {
        clrscrn();
        break;
        }
    else
        {
        printf("%c",7);
        }
    }
clrscrn();
}
```

First, you deliberately set up an infinite loop with the condition **while(1==1)**. Because it is always true that 1 is equal to 1, this loop will continue forever, but the statement **break;** is executed if the user chooses menu option 3. The flow of the program does not return to the top of the **while** loop to evaluate the condition again; instead, it breaks out of the loop and continues with the next statement after the loop's final curly bracket. In this example, of course, there is no next statement, and the program simply ends.

Looking at these two versions of the menu, you can probably see that it is easier to take in at a glance what the program is doing in the version using **break;** because everything that is happening is within the **if-else** ladder.

Another statement that is a bit like **break;** is **exit();**. The difference is that, while **break;** only takes you out of the current loop, **exit();** takes you out of the program entirely, and you are returned to the operating system. In the example you just examined, there would be one difference if you used **exit();** instead of **break;**. The program would not execute the **clrscrn();** command that follows the final } of the **while** loop. Instead of just exiting the loop, it would exit the entire program.

The statement **continue;** is almost the opposite of **break;**. Rather than breaking you out of the bottom of the loop, it takes you immediately back to the top of the loop and checks the condition there again. One place that this statement can be useful is when you are performng error-trapping and do not want to nest the entire program inside of an **if-else** statement. The difficult way to do this sort of error trapping would be as follows:

```
while(condition)
    {
    GET INPUT FROM USER
    if(errorCondition)
        {
        PRINT ERROR MESSAGE
        }
    else
        {
        DO 500 LINES OF CODE
        }
    }
```

Like the ASCII chart program, the previous program should not be executed if the user does the wrong thing. Because this is a much longer program, however, it is confusing to put it all within the **else** portion of an **if-else** statement. By the time you reach the end, you forget why it is doubly indented. The program is easier to read and understand in the following form:

```
while(condition)
    {
    GET INPUT FROM USER
    {
    if(errorCondition)
        {
        PRINT ERROR MESSAGE
        continue;
        }
    DO 500 LINES OF CODE
    }
```

In case of an error, the error message is displayed and the statement **continue;** directs the flow of the program back to the **while**() at the top of the loop, bypassing the 500 lines of code you want to avoid (without nesting the 500 lines within an **if-else** statement).

Finally, most discussions of controlling program flow in C end with a slightly shame-faced confession that C does actually contain a **goto** statement, which must be used in combination with a **label**, as follows:

```
if(condition)
    {
    goto nextstep;
    }
50 LINES OF CODE
nextstep:
500 MORE LINES OF CODE
```

If the condition is true, the program's flow of control will skip over the 50 lines of code and move to the label **nextstep:**. C knows this is a label because it ends with a colon. You will see similar use of **goto** and labels in Assembly Language and in MS-DOS batch command language, so it is good to be familiar with it.

The use of **goto** has been generally discredited by the rise of structured programming, and most C programmers never use it. The example you just looked at is terrible programming style, yet there are times when **goto** can be useful. You can use it to escape from a deeply nested series of loops, for example, as follows:

```
while(condition}
     {
     DO CODE
     while(condition)
          {
          DO MORE
          while(condition)
               {
               DO YET MORE
               while(condition)
                    {
                    DO EVEN MORE
                    if(errorCondition)
                    {
                    goto end;
                    }
               DO YET MORE
               }
          DO MORE
          }
     DO CODE
     }
end:
```

If you used **break;** instead of **goto end;**, that would only take you out of the innermost loop, and you would need to write some tricky code in four places to break out of all four loops. Only in a situation like this are you beginning to reach a point at which you might be justified in considering using a **goto** statement.

SUMMARY

Structured programming uses the following three methods of controlling program flow:

- sequence
- selection
- iteration

Sequence means performing one statement after another in the same order in which the statements appear in the program.

Iteration means repeating (or reiterating) the same procedure and can be done in C using the **while** loop, which takes the following form:

```
while(condition)
    {
    statement;
    statement;
    }
```

If the condition is true, the program performs the statements within the curly brackets. When it encounters the final bracket, it loops back up to the condition; if the condition is still true, the program performs these statements again. If the condition is false, the program continues to whatever statements follow the final curly bracket. There must be some statement within the curly brackets that eventually makes the condition false, or else the loop will continue indefinitely.

Selection can be performed using the **if-else** statement, which takes the following form:

```
if(condition)
     {
     statement;
     statement;
     }
else
     {
     statement;
     statement;
     }
```

If the condition is true, the statements in the curly brackets following it are executed; if it is false, the statements in the curly brackets following **else** are executed. The **else** may be omitted, and nothing will be done if the condition is false.

You may choose among a larger number of options, using the **if-else-if** ladder.

In either the **while** loop or the **if-else** statement, the conditions must include logical operators, which are evaluated as true or false. The following chart summarizes these operators:

Symbol	Meaning
&&	and
||	or
!	not
==	is equal to
!=	is not equal to
>	is greater than
<	is less than
>=	is greater than or equal to
<=	is less than or equal to

You may combine other operators in a single condition, using **&&** or **||**. If **&&** is used, both (or all) conditions must be true for the entire statement to be true. If **||** is used, either (or any) condition may be true and the entire statement is true.

The following statements are used for controlling program flow:

break;   breaks out of the loop and executes the command following its final curly bracket.

exit();   terminates the program and returns the user to the operating system.

continue;   immediately returns to the **while** at the beginning of the loop and checks its condition again.

goto labelName;   must be used in combination with a label followed by a colon elsewhere in the program and should be avoided.

while loops and **if-else** statements may be nested within one another, and — though the compiler does not require it — it is very important to indent them properly in order to follow their logic.

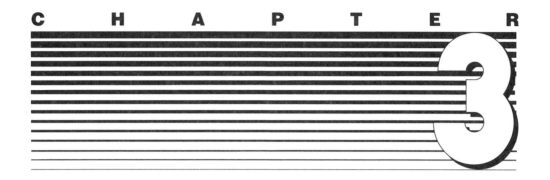

CHAPTER 3

NUMBERS AND ARRAYS

THE ARRAY

The **array** is a basic element of computer programming and is particularly important in the C language. Yet it is really nothing more than an easy way to keep
track of lists.

Keeping track of long lists — for example, data about all of a business's employees
or all of an organization's members — is one of the most common uses of computers, but it would be very unwieldy to keep track of this information by using
the methods you have already learned.

Imagine, for example, that you need a program that will let you enter an
employee's weekly wages for every week of the year. To create this program using
ordinary variables, the type that you have already learned about, you would need
to begin by declaring 52 variables, with names like **wageWk1**, **wageWk2**, **wageWk3**,
and so on, and then you would need to write over 100 lines of code to allow your
data entry person to enter an amount for each week. The program would look
like the following:

```
main()                          /* enter wages for each week */
{                                    /* written the hard way */
float wageWk1, wageWk2, wageWk3 . . .
         FORTY SEVEN MORE VARIABLES
         . . . wageWk51, wageWk52;

printf("\nEnter the wage for week 1 > ");
scanf("%f",&wageWk1);
printf("\nEnter the wage for week 2 > ");
scanf("%f",&wageWk2);
printf("\nEnter the wage for week 3 > ");
scanf("\n%f",&wageWk3);
. . .
NINETY-FOUR MORE LINES OF CODE
. . .
printf("\nEnter the wage for week 51 > ");
scanf("%f",&wageWk51);
printf("\nEnter the wage for week 52 > ");
scanf("%f",&wageWk52);

}
```

This program requires a great deal of unnecessary work, and it is just the sort of repetitive work that the computer can do for you.

All you need to do to make your life easier is declare all these variables as an array, using the following statement:

```
float wageWk[52];
```

This statement automatically creates 52 variables, with names ranging from **wage-Wk[0]** through **wageWk[51]**. Each of these variables is called an element of the array. The number in brackets is sometimes called a subscript, and you can read these names as "wageWk sub zero" and "wageWk sub fifty-one."

You must declare the array as one of the ordinary data types so the compiler will know how much space to reserve in memory for each element of the array; you use **float** in this case because you are keeping track of money, but in other cases, you will create arrays of **int**s, **long**s, and **char**s. Then, to tell the compiler how many elements the array has, you must give the array a name that ends with a number in square brackets.

The one slightly tricky thing about working with arrays in C is that the number in the declaration is one greater than the index number of the highest numbered variable you create. In this example of weekly wages, for instance, the variable is declared as **wageWk[52]**, but the elements are numbered up to **wageWk[51]**. The declaration tells you the actual number of elements in the array, but because numbering begins with **wageWk[0]**, the program only needs to go up to **wageWk[51]** for the array to have 52 elements all together. In more advanced applications, it is often very convenient to have the numbering of arrays begin with 0; when you are first learning, it is a bit tricky, but you get used to it rather quickly.

Note how much easier it is to write the weekly wage program you looked at previously, using an array:

```
/* CHAPTER 3, EXAMPLE 1 */
#include <stdio.h>

main()                      /* enter wages for each week */
{                              /* written the easy way */
float wageWk[52];
int cntr, numOfWks;

printf("\nHow many weeks of wages do you want to enter? ");
scanf("%d",&numOfWks);
cntr = 0;
while(cntr < numOfWks && cntr < 52)
    {
    printf("\nEnter the wage for week %d > ",cntr+1);
    scanf("%f",&wageWk[cntr]);
    cntr = cntr + 1;
    }
}
```

You simply use a **while** loop to go through all of the elements of the array. The same variable, **cntr**, that you use for controlling the number of times you pass through the loop can also be used to index the array and give it values from **wageWk[0]** through **wageWk[51]**. This example also lets you enter a smaller number of weeks, so you can test the program without having to go through the loop 52 times. Note that the condition of the **while()** statement requires the number of times through the loop both to be smaller than 52 *and* to be smaller than the number of weeks you entered.

The one slightly tricky thing about this program is its use of **cntr + 1** as the number of the week. Again, this is because you begin numbering the array with 0, but you want to ask the user to enter values beginning with week number 1. If you find this a bit confusing, look at this slightly longer version of the program, which is easier to understand:

```
/* CHAPTER 3, EXAMPLE 2 */
#include <stdio.h>

main()                      /* enter wages for each week */
{                           /* the easy-to-understand way */
float wageWk[52];
int cntr, numOfWks, weekNmbr;

printf("\nHow many weeks of wages do you want to enter? ");
scanf("%d",&numOfWks);

cntr = 0;
weekNmbr = 1;
while(cntr < numOfWks && cntr < 52)
    {
    printf("\nEnter the wage for week %d > ",weekNmbr);
    scanf("%f",&wageWk[cntr]);
    cntr = cntr + 1;
    weekNmbr = weekNmbr + 1;
    }
}
```

Here, you create a separate variable, **weekNmbr**, which is only used in the **printf**() statement that asks the user to enter the wages for a given week, numbered from 1 to 52. If the first version of this program puzzled you, look at this version carefully, and you will see that the variable **weekNmbr** is always one greater than the variable **cntr**.

Using an array saved you the trouble of writing close to 100 lines of code in this sample program alone. Of course, in an actual program, you would not just be getting the figures for each week's wages, but you would be doing things with these figures as well, and you would save yourself the same trouble each time you worked with them. Perhaps later in the program, you will need to add all the weekly wage figures in order to get a figure for the total yearly wages. You could do that very easily by adding a few extra lines to the program, as follows:

```
/* CHAPTER 3, EXAMPLE 3 */
#include <stdio.h>

main()                      /* enter wages for each week */
{                           /* and calculate yearly wage */
float wageWk[52];
int cntr, numOfWks;
float yrlyWage;

printf("\nHow many weeks of wages do you want to enter? ");
scanf("%d",&numOfWks);

cntr = 0;                   /* get each week's wages */
while(cntr < numOfWks && cntr < 52)
    {
    printf("\nEnter the wage for week %d > ",cntr+1);
    scanf("%f",&wageWk[cntr]);
    cntr = cntr + 1;
    }


yrlyWage = 0;                    /* add all weekly wages */
cntr = 0;
while(cntr < numOfWks && cntr < 52)
    {
    yrlyWage = yrlyWage + wageWk[cntr];
    cntr = cntr + 1;
    }
printf("\n\nThe total yearly wage is %f",yrlyWage);
}
```

The new addition to the program starts with a yearly wage of 0; then it adds the wage for week 0, the wage for week 1, and so on through week 51 to get the entire year's wage. When you test this program, you may find more examples of rounding errors, which occur when the computer converts the binary numbers it uses into the decimal numbers it displays; for example, if you enter a wage of **10.10** per week for four weeks, the program might say the total is **40.400002**. This degree of precision is adequate for working with money. Chapter 8 explains how to use double-precision floats and how to use **printf**() to make floats display only two decimal points.

Remember that simply adding the wages for the year would take over 50 lines of extra code if you were using ordinary variables instead of an array, and you can begin to appreciate how much programming time and effort you can save by using arrays.

AN ARITHMETIC QUIZ PROGRAM

Arrays are most often used for going through a list from top to bottom, as in the previous example, but they can also be used in more creative ways. In the rest of this chapter, you will develop a simple arithmetic quiz program, using an array of ten numbers to simulate a much longer list of numbers. The program will begin with a menu that gives users the choice of whether they want addition, subtraction, multiplication, or division problems. Because this is a simple program, the problems will all use one-digit numbers — that is, numbers from zero to nine.

The problem for the programmer is how to give a long series of these problems without there being any obvious repetition. Your first impulse might be to use a long list of numbers, perhaps a list of 100 numbers between zero and nine, arranged in random order, so the program could go through this whole list for its examples. You would begin the program by declaring an array, a counter to take you through the array, and a variable to get the answer from the user:

```
int nmbr[100];
int cntr;
int answer;
```

Then you would need a module to **initialize** the array—to give each of the variables from **nmbr[0]** to **nmbr[99]** a value. The modules that pose the problems could then contain loops that look something like the following:

```
cntr = 0
while(cntr<98)
      {
      printf("%d + %d = ",nmbr[cntr],nmbr[cntr+1]);
      scanf("%d",&answer);
      if(answer==nmbr[cntr]+nmbr[cntr+1])
            {
            printf("\nRIGHT!!");
            cntr = cntr + 2;
            }
      else
            {
            printf("\nwrong");
            }
      }
```

Note that when you use the symbols + and = here as parts of the string within quotation marks displayed by the **printf()** statement, the program simply uses them as characters and does not use them to perform any arithmetic operations. If **nmbr[cntr]** happens to equal 6, for example, and **nmbr[cntr+1]** happens to equal 3, the statement

```
printf("%d + %d = ",nmbr[cntr],nmbr[cntr+1]);
```

will simply display the following on the screen,

```
6 + 3 =
```

and the **scanf()** statement that follows the **print()** statement will display the cursor where the answer should go and will wait for the user's response.

This example is a stripped-down version of the program. The actual program would include a title at the top of the screen and could also give clues in case of a wrong answer. This version simply shows how you would go through the list of numbers to use them in your problems.

More repetition becomes possible when you start to write the other modules. If you begin them with **nmbr[0]** and go right through the list, as you did with addition, what you are doing will be fairly obvious even to children who are still learning arithmetic. They will not be overly impressed when they see that the first addition problem is, say, 7 plus 4, the first subtraction problem is 7 minus 4, the first multiplication problem is 7 times 4, and the first division problem is 7 divided by 4 — and that there is a similar mysterious correspondence among the other problems. The obvious solution is to begin each different module with a different value for **cntr**, so each begins at a different point in the list, and to make some modules work with **nmbr[cntr]** and **nmbr[cntr+2]** or **nmbr[cntr+3]**, rather than having all of them use **nmbr[cntr]** and **nmbr[cntr+1]**.

Now, you can actually apply this idea of varying the value of **cntr** more generally and make this program easier to write. Instead of using an array of 100 numbers, use an array of just 10 numbers: all of the numbers from zero to nine arranged in random order. Then you can go through that list over and over again, varying the value of the counters so that it is not obvious that you are just going through the same array of nine numbers each time.

The module to initialize the values of the nine variables in the list would not be difficult to write. It would look something like the following:

```
initlze()
{
nmbr[0] = 3;
nmbr[1] = 5;
nmbr[2] = 0;
nmbr[3] = 9;
nmbr[4] = 6;
nmbr[5] = 1;
nmbr[6] = 7;
nmbr[7] = 2;
nmbr[8] = 8;
nmbr[9] = 4;
}
```

That strategy is much less work than initializing 100 variables and trying to make sure that the numbers are random while you are doing it.

It is easy to go through the list over and over again. If you add the following bit of code within the loop you use to go through the array of 100 variables,

```
if(cntr>9)
     {
     cntr = cntr - 10
     }
```

then the program will keep increasing the value of **cntr** by two each time through the loop, as it did before; but when the value of **cntr** reaches 10, this extra bit of code will make it equal to zero and start again at the beginning of the array, with **nmbr[0]**.

You also need to worry about **cntr + 1** being greater than nine. And it would be good to vary the spacing between the two numbers that the problems use. There is no need to always work with **nmbr[cntr]** and **nmbr[cntr + 1]**; the program would do better at avoiding repetition if it could switch to working with **nmbr[cntr]** and **nmbr[cntr + 2]** and later to working with **nmbr[cntr]** and **nmbr[cntr + 3]**.

The easiest way to deal with these problems is by using two counters, **cntrA** and **cntrB**, along with a third variable, which could be called **diff** (for difference). Then, it would not be difficult to vary the value of **diff**, to make **cntrB** equal **cntrA** plus **diff**, and to check **cntrA** and **cntrB** separately to see if either of them is greater than 9. Of course, you would also need to check **diff** to make sure it did not become too large.

With these changes, the stripped-down version of the addition module that you looked at previously would be as follows:

```
cntrA = 0;
diff = 1;
cntrB = cntrA + diff;

while(1==1)
    {
    printf("%d + %d = ",nmbr[cntrA],nmbr[cntrB]);
    scanf("%d",&answer);
    if(answer==nmbr[cntrA]+nmbr[cntrB]
        {
        printf("\nRIGHT!!");
        }
    else
        {
        printf("\nwrong");
        continue;
        }


    cntrA = cntrA + 2;
    if(cntrA>9)
        {
        cntrA = cntrA - 10;
        diff = diff + 1;
        }
    if(diff>9)
        {
        diff = 2;
        }
    cntrB = cntrA + diff;
    if(cntrB>9)
        {
        cntrB = cntrB - 10;
        }
    }
```

The logic here is not all that difficult to follow, but it is worthwhile to look at it carefully because much of what computer programmers do involves thinking up clever ways of writing code to eliminate repetitious programming work, as this code does.

The first half of the module does the same thing as the earlier fragmentary example: it displays the problem with the current values of the variables, for example,

```
3 + 5 =
```

followed by a blinking cursor, and then it waits for the answer and checks if the answer is right or wrong.

The entire second half of the program is devoted to changing the value of the variables. The first time through, the program would just make **cntrA** equal 2 and **cntrB** equal 3, and the other conditions would not apply. The fifth time through, however, after the program goes through the entire list once, **cntrA** would be equal to 10, so the first **if()** condition would apply. **cntrA** would be made 0 again, and **diff** would be made 2. The second **if()** condition would not apply, so **cntrB** would remain 9, and the problem would be **nmbr[0]** plus **nmbr[9]**, a combination you did not have before. The next time through, **cntrA** would be incremented by the usual 2, so it would increase from 0 to 2, but since **diff** has been increased from 1 to 2, the statement **cntrB = cntrA + diff;** would make **cntrB** equal to 4 this time; the problem would be **nmbr[2] + nmbr[4]**, another combination you did not have before. So the program would go, with new combinations coming up all the time. Trace in your own mind how the combinations go as **diff** becomes larger at the end of every five loops.

Again, this is just a stripped-down version of the addition module, used to show its logic. The actual module will have a better screen display, and the user will even have the option of exiting rather than remaining in this infinite loop forever. (Ironically, there is a nationally distributed public domain program that is a bit like this one. It has at least a dozen options on the main menu but does not include the option of leaving the program and returning to DOS. It is written in BASIC, and you can only get out of it if you know enough, first, to press ESCAPE to get back to the BASIC interpreter and, second, to enter the SYSTEM command to get out of BASIC and back into DOS. If you do not happen to know the SYSTEM command, your only choice is to turn off your computer.)

The Arithmetic Operators

Before you write this program, you will need to learn the **arithmetic operators** in C. Most of these operators will look familiar to you: in fact, you have already been using one, + for addition, without even thinking about it. The arithmetic operators are as follows:

+ addition
− subtraction
* multiplication
/ division
% modulo division (remainder)

These symbols are the same ones used in most computer languages and in programs such as spreadsheets. The symbols for the four basic operations are for the most part the same ones you used in elementary arithmetic, the exception being that the asterisk * is used for multiplication instead of the usual times sign (×) in order to avoid confusion with the letter "x."

Modulo division is the only symbol that needs any explanation, and it simply gives you what elementary school teachers call the "remainder" from division. For example, **20 % 6** is equal to **2**. That is, 20 divided by 6 is 3 with a remainder of 2; and the equation **20 % 6** gives you just the remainder from the division equation.

Keep in mind that the result of the division problem depends on whether the number you are dividing is declared as an integer or a float. For example, the following program would print **10.000000 / 3.000000 = 3.333333** on the screen, which is just what you would expect if you remembered that the default display for floats is six decimal points.

```
/* CHAPTER 3, EXAMPLE 4 */
#include <stdio.h>

main()                      /* sample of float division */
{
float dividend, divisor, answer;
dividend = 10;
divisor = 3;
answer = dividend/divisor;
printf("\n%f / %f = %f",dividend,divisor,answer);
}
```

On the other hand, this next program would print **10 / 3 = 3** on the screen. It works only with integer values and drops any decimals.

```
/* CHAPTER 3, EXAMPLE 5 */
#include <stdio.h>

main()                      /* sample of integer division */
{
int dividend, divisor, answer;
dividend = 10;
divisor = 3;
answer = dividend/divisor;
printf("\n%d / %d = %d",dividend,divisor,answer);
}
```

There are times when programmers actually want only integer results, but in this simple quiz program, you will use a method that gives the remainder as well, something like the following:

```
/* CHAPTER 3, EXAMPLE 6 */
#include <stdio.h>

main()                      /* sample of integer division */
{                                   /* with remainder */
int dvidnd, dvisr, answr, remndr;

dvidnd = 10;
dvisr = 3;
answr = dvidnd / dvisr;
remndr = dvidnd % dvisr;
printf("\n%d / %d = %d  R %d", dvidnd,dvisr,answr,remndr);
}
```

This program will print **10 / 3 = 3 R 1** on the screen.

There is one other term about computer arithmetic that probably needs clarification. In computer jargon, this term is **precedence of operation**, which means deciding what operation to perform first. In ordinary arithmetic, for example, you might interpret the following problem in two different ways:

```
3 * 4 + 1 =
```

You could multiply 3 times 4 first, getting 12, and than add 1 for a final answer of 13. Or you could add 4 plus 1 first, getting 5, and then multiply by 3 for a final answer of 15. Precedence makes a difference: if you multiply first, you will not receive the same answer you will if you add first.

In arithmetic, you can either add or multiply first. In algebra, however, there is a set order of precedence, which you probably know without thinking about it. For example, if you knew that **n = 4**, you would, without any hesitation, say that the value of **3n + 1** is equal to **13**. In algebra, you generally perform multiplication and division before addition and subtraction.

The same is true in C and in most computer languages and applications you will ever come across. The problem **3 * 4 + 1** does not have two different answers: the answer is 13 because C gives precedence to multiplication and division over addition and subtraction. First it multiplies 3 times 4 to get 12; then it adds 1 to that result for a final answer of 13.

You can alter this order of precedence in C by using parentheses, just as you can in ordinary mathematics. For example, in mathematics, if the problem were **(3 * 4) + 1 =**, you would know that you had to perform the multiplication first so that the answer is 13; but if the problem were **3 * (4 + 1) =**, you would know that you had to perform the addition first, with the result being 15. You can also use parentheses this way in C and in most computer languages and applications to control precedence. If you rewrote the previous C formula as **3 * (4 + 1)**, the answer would be the expected 15.

It is generally better programming style to use parentheses in any complex calculation, even if they just tell the computer to do things in the same order as it would through its normal order of precedence. Such notation will make things easier to understand for any humans who must read the program at a later time For example, **(3 * 4) + 1** is better style than **3 * 4 + 1**, even though the answers are the same.

Incidentally, you can also use parentheses with logical operators to alter precedence. For example, **if(x= =1 && (y= =2 || z= =3))** would be true only if it is true that **x= =1** *and* it is also true that either **y= =2** or **z= =3**. On the other hand, **if((x= =1 && y= =2) || z= =3)** would be true if it is true both that **x= =1** and that **y= =2** *or* it is true that **z= =3**. Without parentheses, the **&&** has precedence, but with logical conditions, it is always better to use parentheses to reduce — if not avoid — confusion.

Global and Local Variables

Before you begin to write the arithmetic quiz program, there is one more very basic programming concept you will need to handle this program's variables. In all of the programs you have looked at so far, each variable has been used by only one function. In this program, there are variables that will be used by many functions. The array of numbers must be given values by the **initlze()** function and must also be accessible to the functions that display the addition, subtraction, multiplication, and division problems.

Ordinary variables, the type you have used so far, are not shared between modules in this way, and the reason is fairly obvious. Because C is a structured language, it is necessary to keep modules as independent from each other as possible. This is particularly important in making it an extensible language, which you can add to by writing libraries of new functions. Often, programmers work with libraries of functions that they have not studied in detail, just as you have used the functions such as **printf**() and **scanf**() without looking at the details of how they are written. What if one of these functions happens to have a variable with the same name as one of the variables in another module you were writing?

If the variables in each function were not strictly segregated from each other, the results could be disastrous. For example, consider the program from the beginning of this chapter, which had the user enter a worker's wages for each week of the year. Imagine that you suddenly remember that you wrote a function called **clrscrn**() for another project a few months before and put it into a library, that you decide the wage entry program would look nicer if it cleared the screen after each week's wages, and that you write an **#include** statement so you can use that library and function in the program.

If you wrote both the new program and the library function together, so you could look at them more closely, the code would look like the following:

```
/* CHAPTER 3, EXAMPLE 7 */

#include <stdio.h>
main()                  /* enter wages for each week */
{                       /* written with clrscrn() */
float wageWk[52];
int cntr, numOfWks;

printf("\nHow many weeks of wages do you want to enter? ");
scanf("%d",&numOfWks);
```

continued...

...from previous page

```
cntr = 0;
while(cntr < numOfWks && cntr < 52)
     {
     printf("Enter the wage for week %d > ",cntr+1);
     scanf("%f",&wageWk[cntr]);
     cntr = cntr + 1;
     clrscrn();
     }
}


clrscrn()                    /* clear the screen */
{
int cntr;

cntr = 0;
while(cntr < 25)
     {
     printf("\n");
     cntr = cntr + 1;
     }
}
```

Within this program, you have set up a nice little loop to read the wage for every week, incrementing the variable **cntr** each time through to control the loop, but you cannot be expected to remember that **clrscrn**() also used the variable **cntr**.

If variables in different modules were not segregated from each other, this program would be a mess. At the end of each loop in the **main**() module, **clrscrn**() would be used and would leave **cntr** equal to 25. Starting with the second time through, the program would go on endlessly asking for the wages for week 26 and storing the input in **wageWk[25]**. It would always satisfy the condition of the main loop, **while**(**cntr** < **52**), so it would never terminate. Or if the user entered a number of weeks that is less than 25, the other half of the condition of the main loop, **while**(**cntr** < **numOfWks**), would not be satisfied, and the program would end without getting wages for a second week. The problem is easy to see in this short program, but you can imagine how difficult it could be to find and debug problems like this in a program that is 50 pages long, if variables in different functions were not strictly segregated from each other.

In reality, however, these variables are segregated from each other, so anything done to a variable in one function will have no effect on its value in other functions, and this example program would not have any problems at all. The value of the variable **cntr** in the **clrscrn**() module has absolutely no effect on the value of the variable **cntr** in the **main**() module, so **main**() will run just as it was intended to. You should compile and run this program — even though it just gets 52 numbers from you and does nothing else with them — to impress that fact on your mind. Intuitively, you would tend to think that every time the variable **cntr** is used in this program, it refers to the same thing; it is important to fully realize that, in this program, **cntr** is the name of two entirely different variables.

Variables of this type, which exist only within their own functions, are called **local variables** for the obvious reason that they exist only locally in one part of the program. The opposite of a **local variable** is a **global variable**, which can be used by any module of the program. The way in which you make a variable global is quite simple and reasonable. As you have seen many times, a **local variable**, which is used only by one function, is declared in that function after its opening curly bracket. By contrast, a **global variable**, which can be used by the whole program and is not confined to one function, is declared outside of any function, before the program begins, above the **main**() function.

Look again at the example of local variables in the program that was just given to enter weekly wages for a year. In both modules of that program, the statement **int cntr;** that declares the variable is enclosed within the curly brackets of the function, and the declaration creates a **local variable** that exists only in that function and has no connection with any other variables of the same name that might exist in other functions.

By contrast, when you are writing the arithmetic quiz program, you will need to begin it with the following:

```
int nmbr[10]

main()
{
DECLARATION OF VARIABLES
MANY LINES OF CODE
}

addtest()
{
DECLARATION OF VARIABLES
MANY LINES OF CODE
}
```

The variables declared within each function will be local, but the declaration **int nmbr[10];** creates an array of global variables that can be used by any function. It should be easy for you to remember that if a variable is declared within a function, it works only in that function, and if a variable is declared at the top of the program, it applies to all functions.

Writing the Code

You have already written a version of the **initlze()** module of this program, which gives values to the variables in the array. The other modules should be easy to write.

The **main()** module is just a menu similar to the one used by the ASCCHRT program. It gives users the choice of taking tests in addition, subtraction, multiplication, or division or quitting the program. It then uses a **scanf()** statement to get the user's input and assign that input to a variable. The program then uses an **if-else-if** ladder to branch to the program that runs the test that the user chose. As in the final ASCCHRT program, this menu is placed within a loop so that, after finishing one test, the user has the option of choosing another test or quitting the program.

The only new point about this part of the program is that an array of global variables is declared before the main module begins and the variables are initialized before the menu is presented, as follows:

```
/* AN ARITHMETIC QUIZ PROGRAM */

nmbr[10]                /* array of numbers used by all */
                        /* modules */
main()
{
char choice;
initlze();              /* initialize array of numbers */
while(1==1)
    {
    printf("\n\n\n\t\t\tARITHMETIC QUIZ");
    printf("\n\n\n\n\n");
    printf("\t\t1 - Addition test\n\n");
    printf("\t\t2 - Subtraction test\n\n");
    printf("\t\t3 - Multiplication test\n\n");
    printf("\t\t4 - Division test\n\n");
    printf("\t\t5 - Quit\n\n");
    printf("\n\n\n\n\n\n\t\t\tWHAT IS YOUR CHOICE > ");
    scanf("\n%c",&choice);

    if(choice=='1')
        {
        addtest();
        }
    else if(choice=='2')
        {
        subtest();
        }
    else if(choice=='3')
        {
        multest();
        }
    else if(choice=='4')
        {
        divtest();
        }
    else if(choice=='5')
        {
        break;
        }
```

continued...

83

...from previous page

```
    else
        {
        printf("%c",7);
        }
    }
}
```

The final **else** of the **if-else-if** ladder is handy for error testing, as always. If the user's choice is not 1, 2, 3, 4, or 5, the computer simply beeps and the program's flow of control loops back up to **while(1==1)** and displays the menu again. Likewise, if any of the tests is chosen, then after that test is done, the program's flow of control returns to **main()** at the point right after the point where the program left it, falls through all the other conditions to the bottom of the **while** loop, loops back to the top, and displays the menu again. The program will **break** out of the loop and return to MS-DOS (or whatever other operating system is being used) only if **5** is chosen from the menu.

You have already developed a stripped-down version of the module that tests for addition while looking at how to change the value of the counters that take you through the array. Look at this fragment again carefully and be sure you understand it:

```
cntrA = 0;
diff = 1;
cntrB = cntrA + diff;

while(1==1)
    {
    printf("%d + %d = ",nmbr[cntrA],nmbr[cntrB]);
    scanf("%d",&answer);
    if(answer==nmbr[cntrA]+nmbr[cntrB]
        {
        printf("\nRIGHT!!");
        }
```

continued...

...from previous page

```
else
     {
     printf("\nwrong");
     continue;
     }

cntrA = cntrA + 2;
if(cntrA>9)
     {
     cntrA = cntrA - 10;
     diff = diff + 1;
     }
if(diff>9)
     {
     diff = 2;
     }
cntrB = cntrA + diff;
if(cntrB>9)
{
cntrB = cntrB - 10;
     }
}
```

If you have forgotten the logic behind this fragment, look again at the discussion of it earlier in this chapter.

Once you understand this fragment, it should be easy for you to grasp the rest of this program. The module that gives the addition test simply adds a better screen display and gives the user the option of quitting after each problem:

```
addtest()                    /* test of addition */
{
int cntrA, cntrB, diff, answer;
char again;

cntrA = 0;
diff = 1;
cntrB = cntrA + diff;

while(1==1)
    {
    printf("\n\n\n\n\n\n");
    printf("\t\t\t\ADDITION QUIZ");
    printf("\n\n\n\n\n\n\n\n\n\n\n\n\n\n\n\n\n\n\n");
    printf("\t%d + %d = ",nmbr[cntrA],nmbr[cntrB]);
    scanf("%d",&answer);
    if(answer==nmbr[cntrA]+nmbr[cntrB])
        {
        printf("\nTHAT IS RIGHT!!");
        }
    else
        {
        printf("\nThat is wrong\n");
        printf("The answer is %d",nmbr[cntrA]+nmbr[cntrB]);
        }
    printf("\n\nDo you want to try another ? Y/N > ");
    scanf("\n%c",&again);

    if(again != 'Y' && again != 'y')
        {
        break;
        }
    else
        {
        cntrA = cntrA + 2;
        if(cntrA>9)
            {
            cntrA = cntrA - 10;
            diff = diff + 1;
            }
```

continued...

...from previous page

```
    if(diff>9)
        {
        diff = 2;
        }
    cntrB = cntrA + diff;
    if(cntrB>9)
        {
        cntrB = cntrB - 10;
        }
    }
}
```

If the answer is wrong, the program displays the right answer. Whether the answer is right or wrong, the program asks users whether they want to try another problem. Then, if the user does not enter a 'Y', either upper- or lowercase, the program's flow of control **break**s out of the loop and returns to the menu in **main**(). If the user does enter a 'Y', the program makes the changes in the value of the counters that were described earlier, and the flow of control loops back to let the user go again. To give the user this choice, you nest the **if** statements used to change the values of the counters within a larger **if-else** that checks whether or not the user wants to go again. This series of nested **if** statements might seem a bit confusing at first, but if you begin by understanding the **if** statements that are used to change the value of the counters, it is not difficult to also understand why the larger **if-else** is added around them.

The subtraction module is almost identical to the addition module. So that the subtraction problems do not just look like repetitions of the addition problems, the initial value of **cntrA** and of **diff** is changed. Also, because a simple arithmetic test should not have questions with negative answers, you use problems only if **nmbr[cntrA]** is larger than **nmbr[cntrB]**. You can do this by using an **if** statement to make the part of the module that displays the problem conditional, as follows:

```
subtest()              /* test of subtraction */
{
int cntrA, cntrB, diff, answer;
char again;

cntrA = 2;
diff = 3;
cntrB = cntrA + diff;

while(1==1)
     {
     if(nmbr[cntrA]<nmbr[cntrB])
     {
     again = 'Y';
     }
else
     {
     printf("\n\n\n\n\n\n\n\n\n");
     printf("\t\t\t\SUBTRACTION QUIZ);
     printf("\n\n\n\n\n\n\n\n\n\n\n");
     printf("\t%d - %d = ",nmbr[cntrA],nmbr[cntrB]);
     scanf("%d",&answer);
     if(answer==nmbr[cntrA]-nmbr[cntrB])
          {
          printf("\nTHAT IS RIGHT!!");
          }
     else
          {
          printf("\nThat is wrong\n");
          printf("The answer is %d",
                      nmbr[cntrA]+nmbr[cntrB]);
          }
     printf("\n\nDo you want to try another? Y/N > ");
     scanf("%c",&again);
     }

if(again != 'Y' && again != 'y')
     {
     break;
     }

     continued...
```

...from previous page

```
else
     {
     cntrA = cntrA + 2;
     cntrB = cntrA + diff;
     if(cntrA>9)
          {
          cntrA = cntrA - 10;
          diff = diff + 1;
          }
     if(cntrB>9)
          {
               cntrB = cntrB - 10;
          }
     if(diff>9)
          {
               diff = 2;
          }
     }
}
```

If **nmbr[cntrA]** is less than **nmbr[cntrB]**, you do not display that problem or get the answer; instead, you just make **again** equal to 'Y' so that the program will change the value of the counters and loop back to the top again. You run through the program as usual only if **nmbr[cntrA]** is greater than **nmbr[cntrB]**. Thus, all the problems that would have a negative answer are filtered out, and only those with a positive answer are displayed.

The multiplication module is virtually identical to the addition module. The division module is similar to the subtraction module but has one more possibility that it must filter out: you do not want users of this simple test to divide a number by a larger number, as with subtraction, and you also must avoid division by zero, which is meaningless mathematically. Furthermore, the division module must get two answers from the user, the answer and the remainder. Look for these changes in the listing of the entire program, which follows:

```
/* CHAPTER 3, EXAMPLE 8 */
/* AN ARITHMETIC QUIZ PROGRAM */
#include <stdio.h>

nmbr[10];               /* ARRAY OF NUMBERS USED BY ALL */
                        /* MODULES */
main()
{
char choice;
initlze();              /* INITIALIZE ARRAY OF NUMBERS */
while(1==1)
    {
    printf("\n\n\n\t\t\tARITHMETIC QUIZ");
    printf("\n\n\n\n\n");
    printf("\t\t1 - Addition test\n\n");
    printf("\t\t2 - Subtraction test\n\n");
    printf("\t\t3 - Multiplication test\n\n");
    printf("\t\t4 - Division test\n\n");
    printf("\t\t5 - Quit\n\n");
    printf("\n\n\n\n\n\n\t\t\tWHAT IS YOUR CHOICE > ");
    scanf("\n%c",&choice);

    if(choice=='1')
        {
        addtest();
        }
    else if(choice=='2')
        {
        subtest();
        }
    else if(choice=='3')
        {
        multest();
        }
    else if(choice=='4')
        {
        divtest();
        }
    else if(choice=='5')
```

continued...

...from previous page

```
        {
        break;
        }
    else
        {
        printf("%c",7);
        }
    }
}
```

```
initlze()
    {
    nmbr[0] = 3;
    nmbr[1] = 5;
    nmbr[2] = 0;
    nmbr[3] = 9;
    nmbr[4] = 6;
    nmbr[5] = 1;
    nmbr[6] = 7;
    nmbr[7] = 2;
    nmbr[8] = 8;
    nmbr[9] = 4;
    }
```

```
addtest()              /* test of addition */
{
int cntrA, cntrB, diff, answer;
char again;

cntrA = 0;
diff = 1;
cntrB = cntrA + diff;
```

continued...

...from previous page

```
while(1==1)
     {
     printf("\n\n\n\n\n\n");
     printf("\t\t\tADDITION QUIZ");
     printf("\n\n\n\n\n\n\n\n\n\n\n\n\n\n\n\n\n\n\n");
     printf("\t\t\t\t%d + %d = ",nmbr[cntrA],nmbr[cntrB]);
     scanf("%d",&answer);
     if(answer==nmbr[cntrA]+nmbr[cntrB])
          {
          printf("\nTHAT IS RIGHT!!");
          }
     else
          {
          printf("\nThat is wrong\n");
          printf("The answer is %d",nmbr[cntrA]+nmbr[cntrB]);
          }
     printf("\n\nDo you want to try another ? Y/N > ");
     scanf("\n%c",&again);

     if(again != 'Y' && again != 'y')
          {
          break;
          }
     else
          {
          cntrA = cntrA + 2;
          if(cntrA>9)
               {
               cntrA = cntrA - 10;
               diff = diff + 1;
               }
          if(diff>9)
               {
               diff = 2;
               }
          cntrB = cntrA + diff;
          if(cntrB>9)
               {
```

continued...

...from previous page

```
              cntrB = cntrB - 10;
              }
        }
    }
}




subtest()              /* test of subtraction */
{
int cntrA, cntrB, diff, answer;
char again;

cntrA = 2;
diff = 3;
cntrB = cntrA + diff;

while(1==1)
     {
     if(nmbr[cntrA]<nmbr[cntrB])
         {
         again = 'Y';
         }
     else
         {
         printf("\n\n\n\n\n\n");
         printf("\t\t\tSUBTRACTION QUIZ");
          printf("\n\n\n\n\n\n\n\n\n\n\n\n\n\n\n\n\n\n\n\n");
         printf("\t\t\t\t%d - %d = ",nmbr[cntrA],nmbr[cntrB]);
         scanf("%d",&answer);
         if(answer==nmbr[cntrA]-nmbr[cntrB])
             {
             printf("\nTHAT IS RIGHT!!");
             }
         else
             {
             printf("\nThat is wrong\n");
             printf("The answer is %d",
                          nmbr[cntrA]+nmbr[cntrB]);
             }
```

continued...

...from previous page

```
          printf("\n\nDo you want to try another ? Y/N > ");
          scanf("\n%c",&again);
          }

     if(again != 'Y' && again != 'y')
          {
          break;
          }
     else
          {
          cntrA = cntrA + 2;
          if(cntrA>9)
               {
               cntrA = cntrA - 10;
               diff = diff + 1;
               }
          if(diff>9)
               {
               diff = 2;
               }
          cntrB = cntrA + diff;
          if(cntrB>9)
               {
               cntrB = cntrB - 10;
               }
          }
     }
}


multest()      /* test of multiplication */
{
int cntrA, cntrB, diff, answer;
char again;

cntrA = 4;
diff = 5;
cntrB = cntrA + diff;
```

continued...

...from previous page

```
while(1==1)
    {
    printf("\n\n\n\n\n\n");
    printf("\t\t\tMULTIPLICATION QUIZ");
    printf("\n\n\n\n\n\n\n\n\n\n\n\n\n\n\n\n\n\n");
    printf("\t\t\t\t%d x %d = ",nmbr[cntrA],nmbr[cntrB]);
    scanf("%d",&answer);
    if(answer==nmbr[cntrA]*nmbr[cntrB])
        {
        printf("\nTHAT IS RIGHT!!");
        }
    else
        {
        printf("\nThat is wrong\n");
        printf("The answer is %d",nmbr[cntrA]*nmbr[cntrB]);
        }
    printf("\n\nDo you want to try another ? Y/N > ");
    scanf("\n%c",&again);

    if(again != 'Y' && again != 'y')
        {
        break;
        }
    else
        {
        cntrA = cntrA + 2;
        if(cntrA>9)
            {
            cntrA = cntrA - 10;
            diff = diff + 1;
            }
        if(diff>9)
            {
            diff = 2;
            }
        cntrB = cntrA + diff;
            }
```

continued...

...from previous page

```
        if(cntrB>9)
            {
            cntrB = cntrB - 10;
            }
        }
    }
}



divtest()            /* test of division */
{
int cntrA, cntrB, diff, answer, remaindr;
char again;

cntrA = 3;
diff = 4;
cntrB = cntrA + diff;

while(1==1)
    {
    if(nmbr[cntrA]<nmbr[cntrB] || nmbr[cntrB] == 0)
        {
        again = 'Y';
        }
    else
        {
        printf("\n\n\n\n\n");
        printf("\t\t\t\DIVISION QUIZ");
         printf("\n\n\n\n\n\n\n\n\n\n\n\n\n\n\n\n\n\n\n");
        printf("\t%d / %d = ",nmbr[cntrA],nmbr[cntrB]);
        printf("\nWhat is the answer > ");
        scanf("%d",&answer);
        printf("\nWhat is the remainder > ");
        scanf("%d",&remaindr);
        if(answer==nmbr[cntrA]/nmbr[cntrB]
                && remaindr ==nmbr[cntrA]%nmbr[cntrB])
            {
            printf("\nTHAT IS RIGHT!!");
            }
```

continued...

...from previous page

```
            else
                  {
                  printf("\nThat is wrong\n");
                  printf("The answer is %d remainder %d",
nmbr[cntrA]/nmbr[cntrB],nmbr[cntrA]%nmbr[cntrB]);
                  }
            printf("\n\nDo you want to try another ? Y/N > ");
            scanf("\n%c",&again);
            }

    if(again != 'Y' && again != 'y')
            {
            break;
            }
    else
            {
            cntrA = cntrA + 2;
            if(cntrA>9)
                  {
                  cntrA = cntrA - 10;
                  diff = diff + 1;
                  }
            if(diff>9)
                  {
                  diff = 2;
                  }
            cntrB = cntrA + diff;
            if(cntrB>9)
                  {
                  cntrB = cntrB - 10;
                  }
            }
      }
}
```

This program should be quite easy for you to understand, largely because it is repetitious. Up to now, this book has generally used this repetitious style of programming—a **main**() menu module calling several similar subordinate modules—as a teaching device because it makes programs easy for beginners to grasp. It is better programming style, however, to break down the modules further and create separate functions to perform repeated tasks. In this program, for example, it would be better style to have a separate function to change the values of the counters, rather than repeat the same code four times (though it would require techniques that you will not learn until Chapter 6), not only because it would be more elegant but also because it would make the program easier to modify and maintain. Now that you have had practice with repetitious code that is easier to understand, you will learn to develop more compact and elegant—and sometimes more cryptic—code in the rest of this book.

One thing you will notice when you run this program is that its screen display leaves something to be desired. As in all of the programs in this book, the display simply scrolls up the screen one line at a time, and the **scanf**() that gets user input is on the bottom line of the screen. In some cases, the screen looks good even with this condition, but in this program, where there is only a heading and an arithmetic problem, the screen looks empty and unbalanced. This is the sort of problem that would be very easy for you to fix after you get a library of screen control functions.

TWO-DIMENSIONAL ARRAYS

The arrays you have looked at so far have just been lists, but it is also possible to create arrays that represent tables. Imagine—to return to the example at the beginning of this chapter—that you did not just want to keep a list of the employee's wages for each week, but instead you wanted a more complete list of the employee's weekly wages, tax deductions, social security deductions, net wages after deductions, and the amount the employer paid for benefits.

You want to keep a record of five different figures for each of the 52 weeks, and you can declare an array to keep track of them as follows:

```
float wageTot[52][5];
```

This creates an array of floats that you can think of as a table that is 52 down and 5 across. Conventionally, the first index number is thought of as the row number and the second as the column number, so this array represents a table with 52 rows and 5 columns.

The computer's memory, however, just consists of a sequence of bytes, each with its own address number, and when you declare this two-dimensional array, the compiler simply reserves enough of these addresses — all in a row — to accommodate all the variables being created. But it is convenient for humans to think of it as a two-dimensional table that looks like the following,

```
                WAGES       TAXES       FICA      NET PAY     BENEFITS
              ----------------------------------------------------------
WEEK  1          |           |           |           |
              ---------+-----------+-----------+-----------+-----------
WEEK  2          |           |           |           |
              ---------+-----------+-----------+-----------+-----------
WEEK  3          |           |           |           |
              ---------+-----------+-----------+-----------+-----------
WEEK  4          |           |           |           |
```

and so on, down to week 52. Once you visualize the array as having two dimensions, it becomes easier to write programs for it.

You can revise the program for entering each week's wages (which you looked at in the beginning of this chapter), for example, by thinking in terms of columns (that hold figures for WAGES, TAXES, etc.) and rows (that hold the different weeks). Remember, the one tricky point is that an array declared as **wageTot[5]** is numbered from **wageTot[0]** to **wageTot[4]**. Then look back at the program at the beginning of the chapter, and it should be easy to understand how the program is revised as follows:

```
/* CHAPTER 3, EXAMPLE 9 */
#include <stdio.h>

float wageTot[52][5];
int numOfWks;

main()                  /* enter wages, taxes, FICA */
{                       /* and benefits  for each week */
int cntr;

printf("\nHow many weeks of data do you want to enter? ");
scanf("%d",&numOfWks);

cntr = 0;
while(cntr < 52 && cntr < numOfWks)
     {
     printf("Enter the gross wages for week %d > ",cntr+1);
     scanf("%f",&wageTot[cntr][0]);

     printf("Enter the taxes deducted for week %d > ",cntr+1);
     scanf("%f",&wageTot[cntr][1]);

     printf("Enter the FICA deducted for week %d > ",cntr+1);
     scanf("%f",&wageTot[cntr][2]);

     wageTot[cntr][3] = wageTot[cntr][0] - wageTot[cntr][1] -
                                          wageTot[cntr][2];

     printf("Enter the benefits paid for week %d > ",cntr+1);
     scanf("%f",&wageTot[cntr][4]);

     cntr = cntr + 1;
     }
}
```

Note that the array that holds the wages and the variable that holds the number of weeks are declared as global variables, so other modules added to this program can have access to the data. The net wages for each week (**wageTot[cntr][3]**) are calculated by taking the gross wages for that week (**wageTot[cntr][0]**) and subtracting from it the tax deductions for that week (**wageTot[cntr][1]**) and the FICA deductions for that week (**wageTot[cntr][2]**).

It becomes easier to manipulate the figures when you think of them as being in the form of a table. For example, if you wanted to total an employee's FICA deductions for the year, you could do it by adding this module to the previous example, and adding the command **totfica();** before the final }.

```
/* CHAPTER 3, EXAMPLE 10 */
/* to be used with CHAPTER 3, EXAMPLE 9 */
/* add the statement totfica(); before its final } */
/* and add this function after its final } */

totfica()
{
int cntr;
float sum;

cntr = 0;
sum = 0;
while(cntr < 52 && cntr < numOfWks)
      {
      sum = sum + wageTot[cntr][2];
      cntr = cntr + 1;
      }
printf("\n\nTotal FICA is %f\n\n",sum);
}
```

This example takes advantage of the fact that **wageTot[52][5]** was declared as a global array, not as part of the **main()** module, so that all modules can access it.

Similarly, it is easy to look up the record for an employee for a particular week, as follows:

```
/* CHAPTER 3, EXAMPLE 11 */
/* to be used with CHAPTER 3, EXAMPLE 9 */
/* add the command lookupwk(); before its final } */
/* and add this function after its final } */

lookupwk()
{
int wkToFind;

printf("\nWhat number week do you want to find > ");
scanf("%d",&wkToFind);
if(wkToFind < 1 || wkToFind > 52 || wkToFind > numOfWks)
    {
    printf("%c",7);
    }
else
    {
    wkToFind = wkToFind - 1;
    printf("\nGross Wages: %f",wageTot[wkToFind][0]);
    printf("\nTaxes: %f",wageTot[wkToFind][1]);
    printf("\nFICA: %f",wageTot[wkToFind][2]);
    printf("\nNet Wages: %f",wageTot[wkToFind][3]);
    printf("\nBenefits: %f",wageTot[wkToFind][4]);
    }
}
```

Again, the only trick about this program is remembering to subtract 1 from the week number the user enters to get the week number the computer uses, because humans begin numbering with 1 and the computer begins numbering with 0. An actual program would not just get the wages, then sum the FICA payments, then let the user look up one week, then terminate. These steps are put in sequence purely as an example of ways of using two-dimensional arrays. As an exercise, you might want to rewrite the program as a menu-driven system.

So far, these examples have used a variable to represent the row and constants to represent the columns. Things do get more complicated when you want to use two counters, one for the rows and one for the columns of the array. For example, imagine that you wanted to print out all the wage data for one employee for a year. You could declare two variables as follows:

```
int rowCntr, colCntr;
```

Then, after printing out a heading that includes the words GROSS WAGES, TAXES, FICA, NET WAGES, and BENEFITS, carefully spaced so they will appear above the proper columns, you could print out the entire year's figures in tabular form with the following code:

```
rowCntr = 0;
while(rowCntr<52)
{
printf("\n\nweek %d:",rowCntr+1);
colCntr = 0;
while(colCntr<5)
     {
     printf("\t\t%f",wageTot[rowCntr][colCntr]);
     colCntr = colCntr + 1;
     }
rowCntr = rowCntr +1;
}
```

This program is elegant and concise. The first time through, when **rowCntr** equals 0, it will begin by printing **week 1:** on a new line. Then it will make **colCntr** equal 0 and will print, on the same line but after tabs, **wageTot[0] [0]**, the gross wage for the first week. Then the program will make **colCntr** equal 1 and will print, on the same line but after tabs, **wageTot[0] [1]**, the taxes for the first week. The program will keep incrementing **colCntr** and print all the values for the first week across the first line. Then, when **colCntr** equals 5, the program will break out of the inner loop, make **rowCntr** equal to 1, loop back up to the top of the outer loop, print **week 2:** on a new line, and go through the inner loop another five times, printing the values for the second week across the line. And it will keep doing this until **rowCntr** equals 52, meaning that it has printed out all 52 weeks worth of data.

You can see how powerful a two-dimensional array can be, and how much it can do with just a few lines of programming, but you can also see that a two-dimensional array can be a bit hard to follow. Beyond that, there are higher dimensional arrays. For example, this company probably does not have just one employee. If the company has 100 employees and you want to keep these same records for each employee, you could declare the following three-dimensional array:

```
float wageTot[100][52][5];
```

That declaration will create 100 of the 5-column-by-52-row table you have been working with. You would be able to print out yearly records for all the workers, using the same program you just looked at with only a few lines added to create an outer loop that prints the worker number (from 1 to 100) and a heading and, after all 52 rows were printed for that worker, adds 1 to the worker number and does it again and again until all 100 tables are printed out. Just a few extra lines of code, less than two dozen lines in all, and you have a program that will print out hundreds of pages of data.

SUMMARY

To declare an **array**, you can use a statement such as the following:

```
char samplAry[100];
```

This statement creates 100 character variables, with names ranging from **samplAry[0]** to **samplAry[99]**. Each of these variables is called an element of the array. It is important to remember that, because the declaration gives the total number of elements in the array and the elements are numbered beginning with 0, the subscript of the highest numbered element of the array is 1 less than the number in the declaration.

You can create arrays of any data type. The declaration simply consists of the data type and the name of the variable with the number of elements in the array enclosed in square brackets (and ends with a semicolon, like any declaration).

It is also possible to create higher dimensional arrays. For example, the declaration,

```
char samplAry[100][5];
```

will create an array with 500 elements, numbered from **samplAry[0][0]** to **samplAry[99][4]**. It is easiest to think of two-dimensional arrays as tables. The example above could be be visualized as a table with 5 columns across and 100 rows down. The following declaration,

```
char samplAry[20][100][5];
```

would create a three-dimensional array with 10,000 elements.

The arithmetic operators are as follows:

+   addition
−   subtraction
*   multiplication
/   division
%   modulo division (remainder)

Modulo division (%) gives the remainder of integer division.

When arithmetic operations are evaluated, multiplication and division are given precedence over addition and subtraction, so **3 * 4 + 1** would be evaluated as 13. It is possible to alter the precedence by using parentheses: **3 * (4 + 1)** would be evaluated as 15. The addition would have precedence because it is enclosed in parentheses.

Parentheses can also be used to alter the precedence of logical operators. For example, **x= =1 && (y= =2 || z= =3)** would be evaluated as true only if it is true that x equals 1 *and* it is true that either y equals 2 or z equals 3. On the other hand, **(x= =1 && y= =2) || z= =3** would be evaluated as true if it is true that x equals 1 and y equals 2 *or* it is true that z equals 3. If **z= =3** was the only one of these three statements that was true, then the first example would be evaluated as false and the second would be evaluated as true. Without parentheses, **&&** has precedence over **||** in C, but it is best to always use parentheses in complex logical conditions to minimize confusion.

Earlier programs in this book used only **local variables**, which are known only to the module that declares them. It is also possible to create **global variables** that are known to all the modules of a program. **Global variables** are declared at the beginning of the program, before the **main**() module begins; **local variables** are declared within the curly brackets of the module they are used by. If two modules have **local variables** with the same name, the program will consider them to be totally different variables; this makes C a more structured and extensible language.

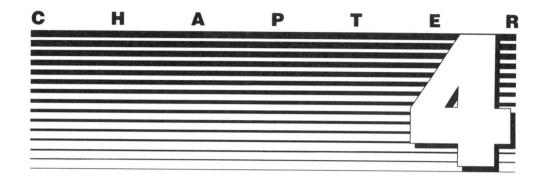

C H A P T E R

4

WORKING WITH ARRAYS: TIC-TAC-TOE

ANALYZING THE PROGRAMMING PROBLEM

Because higher dimensional arrays are powerful but a bit difficult to master, this chapter will give you more practice with them by developing a program that plays tic-tac-toe. You will simply use a two-dimensional array of nine characters — **char sqr[3][3];** — to represent the nine squares of the tic-tac-toe board. Before the game begins, the program will initialize each of the nine elements of the array with a blank. As the game goes on, it will make these elements equal to X's and O's, and it will check to see if either side won the game; if **sqr[0][0]**, **sqr[1][0]**, and **sqr[2][0]** are all equal to X, for example, then X wins.

In addition to being more fun to write than a program that keeps records of workers' wages, a tic-tac-toe program is more complex than any of the programs you have worked on so far in this book. Earlier programs in this book were simple enough to write off the top of your head, without planning them out in advance. This tic-tac-toe program is complex enough to serve as a good introduction to the type of analysis programmers generally perform before beginning the actual work of writing code.

In some large-scale corporate applications, analysis is a complex process performed by many people using an elaborate division of labor; often analysis takes more time than the programming itself does. But most work with microcomputers uses a relatively simple and natural method of analysis based on a **top-down** approach using **pseudocode**.

The **top-down** approach involves looking at the problem as a whole and breaking it up into its larger component parts before breaking it down further and looking at the details of how each part works. Earlier chapters in this book tended to develop programs using a **bottom-up** approach, looking at individual details first — for example, at the addition module of the arithmetic flashcards or at the utility that gives the ASCII value of characters — and building them up into more complex programs. Often, this strategy resulted in repetitive code, with many modules that were copied from one another with only slight variations. The bottom-up method is an excellent way of introducing programming concepts to beginners, who need to study some of the individual trees before they can look at the whole forest. By now, you are advanced enough that you can learn to analyze the program as a whole and come up with a final version of it that is more complex, more elegant, and easier to modify and maintain than earlier programs.

Writing **pseudocode** is simply a matter of thinking about the problem you have to work on in the same step-by-step way that you use in computer programming, but without worrying about every detail the program will have to take care of or about the exact syntax of the programming language. It is very much like an artist drawing a rough sketch of a painting that he will be working on: the idea is to get all the basic shapes in the right place without worrying about the fine details or the colors. It is easy for the artist to modify the sketch as he sees what the composition of the whole picture will be; and it is easy for programmers to modify the pseudocode as they see what the whole program will look like and how best to break it down into modules. In any real programming job, the time you spend in analysis will be amply repaid in the time you save in debugging and rewriting your final program.

Using a top-down approach, you would start with pseudocode that describes the flow of the whole program, and then you would work out more and more detailed pseudocode, which might ultimately need very little adjustment to be translated into the final program — just as the artist might work on more and more detailed sketches that come closer and closer to the final picture. This process naturally fits in with structured programming, which encourages a top-down approach: the first rough sketch of the program corresponds to the **main**() module, and the details are handled in the other modules.

What, then, does a tic-tac-toe program need to do? Much of it, obviously, is a matter of getting moves from the opponent, making moves yourself, seeing if the opponent has a chance to win, and seeing if there is a chance for you to win. Think about what you do more clearly, in terms of the step-by-step logic that computers use, and your first attempt at pseudocode could look like the following:

```
REPEAT UNTIL THE END OF THE GAME:
    GET A MOVE FROM THE OPPONENT
    CHECK TO SEE IF THE OPPONENT HAS WON
    IF SO
        DISPLAY THE UPDATED BOARD
        CONGRATULATE HIM
        END THE GAME
    OTHERWISE
        CHECK TO SEE IF YOU CAN WIN
        IF SO
            MAKE THE MOVE THAT WINS
            DISPLAY THE UPDATED BOARD
            END THE GAME
        OTHERWISE
            CHECK TO SEE IF OPPONENT CAN WIN
            IF SO
                BLOCK HIM
            OTHERWISE
                MAKE SOME MOVE
            DISPLAY THE UPDATED BOARD.
```

Writing this pseudocode is simply a matter of thinking systematically about what you actually do when you are playing tic-tac-toe and it is your turn to move. First, you see if the opponent has won. If not, you see if there is anywhere you can move to win. If not, you see if the opponent is threatening to win and if you need to block him. Only after doing all these things do you look for another possible move. Add to these thoughts the things the computer must do, such as displaying the screen, and you create a sketch of the program.

In an actual game, however, you do all the thinking you need in an instant and do not even know what sequence you are considering these issues in. You need to think for a while about what you actually do in a game before you realize, for example, that you check if you can win first and then see if you need to block your opponent from winning.

When you first are working on pseudocode, you might well jot the tasks down in the wrong order or leave out a task. Then, as you look through the pseudocode again, you will suddenly realize that you made a mistake and will correct it. Do not let this worry you; it is a trait you will share with virtually every other computer programmer in the world. It is important to remember that analysis is what is called an "iterative" process — just the programmer's way of saying that you need to go through the pseudocode again and again and figure out more things about it each time.

Even from the bit of pseudocode from the previous example you can see that there should probably be a separate module to display the board and another that can check for an actual or potential win for either X or O so that you do not need to write the same code twice.

As you consider the pseudocode and think about what to do next, it becomes clear that you must choose whether you want the program to be able to play both X and O or just one. For the sake of simplicity, make it play only X for now. It is also obvious that you need to start off the pseudocode by filling all the squares with blanks. And there is no need to check for wins after the first move: the opponent can threaten to win only after his second move, and you can have the chance of winning only when your third move comes, so you can have a separate set of commands for the earliest moves. The best initial move for X is to move to the center.

Note that in addition to checking for wins, you must handle the possibility of a draw, which is actually more than just a possibility because most tic-tac-toe games end in a draw. One way of checking for a draw would be to scan the whole board and see if all the spaces are filled, but it is easier just to count the moves. If you and your opponent make nine moves and fill all the squares without either of you winning, then you have a draw. Because you have X and make the first move, any draw would occur after your move, so that is when the program should check the move counter.

At some point, probably after you have rewritten the pseudocode several times, you will realize that when you get the opponent's move in the program, he might enter a number greater than 8 or might enter the number of a square that is already filled. So you not only need to get the move, but you do need to check it for validity and, if it is invalid, give the user an error message and get another move. You could become aware of this type of problem at any time. You simply must go back to your editor and revise the pseudocode accordingly. Analysis really just means looking at the problem again and again, and writing down your ideas until you have the process all clear in your mind. It is easier to correct your errors in the planning phase than when you are actually writing code.

Finally, the program should end by asking the opponent if he wants to play another game. To do this, you will put the whole program inside of a loop—a second, larger loop in addition to the central loop that *REPEATS UNTIL THE END OF THE GAME*. If the opponent wants to play another game, you loop the opponent back to the beginning; if not, you **break;** him out of the large loop.

If you add these features to the pseudocode, you get the following:

REPEAT WHILE THE USER WANTS TO KEEP PLAYING:
    MAKE ALL NINE SQUARES EQUAL TO BLANK
    PUT AN 'X' IN THE CENTRAL SQUARE
    DISPLAY THE BOARD
    GET A MOVE FROM THE OPPONENT
    MAKE SOME MOVE
    DISPLAY THE BOARD
    MAKE THE MOVE COUNTER EQUAL TO THREE
    REPEAT UNTIL THE END OF THE GAME:
        GET A MOVE FROM THE OPPONENT
        ADD ONE TO THE MOVE COUNTER
        CHECK TO SEE IF THE OPPONENT HAS WON
        IF SO
            DISPLAY THE UPDATED BOARD
            CONGRATULATE HIM
            END THE GAME
        OTHERWISE
            CHECK TO SEE IF YOU CAN WIN
            IF SO
                MAKE THE WINNING MOVE
                DISPLAY THE UPDATED BOARD
                END THE GAME
            OTHERWISE
                CHECK TO SEE IF OPPONENT CAN WIN
                IF SO
                    BLOCK HIM
                OTHERWISE
                    MAKE SOME MOVE
                DISPLAY THE UPDATED BOARD.
                ADD ONE TO THE MOVE COUNTER.
                IF THE MOVE COUNTER EQUALS NINE
                    END THE GAME AS A DRAW
  AFTER THE END OF THE GAME,
  ASK IF THE OPPONENT WANTS TO PLAY ANOTHER GAME.

Some programmers would then analyze the program in more detail and write more specific pseudocode, but most would consider the pseudocode above to be adequate.

Now, you need to analyze some of the repeated tasks that will go into separate modules. To display the board, it is probably best to use the underline and the "pipe" character (|) above the backslash on your keyboard. The program would actually look better if you used the graphics characters that are in the extended ASCII character set of the IBM-PC, but using the underline and pipe is a bit simpler and is portable to other systems. The board will look something like the following when it is time for the opponent's first move:

```
                   COLUMN
                 1   2   3

         1        |   |
   R           -----------
   O     2        | X |
   W           -----------
         3        |   |


   Which row do you put your 'O' in?
          Enter a number from 1 to 3 >
```

After the column number is entered, the program will ask for the row number in the same way.

Analysis in this case consists mainly of fiddling around with your editor until you get a nice looking screen and then counting how many tabs, spaces, and skipped lines you used to get the effect you wanted. In the program, you will simply use a series of **printf()** statements to display this screen line by line.

With the screen sketched out, writing the module to check if the opponent has actually won is relatively simple. You just need to write a long series of conditions, similar to the following:

```
IF SQR[0][0] = 'O' AND SQR[0][1] = 'O' AND SQR[0[2]] = 'O'
      'O' WINS
OTHERWISE,
IF SQR[1][0] = 'O' AND SQR[1][1] = 'O' AND SQR[1][2] = 'O'
      'O' WINS
```

Continue the list with the other row and the three columns and end with the diagonals:

```
OTHERWISE,
IF SQR[0][0] = 'O' AND SQR[1][1] = 'O' AND SQR[2][2] = 'O'
      'O' WINS
OTHERWISE,
IF SQR[0][2] = 'O' AND SQR[1][1] = 'O' AND SQR[2][0] = 'O'
      'O' WINS
```

You also need to have this module check for 'X' winning as well as for 'O' winning. When you actually write the code, you will see how to check for a winner, and you will also use loops to replace some of the repetition in the pseudocode.

The module to get a valid move is similar enough to parts of other programs you have looked at that the pseudocode should come easily:

```
REPEAT UNTIL THE MOVE IS VALID:
      GET A MOVE
      IF THE COLUMN IS LESS THAN '0' OR MORE THAN '2'
      OR IF THE ROW IS LESS THAN '0' OR MORE THAN '2'
      OR IF THE SQUARE IS NOT A BLANK
            GIVE THE USER AN ERROR MESSAGE
      OTHERWISE
            THE MOVE IS VALID
```

You simply do not let the user out of the loop if there is something wrong with the move he or she enters.

The module to check for future wins will be developed later in the chapter. The only other statement that is repeated in the pseudocode frequently enough that it obviously needs a module of its own is the vague *MAKE SOME MOVE*, which is executed when none of the other conditions applies. For this execution to take place, the module can simply go through all the squares on the board and put an 'X' in the first blank square it finds. Because it is usually a better strategy to move in the corner squares, the *MAKE SOME MOVE* module will look at these squares first. Finally, though it is not repeated, the code will be clearer if you write a separate module to *MAKE ALL NINE SQUARES EQUAL TO BLANK*; this module also will just go through all the squares.

PASSING PARAMETERS

The pseudocode is now at a point where you can begin translating it into an actual C language program. First, however, you must learn one more basic programming concept, which you will need to handle the variables in this program.

So far, you have learned about **global** and **local variables**. In this program, the variables that represent the board, **sqr[0][0]** through **sqr[2][2]**, must be used by almost all of the modules in the program and should be **global**. Most variables within the modules will be **local**.

But there are also variables in this program that need to be used by only two modules. For example, instead of writing one set of modules to check for wins and potential wins for 'X' and another set to check for 'O', suppose the analysis came up with the idea of using a variable called **toCheck,** which can be made to equal either 'X' or 'O', so the same modules can check both. This **toCheck** variable would need to be given the value of 'X' or 'O' by the **main**() module, which controls the order in which wins are checked, and then that value would need to be passed to the module that does the checking. This value passing could be done by making **toCheck** a global variable, but it is much better programming style to use what is called a **parameter**, a local variable that is passed between functions.

The way parameters are passed from one function to another in C may seem a bit strange at first, but it should become clear that such parameter passing is necessary, like the segregation of local variables, to make the language fully structured and extensible.

Imagine, for example, that for some reason you wanted to write a function that would add integers, which might be called **addint**(). Following is how the function would be used with a simplified **main**() module.

```
/* CHAPTER 4, EXAMPLE 1 */
#include <stdio.h>

main()                      /* sample program */
{                           /* passing parameters */
int numbr1, numbr2, total;
numbr1 = 5;
numbr2 = 3;
total = addint(numbr1,numbr2);
printf("%d plus %d equals %d",numbr1,numbr2,total);
}


addint(x,y)                 /* add two integers */
int x,y;
{
return x + y;
}
```

Note that you declare the parameters of **addint**() — the variables that appear within the parentheses of the function — after the name of the function but before the opening curly bracket that begins the body of the function. These variables are known as **formal arguments**. (Chapter 8 will discuss another way of declaring these formal arguments.) By contrast, the arguments of **addint** that are used within **main**() (or within any function that calls **addint**()) are known as **actual arguments**, and are declared within the curly brackets of the function, like any other variables.

You now know all three locations where variables can be declared. **Local variables**, used only in one function, are declared within the body of that function. **Global variables**, used by all functions, are declared at the very top of the program, outside of any function. And **parameters**, which are passed between functions, appear between the name and the body of the function they are passed to; these are actually ordinary local variables within the function that passes them (the **main**() function in the example) and are **parameters** of the function they are passed to, where they appear within the parentheses following the function they are passed to. These declarations are all in plausible places; their locations pretty much convey how that type of variable fits in the program.

Parameters are declared as ordinary local variables within the function that calls another function. The names of the variables in the two functions are not related to each other. The values of the variables in the calling function are copied into the parameters of the function that is called. What initially seems strange about passing parameters is that the names of the variables in the function that does the passing (**main**() in the example) are different from the variable names in the function they are passed to. If you think about it, you will see that this difference is absolutely necessary for C to work as an extensible, structured language. If you write a library of functions to perform special mathematical calculations, for example, the people who use this library should not be forced to change the names of all the variables in their programs to match the variable names in your library. Even if you are developing a large program by yourself, it is very handy to be able to concentrate on the module you are writing without having to worry about all the variable names in the rest of the program. It might be useful to be able to borrow a function from a program you wrote before without needing to change the variable names. COBOL is a miserable language to program in because it requires you to declare all the variables for the entire program before you begin writing any of its modules; it has only global variables, which is why it is not a genuinely structured language — and why everyone is trying hard to abandon it.

You could use the same name for the parameter in both modules if you wanted to, and the program would work, but the compiler would not be affected by the fact that the parameters have the same name. The variables in the two modules are segregated from each other, like local variables. The program would work regardless of the fact that the variables had the same name, just as the example that used local variables to enter weekly wages worked regardless of the fact that variables in two modules both happened to be named **counter**. It is best to use different names for stylistic reasons, to remind you that variables in different modules are segregated from each other and that parameters must be passed back and forth explicitly.

The example of **addint**() makes it very clear how variables are passed to a function as its parameters: you simply use that function (in this case, **addint**()) with the variables you want it to work on, and the compiler automatically copies those variables into the variables declared as the function's parameters. Likewise, it is clear from the example that a value is passed back, using the statement **return**. The function itself takes on the value that is returned, so you can then use that value by making other variables equal to the value returned by the function, as in the example.

If nothing else is specified, a function returns an integer. It is possible to declare a function to make it return another data type, and you will look more closely at this and other special features of functions later in Chapter 8. You already know enough about functions to complete the tic-tac-toe program and the other sample programs in this book.

A DUMB TIC-TAC-TOE PROGRAM

Your analysis of the tic-tac-toe program has gone far enough that you can almost translate directly from pseudocode to the C language. You still need to learn a bit more about passing parameters to complete a few places where the **main**() module works with other modules, but you can just leave these areas as pseudocode for now, and you will see precisely how the parameters are passed as you write the modules they work with.

Look again at the pseudocode listed earlier in this chapter, and most of the **main**() module should be easy to write. You need to begin by declaring the global variable that represents the board. You could either put the entire program in a loop headed **while(again = ='Y')** or else put it in a **while(1 = =1)** loop and use **break;** at the bottom of the program to get out of the loop. Putting it in a **while(1 = =1)** loop and using **break;** at the bottom makes the program a bit easier to read and will give you more experience with this sort of loop control. It is obvious from the start that you must declare the **again** variable within the **main**() module; other variables this module uses will become apparent as you write the program.

You should use more comments here than you have used so far because this program is more complicated and could be difficult for other programmers to understand. The pseudocode itself is the best tool for making the code clearer, and you can use it as the basis of your comments as you run through the pseudocode and translate it into C code.

The only parts of the program that will be a bit difficult for you are the modules to check for a win or potential win; these modules must get parameters from the main module and return values to it. So you can be introduced to this concept gradually, the first version of the program will only include one of these modules: the module to check for a win. The module to check for a future win will be added later, and the parts of the program that call it will be left as comments in pseudocode in the first version. This will give you a dumb tic-tac-toe program that cannot block the opponent's win or even see if it can win itself. In the first version, this program will simply get the opponent's move and make its own move in the first empty space available.

To check for the opponent's win, the program will use the command **check-win('O');**. After writing the **main**() module, you will write the **checkwin**() function to receive parameters from **main**() and to return information to the **main**() module about whether O won or not. This version of **main**() will use what programmers call a **flag**, which is simply a variable that is set to one value until a certain condition applies, and then it is changed to act as a signal that this particular condition is in effect. **winFlag** would be a good name for this variable. **main**() will get information back from **checkwin**() by using the command **winFlag = checkwin('O');**. Then, it can test the value of **winFlag** to see whether or not the opponent won.

In COBOL, it is usual to use characters as flags and start off by setting them equal to "N" (for "no") or "F" (for "false"). When the condition comes into effect, the flag is changed to "Y" (for "yes") or "T" (for "true"). Then the condition is checked using the easy-to-understand statement **IF WINFLAG EQUALS "T"** or **IF WINFLAG EQUALS "Y"**. In C, for reasons that will become clear in Chapter 7, it is common to use integers as flags and to make them equal to 0 if the condition is false and equal to 1 if the condition is true.

One other point must be added to what was sketched out in the pseudocode. Because this first "dumb" version of the program is not checking for its own potential wins — and making its move and claiming a win on the basis of the result — the program will need to check after it moves, to see if it has won. The program will simply need to issue the command **winFlag = wincheck('X');** after its move to see if, by chance, it has made a move that won the game. This should be clear when you look at the code of the **main**() module:

```
/* CHAPTER 4, EXAMPLE 2A */
/* (TO BE COMBINED WITH EXAMPLES 2B, 2C, 2D, 2E, 2F) */

/* TIC-TAC-TOE: DUMB VERSION */

#include <stdio.h>

char sqr[3][3];                 /* array used as board */

main()
{
char again;
```

continued...

...from previous page

```
int moveCntr, winFlag;

while(1==1)                      /* repeat as long as the */
    {                           /* user wants to play */

    initliz();                  /* make squares equal blank */

    sqr[1][1] = 'X';            /* put X in central square */
    dispbord();                 /* display the board */
    getmove();                  /* get a valid move */
    makemove();                 /* make some move */
    moveCntr = 3;               /* three moves made */

    while(1==1)                 /* repeat till end of game */
        {
        dispbord();
        getmove();
        moveCntr = moveCntr + 1;

        winFlag = checkwin('O');
        if(winFlag==1)        /* see if opponent won */
            {                 /* if so end the game */
            dispbord();
            printf("Congratulations!! You win.\n");
            break;
            }

/* TO BE INCLUDED IN NEXT VERSION                              */
/*                                                             */
/*                  OTHERWISE                                  */
/*                      CHECK TO SEE IF YOU CAN WIN            */
/*                      IF SO                                  */
/*                          MAKE THE WINNING MOVE             */
/*                          DISPLAY THE UPDATED BOARD         */
/*                          END THE GAME                       */
/*                      OTHERWISE                              */
/*                          CHECK IF OPPONENT CAN WIN         */
/*                          IF SO                              */
/*                              BLOCK HIM                      */
/*                                                             */
/* TO BE INCLUDED IN NEXT VERSION                              */
```

continued...

...from previous page

```
        else
            {                   /* otherwise make some move */
            makemove();


/*INCLUDED IN "DUMB" VERSION ONLY                            */
/*                                                           */
/*                                                           */
            winFlag = checkwin('X');
            if(winFlag==1)          /* see if program won */
                {                   /* if so end the game */
                dispbord();
                printf("I  win.\n");
                break;
                }
/*                                                           */
/*                                                           */
/*INCLUDED IN "DUMB" VERSION ONLY                            */



            }

        moveCntr = moveCntr + 1;
        if(moveCntr==9)             /* if nine moves without */
            {                       /* a win, end game: draw */
            dispbord();
            printf("It's a draw. Good game.\n");
            break;
            }
        else                    /* otherwise, do */
            {                   /* the loop again */
            continue;
            }
        }                       /*** game over ***/

    printf("\nDo you want to play again (Y/N)? ");
    scanf("\n%c",&again);
```

continued...

...from previous page

```
    if(again=='Y' || again=='y')
        {                         /* if user wants to */
        continue;                 /* play again, loop */
        }                         /* back to beginning */
    else
        {                         /* Otherwise, */
        break;                    /* end the program */
        }
    }
}
```

The logic of the main, inner loop of this module should be clear if you simply ignore what will be added in the smarter version of the program. First, this module gets a move from the opponent and checks to see if the opponent won; if so, it congratulates the opponent and breaks out of the loop, ending the game. Then it makes a move and checks to see if it won; if so, it claims the win and breaks out of the loop. Then it sees if the move counter equals 9; if so, it says the game is a draw and breaks out of the loop. Once the flow of control has broken out of the inner loop, the program asks if the user wants to play again.

The one problem you still have is to write the **checkwin**() module that gives **main**() the information on whether or not a player won. You could declare another global variable to carry back to the main module information from the modules that check for wins, but it is more elegant and is really not difficult to pass the parameter directly from one module to another.

The module **checkwin();** will simply go through all the rows, columns, and diagonals of the board to see if there are three of the same letter in any of them. Because the module must work for either 'O' or 'X', it will be written in the general form **checkwin(ltr)**, which will check for any **char** you pass to it.

Remember the example of **addint(x,y);** that you looked at early in this chapter. The **addint** module is written using the variables **x** and **y**, but the module that calls it can use any variables. If you use the command **addint(numbr1,numbr2)**, the **addint** module will do the same thing it always does, using the values of **numbr1** and **numbr2** in place of **x** and **y**. Likewise, the module **checkwin** will be written in general form, using the variable **ltr**, so that other modules will be able to use the commands **checkwin('X');** or **checkwin('O');** to check for these specific letters. (Note that the letters must be surrounded by single quotation marks because they are constants rather than variables.)

The program then must send back to the **main()** module information about whether or not that letter won. As you have seen, the program does this by using the statement **winFlag = checkwin('O')**, which also is very similar to the statement used in the first example of parameters you looked at: **total = addint(numbr1,numbr2);**. There, you wrote the **addint** module to **return x+y;**, so you were able to use an assignment statement to make **total** equal **x** plus **y**. Here, you simply write the **checkwin()** module to return a 0 if there is no win and a 1 if there is a win, so you can use the assignment **winFlag = checkwin('O')** to make **winFlag** equal to 1 or 0, as follows:

```
/* CHAPTER 4, EXAMPLE 2B */
/* TO BE ADDED TO EXAMPLE 2A */

checkwin(ltr)
char ltr;
{
int ct;

ct = 0;
while(ct < 3)
    {
    if(sqr[ct][0]==ltr && sqr[ct][1]==ltr && sqr[ct][2]==ltr)
        {
        return 1;
        }
    else                            /* read thru all rows */
        {
        ct = ct + 1;
        }
    }
ct = 0;
while(ct < 3)
    {
    if(sqr[0][ct]==ltr && sqr[1][ct]==ltr && sqr[2][ct]==ltr)
        {
        return 1;
        }
```

continued...

...from previous page

```
    else                          /* read thru all columns */
        {
        ct = ct + 1;
        }
    }
if(sqr[0][0]==ltr && sqr[1][1]==ltr && sqr[2][2]==ltr)
    {
    return 1;                     /* read thru diagonals */
    }
if(sqr[0][2]==ltr && sqr[1][1]==ltr && sqr[2][0]==ltr)
    {
    return 1;                     /* and return 1 if all */
    }                             /* three squares have */
return 0;                         /* same letter: a win */
}                                 /* Otherwise, return 0 */
```

This module simply goes through all the possible combinations that win and, if any of these conditions applies, the program returns 1; otherwise, it returns 0. The first loop in the module uses a counter to go through all three columns of each row and to see if any row has **ltr** in all three of its squares; the second loop reads through all three rows of each column; and the final two statements check the diagonals. One important point to note here is that the **return** statement not only determines what value is passed back; it also breaks out of this function entirely and returns the program flow to the calling function without any other code in this function being executed; thus, if any of the tests shows there is a win, this function returns a 1 and also returns control to **main()** without executing the other statements. In fact, you can use the statement **return;** alone, without any value, simply to redirect program flow. This use of **return;** is a bit like **break;**, except that **return;** breaks you out of the entire function rather than just out of a loop.

The variable **winFlag** in the **main()** function is made equal to whatever value **checkwin()** returns: to 1 if there is a win or to 0 if the module goes through all of the tests without finding a win and manages to reach its final statement.

With this module out of the way, the other modules of this "dumb" version of tic-tac-toe should be easy for you to write.

Writing the final program is often actually easier than performing the analysis. After you have developed good pseudocode, you just need to go through the pseudocode, filling in extra little details and changing the wording to conform to the C language. It would be equally easy to translate the pseudocode into almost any computer language; once you understand the sort of step-by-step logic that computers use, the details of individual languages are not hard to pick up.

You will write the other modules in the order in which they appear in the program. **initliz**() uses two nested **while**() loops to make all the squares equal to a blank at the beginning of the program:

```
/* CHAPTER 4, EXAMPLE 2C */
/* TO BE ADDED TO EXAMPLE 2A */

initliz()                        /* make all the squares */
{                                /* equal to blank */
int rowCntr, colCntr;

rowCntr = 0;
while(rowCntr < 3)
     {
     colCntr = 0;
     while(colCntr < 3)
          {
          sqr[rowCntr][colCntr] = ' ';
          colCntr = colCntr + 1;
          }
     rowCntr = rowCntr + 1;
     }
}
```

First, to make the first three squares blank, the row counter is 0 as the column counter increases from 0 to 2. You can think of the program as going across the three columns of the first row. Then, the row counter is increased to 1 and to 2, and the column counter goes across all the columns or the second and third rows to make the squares blank. This module is a very typical example of how two-dimensional arrays are manipulated.

The module to display the screen is even simpler to write. Look again at the model screen that was laid out early in this chapter. All you need to do is count the new lines, tabs, and spaces and write a series of **printf()** statements to display this model on the screen, along with the contents of each square, depending on whether the variable is 'X' or 'O' or a blank:

```
/* CHAPTER 4, EXAMPLE 2d */
/* TO BE ADDED TO EXAMPLE 2A */

dispbord()                      /* display the board */
{
printf("\n\n\n\n\n\n\n");
printf("\t\t\t\t    COLUMN\n");
printf("\t\t\t\t 1    2    3\n\n");
printf("\t\t\t     1    %c | %c | %c\n",
                           sqr[0][0],sqr[0][1],sqr[0][2]);
printf("\t\t\t     R    -----------\n");
printf("\t\t\t     O 2    %c | %c | %c\n",
                           sqr[1][0],sqr[1][1],sqr[1][2]);
printf("\t\t\t     W    -----------\n");
printf("\t\t\t     3    %c | %c | %c\n",
                           sqr[2][0],sqr[2][1],sqr[2][2]);
printf("\n\n\n\n\n\n\n");
}
```

If you do not like the screen layout here, you can design one of your own. Just remember that, after this **dispbord()** function runs, the function that called it will need to display four more lines on the screen that ask for another move, announce the end of the game, or tell the user his move is invalid. That is why the module above only displays 20 lines instead of the total of 25 lines on the screen. You must not display the board so close to the top of the screen that it will scroll off when the extra lines are displayed.

The module to get a valid move from the opponent should also be easy for you to understand because the method of checking for validity is very similar to what you used in previous programs. You simply put the **scanf()** statement that gets the move within a **while** loop, and you do not let the user out of that loop unless the move is valid.

```
/* CHAPTER 4, EXAMPLE 2E */
/* TO BE ADDED TO EXAMPLE 2A */
getmove()                              /* get a valid move */
{
int rowNmbr, colNmbr;

while(1==1)                            /* get opponent's move */
     {
     printf("\nWhat row will you put O in?");
     printf("\nEnter a number from 1 to 3 > ");
     scanf("%d",&rowNmbr);
     printf("\nWhat col will you put O in?");
     printf("\nEnter a number from 1 to 3 > ");
     scanf("%d",&colNmbr);

     rowNmbr = rowNmbr - 1;
     colNmbr = colNmbr - 1;

     if(rowNmbr < 0 || rowNmbr > 2 || colNmbr < 0 || colNmbr >
2 || sqr[rowNmbr][colNmbr] != ' ')
          {
          printf("%c",7);           /* if move is invalid,*/
          dispbord();               /* beep, redisplay */
          continue;                 /* board and loop back */
          }                         /* to get new move */
     else                           /* if valid, put an o */
          {                                /* there */
          sqr[rowNmbr][colNmbr] = 'O';
          break;
          }
     }
}
```

After the row and column numbers are entered, 1 is subtracted from them to convert them to the actual subscripts used in the array (which, of course, run from 0 to 2 instead of 1 to 3). This function checks for two errors the user can make: entering numbers that are not between 1 and 3 or entering the number of a square that is not blank. (Like the other programs you have looked at so far, this program does not check for the entry of a non-numeric character.) In case of an error, the program redisplays the board before looping back and asking for the move again; otherwise, the board would scroll up the screen an extra two lines each time the user makes an invalid move, and could ultimately disappear completely if the user makes enough errors. The statement **continue;** is not really needed to loop back to the beginning of the module. Even without it, program control would bypass the **else** half of the condition and then flow back to the top, but it is useful stylistically to make clear what is happening here. If the move is valid, the square whose numbers were entered is made to equal 'O.' You do not even need to think about passing this value back to the **main**() module because all of the **sqr[] []**s are global variables, which are automatically accessible to all modules.

All you have left to do is to write the **makemove**() module to MAKE SOME MOVE if none of the other possibilities applies, which is just a matter of going through all the squares, giving priority to the corner squares, and looking for a blank:

```
/* CHAPTER 4, EXAMPLE 2F */
/* TO BE ADDED TO EXAMPLE 2A */

makemove()
{
if(sqr[0][0]==' ')
      {
      sqr[0][0] = 'X';
      }
else if(sqr[0][2]==' ')
      {
      sqr[0][2] = 'X';
      }
else if(sqr[2][0]==' ')
      {
      sqr[2][0] = 'X';
      }

      continued...
```

...from previous page

```
else if(sqr[2][2]==' ')
     {
     sqr[2][2] = 'X';
     }
else if(sqr[0][1]==' ')
     {
     sqr[0][1] = 'X';
     }
else if(sqr[1][0]==' ')
     {
     sqr[1][0] = 'X';
     }
else if(sqr[1][2]==' ')
     {
     sqr[1][2] = 'X';
     }
else if(sqr[2][1]==' ')
     {
     sqr[2][1] = 'X';
     }
}
```

The program skips **sqr[1] [1]**, which cannot be blank because the program put an X there as the first move. It would be nice if the program could have a final **else** statement that declares a draw if none of the squares is blank. In this initial version of the program, this **else** statement would work as the function is used to make all of X's moves. In the final version, however, this function does not run each time the program goes through the loop, as you can see by looking at the pseudocode left in the **main**() function above. The program needs to check for a draw separately, by seeing if **moveCntr** is equal to nine.

That completes the first, "dumb" version of the tic-tac-toe program. Put Program Examples 2A, 2B, 2C, 2D, 2E, and 2F in a single file and compile it; it will play a legal, though decidedly not an inspired, game.

A SMARTER TIC-TAC-TOE PROGRAM

To become a bit smarter, the program needs a function to look for possible wins on the next move. This function must do two things: it must check if X can win and, if so, make the winning move and end the game; and it also needs to check if O can win and, if so, put an X in the square that blocks the win. In either case, the function needs to scan the board only until it finds one square that satisfies the condition it is looking for. This is the way the computer's logic naturally works, using the **return;** statement, and this logic is perfectly appropriate here because there is really no need to see if there is a second square where you can move to win and no point to seeing if there is a second square where you need to move to block the opponent. If there are two squares where the opponent can move to win, the program will block the one that it comes across first; then, if the opponent moves in the other square and wins, the program will notice the move when it is scanning the entire board to see if the opponent has won — one of the first things the program does as it goes through the repeated central loop of its **main**() function.

You could write the module to search for future wins by checking whether any possible combination of two X's (or two O's) and a blank exists on the same line, which would take three lines for each row, column, and diagonal on the board. Fortunately, there is an easier way to search for future wins: make each blank space an 'X' (or an 'O', depending on which you are checking) temporarily, and then run the **checkwin**() module. Then make the square a blank again. The pseudocode would look like the following:

```
FOR EVERY SQUARE
        IF THE SQUARE IS A BLANK
                MAKE THE SQUARE AN 'X'
                CHECK FOR A WIN (USING checkwin())
                IF THERE IS A WIN
                        LEAVE THE X THERE
                        STOP CHECKING OTHER SQUARES
                OTHERWISE
                        MAKE THE SQUARE A BLANK AGAIN
                        KEEP CHECKING OTHER SQUARES
        IF NO WINS WERE FOUND IN ANY SQUARE
                MAKE SOME MOVE
```

If you are checking for 'X', simply leave the X there to make the winning move if this module shows there is one; otherwise, make the square blank again and keep checking.

There is only one difference when using the module to check a future win for O: when the module shows there is a win, put an X in that square in place of the O that you put there temporarily in order to block the win. Otherwise, make the square equal to blank again and keep checking.

```
canwin(xoro)
char xoro;
{
int rowCntr, colCntr;
int winFlag;

rowCntr = 0;
while(rowCntr < 3)
    {
    colCntr = 0;
    while(colCntr < 3)
        {
        if(sqr[rowCntr][colCntr]==' ')
            {
            sqr[rowCntr][colCntr] = xoro;
            WinFlag = checkwin(xoro);
            if(WinFlag==0)
                {
                sqr[rowCntr][colCntr] = ' ';
                }
            else
                {
                if(xoro == 'O')
                    {
                    sqr[rowCntr][colCntr] = 'X';
                    }
                return 1;
                }
            }
        colCntr = colCntr + 1;
        }
    rowCntr = rowCntr + 1;
    }
return 0;
}
```

This function is powerful but not too hard to understand. It uses the familiar nested **while**() loops, with a row counter and a column counter, to go through all the squares on the board. If a square is blank, the program makes it either 'X' or 'O', depending on which is being tested, and runs the **checkwin**() function. Normally, there will be no win. **checkwin**() will return a 0, and the program will make the square a blank again and go on to try an 'X' or 'O' in the next square. On the other hand, sometimes **checkwin**() will find there is a win, making **winFlag** equal to 1. Then, the program does not make **sqr[rowCntr] [colCntr]** a blank again. If the **ltr** being checked is X, the program simply returns a 1, returning control to **main**() and letting that function know it should display the board and declare a victory. If the **ltr** being checked is O, the program puts an X in the square to block the win and returns a 1, letting **main**() know that it does not need to make a move. And if the program goes through all the squares without finding a win, it returns a 0, letting **main**() know that no move has been made and that the program must go on to the next step.

This part of the program should be clear when you look at the entire program listing. There is one other shortcut in the final listing: it cuts out the use of the **winFlag.** Instead of the following,

```
winFlag = checkwin('O');
if(winFlag==1)
```

the program simply uses

```
if(checkwin('O')==1);
```

When you were first learning this program, it was easier to understand if this part of the program was in two steps: first, to check for the win and second, to use the result in a condition. Now that you are used to the program, however, you should be able to see without any trouble that you were able to give **winFlag** the value of 1 or 0 by making it equal to **checkwin('O')** only because **checkwin('O')** itself had the value of 1 or 0. So why not cut out the middleman and use **checkwin('O')** itself in the condition. (You will see this type of nesting of parentheses frequently in C code, and if it is confusing, you should just break it up into two parts by inventing some variable to represent the innermost function, as **winFlag** did above.)

The entire program is long enough that there is an advantage to putting the modules in alphabetical order to make them easier to follow. The complete listing follows:

```
/* CHAPTER 4, EXAMPLE 3 */
/* program to play tic-tac-toe: smarter version */

#include <stdio.h>

char sqr[3][3];                         /* array used as board */

main()
{
char again;
int rowCntr, colCntr;
int moveCntr;
while(1==1)                    /* repeat as long as the */
     {                         /* user wants to play */

     initliz();                /* make squares equal blank */
     sqr[1][1] = 'X';          /* put X in central square */
     dispbord();
     getmove();                /* get a valid move */
     makemove();               /* make some move */
     moveCntr = 3;             /* three moves made */

     while(1==1)               /* repeat until end of game */
         {
         dispbord();
         getmove();
         moveCntr = moveCntr + 1;

         if(checkwin('O')==1)           /* if opponent won */
             {                          /* end the game */
             dispbord();
             printf("Congratulations!! You win.\n");
             break;
             }
```

continued...

...from previous page

```
        else                            /* if you can win */
            {                           /* end the game */
            if(canwin('X')==1)
                {
                dispbord();
                printf("I win.\n");
                break;
                }
            else                        /* if opponent can */
                {                       /* win, block him */
                if(canwin('O')==0)
                    {                   /* otherwise make */
                    makemove();         /* some move */
                    }
                }
            }

        moveCntr = moveCntr + 1;        /* if nine moves */
        if(moveCntr==9)                 /* without a win */
            {                           /* end game : draw */
            dispbord();
            printf("It's a draw. Good game.\n");
            break;
            }
        else                            /* otherwise, do */
            {                           /* the loop again */
            continue;
            }
        }                               /*** game over ***/

    printf("\nDo you want to play again (Y/N)? ");
    scanf("\n%c",&again);
    if(again=='Y' || again=='y')
        {                               /* if user wants to */
        continue;                       /* play again, loop */
        }                               /* back to beginning */
    else
        {                               /* Otherwise, */
        break;                          /* end program */
        }
    }
}
```

continued...

134

...from previous page

```
canwin(xoro)
char xoro;
{
int rowCntr, colCntr;

rowCntr = 0;
while(rowCntr < 3)                /* loop through all squares */
     {                            /* if one is blank, make it */
     colCntr = 0;                 /* X or O temporarily */
     while(colCntr < 3)
          {
          if(sqr[rowCntr][colCntr]==' ')
               {
               sqr[rowCntr][colCntr] = xoro;
               if(checkwin(xoro)==0)    /* if no win, make */
                    {                    /* it blank again */
                    sqr[rowCntr][colCntr] = ' ';
                    }
               else                 /* if there is a win */
                    {                /* either block O or */
                    if(xoro == 'O')  /* just leave X */
                         {
                         sqr[rowCntr][colCntr] = 'X';
                         }
                    return 1;        /* and return 1 to */
                    }                /* let main() know */
               }                     /* a move was made */
          colCntr = colCntr + 1;
          }
     rowCntr = rowCntr + 1;
     }                              /* if no move was */
return 0;                           /* made, return 0 */
}



checkwin(ltr)
char ltr;
{
int ct;
```

continued...

...from previous page

```
ct = 0;
while(ct < 3)
     {
     if(sqr[ct][0]==ltr && sqr[ct][1]==ltr && sqr[ct][2]==ltr)
          {
          return 1;
          }
     else                            /* read thru all rows */
          {
          ct = ct + 1;
          }
     }
ct = 0;
while(ct < 3)
     {
     if(sqr[0][ct]==ltr && sqr[1][ct]==ltr && sqr[2][ct]==ltr)
          {
          return 1;
          }
     else                            /* read thru all columns */
          {
          ct = ct + 1;
          }
     }
if(sqr[0][0]==ltr && sqr[1][1]==ltr && sqr[2][2]==ltr)
     {
     return 1;                       /* read thru diagonals */
     }
if(sqr[0][2]==ltr && sqr[1][1]==ltr && sqr[2][0]==ltr)
     {
     return 1;                       /* and return 1 if all */
     }                               /* 3 squares have same */
                                     /* letter: there is win */
return 0;
}                                    /* Otherwise return 0 */
```

continued...

...from previous page

```
dispbord()                                    /* display the board */
{
printf("\n\n\n\n\n\n\n");
printf("\t\t\t\t    COLUMN\n");
printf("\t\t\t\t 1    2    3\n\n");
printf("\t\t\t    1    %c | %c | %c\n",
                              sqr[0][0],sqr[0][1],sqr[0][2]);
printf("\t\t\t    R    -----------\n");
printf("\t\t\t    O 2    %c | %c | %c\n",
                              sqr[1][0],sqr[1][1],sqr[1][2]);
printf("\t\t\t    W    -----------\n");
printf("\t\t\t    3    %c | %c | %c\n",
                              sqr[2][0],sqr[2][1],sqr[2][2]);
printf("\n\n\n\n\n\n\n");
}


getmove()                              /* get a valid move */
{
int rowNmbr, colNmbr;

while(1==1)                            /* get opponents move */
    {
    printf("\nWhat row will you put O in?");
    printf("\nEnter a number from 1 to 3 > ");
    scanf("%d",&rowNmbr);
    printf("\nWhat column will you put O in?");
    printf("\nEnter a number from 1 to 3 > ");
    scanf("%d",&colNmbr);

    rowNmbr = rowNmbr - 1;
    colNmbr = colNmbr - 1;

    if(rowNmbr < 0 || rowNmbr > 2 || colNmbr < 0
            || colNmbr > 2 || sqr[rowNmbr][colNmbr] != ' ')
        {
        printf("%c",7);             /* if move is invalid */
        dispbord();                 /* beep, redisplay */
        continue;                   /* board and loop back */
        }                           /* to get new move */
```

continued...

4 Working with Arrays

...from previous page

```
    else
        {
        sqr[rowNmbr][colNmbr] = 'O';
        break;
        }
    }
}


initliz()                               /* make all the squares */
{                                       /* equal to blank */
int rowCntr, colCntr;

rowCntr = 0;
while(rowCntr < 3)
    {
    colCntr = 0;
    while(colCntr < 3)
        {
        sqr[rowCntr][colCntr] = ' ';
        colCntr = colCntr + 1;
        }
    rowCntr = rowCntr + 1;
    }
}


makemove()                              /* make some move */
{
if(sqr[0][0]==' ')
    {
    sqr[0][0] = 'X';
    }
else if(sqr[0][2]==' ')
    {
    sqr[0][2] = 'X';
    }

    continued...
```

...from previous page

```
else if(sqr[2][0]==' ')
     {
     sqr[2][0] = 'X';
     }
else if(sqr[2][2]==' ')
     {
     sqr[2][2] = 'X';
     }
else if(sqr[0][1]==' ')
     {
     sqr[0][1] = 'X';
     }
else if(sqr[1][0]==' ')
     {
     sqr[1][0] = 'X';
     }
else if(sqr[1][2]==' ')
     {
     sqr[1][2] = 'X';
     }
else if(sqr[2][1]==' ')
     {
     sqr[2][1] = 'X';
     }
}
```

It is interesting that the logic of the **main**() module of this program obviously requires three nested **if-else** statements. If the opponent wins, congratulate him. Otherwise, look for a potential win. If that win is found, make the winning move. Otherwise, see if the opponent can win. If he can win, block him. Otherwise, make some move. The use of nested **if-else** statements is much more intuitive here than in most cases, and if you study this example closely, looking especially at the indentation and the reverse-indentation of the closing brackets, you should find it easy to work with nested **if-else** statements in the future.

More conditions could be added to this series of **if-else** statements if you wanted to make the program even smarter. This program just checks for a win on the next move. If it does not find anything, it uses the **makemove**() function and simply occupies the first open square it finds. By adding more conditions here, you could make the program look even farther ahead to find the best move.

If you were writing a program to play a difficult game, such as chess, much of the programming would be devoted to developing heuristics to make the best move; **heuristics** are programs that are used as "rules of thumb" to guide you toward the best possibility when there is no precise, step-by-step way of getting to your goal, and they are a major subject of research in artificial intelligence. In tic-tac-toe, the game is simple enough that heuristics are not needed; you can work entirely with what are called **algorithms**, the step-by-step procedures to reach a precise goal that computers most often use.

If you wanted to do the extra work, you could develop a module to check whether it was possible to create what is called a "fork," or a position where you can win in two ways. For example, in the following position,

the program could be intelligent enough to put the X in row 3, column 3 so that it could win on the next move by going in either row 2, column 3 or in row 1, column 1. This would involve looking ahead two moves instead of just one. It is not hard to do in theory: it is simply a matter of putting an 'X' in each blank square temporarily and then using the module that checks for potential wins, **canwin()**, to see if any of those moves creates two different potential wins. If two potential wins were possible, the program would leave the 'X' there; otherwise, it would make the square blank again.

Finally, you could write a module to set up future forks, looking ahead three moves. Then, the program would be as good as any human tic-tac-toe player, which is really no great achievement for artificial intelligence. You can begin to see that when people talk about computers becoming more intelligent and imitating human thought, what they really mean is that programmers are becoming more intelligent and developing sets of rules that let the computer imitate some of the forms of thinking that people do. The intelligence is built into the program, and all that better computers can do is execute the programs more quickly.

SUMMARY

Local variables are used by one function. **Global variables** can be used by all functions. **Parameters** are variables that are passed between two functions.

Local variables are declared within the function they are used in, as follows:

```
main()
{
int samplVar;

MORE CODE
}
```

Global variables are declared outside of any function, before the **main**() module, as follows:

```
int samplVar;

main()
{
MORE CODE
}
```

Parameters are declared after the name of a function and before its opening bracket as they are received by that function from outside:

```
smplfunc(a,b)
int a,b;
{
MORE CODE
}
```

(Chapter 8 will cover another, newer way of declaring parameters in the function that receives them.) Parameters are declared as ordinary local variables within the function that calls another function. The names of the variables in the two functions are not related to each other. The values of the variables in the calling function are copied into the parameters of the function that is called.

Using the statement **return;** plus some value within the called function will make the program return that value to the calling function. That is, the called function will assume that value in the calling function, and the value can be assigned to a variable as follows: **samplVar = smplfunc(1,2);**. This example assigns to **samplVar** the value that **smplfunc** returns if its parameters **a** and **b** have the values 1 and 2.

The statement **return;** also redirects the flow of program control back to the calling function, without any of the remaining instructions of the called function being executed. It can be used without any value simply to redirect control flow in this way.

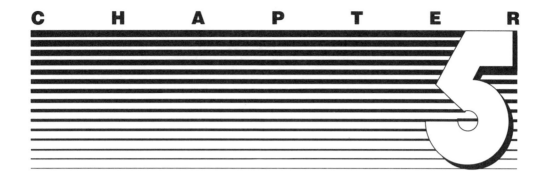

WORKING WITH WORDS

STRINGS OF CHARACTERS

Now that you have experience working with arrays, you are ready to work with "strings" — that is with words and texts — because, in C, a string is an array of characters.

To be more precise, a string is an array of characters terminated by the **null** character. The **null** is the first ASCII character, which has a value of zero. The eight bits that represent this character are set to 00000000. It is not to be confused with the character zero (0), which is ASCII character 48. The **null** character is not actually used in any text in the way that ordinary characters such as '0' or 'A' or '?' and even carriage returns are used; the **null** can be used as a signal to let the compiler know when the text has ended. In C, **null** is represented by the special escape character '**\0**', which is similar to the special characters '**\n**' (for a new line) and '**\t**' (for tab) that have been discussed previously.

Having this sort of marker to tell you when the string ends is useful because it allows you to work with character strings of different lengths. Say, for example, that you are working with names. You can declare the array of characters that will hold a name as follows,

```
char name[16];
```

assuming that the maximum length of a name is fifteen characters and adding one more character for the final **null**. Then, if the program must work with the name "Sam," you can initialize that array as follows:

```
name[0] = 'S';
name[1] = 'a';
name[2] = 'm';
name[3] = '\0';
```

name[4] through **name[15]** are either empty or contain random values they happened to hold when the program began. However, when other parts of the program work with this string, they will simply read the characters until they reach the null; then they will know the string is over.

In the previous example, other parts of the program will read 'S', 'a', and 'm' and then stop. Later in the program, if you want to use the name "Amadeus," for example, you can initialize the same string, **char name[16];**, as follows:

```
name[0] = 'A';
name[1] = 'm';
name[2] = 'a';
name[3] = 'd';
name[4] = 'e';
name[5] = 'u';
name[6] = 's';
name[7] = '\0';
```

Using the **null** terminator allows you to use the same array to hold strings of different lengths, which in turn allows you to give the strings different values — regardless of the strings' lengths — and to use strings more or less like other variables.

It is important to emphasize, however, that a string cannot be initialized like other variables. In general, you cannot say

```
name[16] = "Sam";
```

With some compilers and in some situations you can initialize entire strings by using the equal sign as you do with other variables; however the general rule is that each element of an array — in this case, each character of a string — is a separate variable. If you want to initialize using the equal sign as you do with other variables, you generally must initialize each character in a string individually.

Fortunately, there are standard functions in C that provide easy ways to work with strings. The most common way of initializing a string is using the function **strcpy()** (short for "string copy"), which takes the following form:

```
char name[16];
strcpy(name,"Amadeus");
```

This code will copy the string "Amadeus" into the array **name[16]** and will automatically place the **null** terminator after the string: in just one line, this code accomplishes the same task as the previous seven-line program.

Note that, as in most all string-handling functions, you enter the name of the target string that is being changed first. You can also copy one variable into another. For example, if you had another string declared as **char musician[16];** that had already been given the value **"Amadeus"**, then you could use the statement

```
strcpy(name, musician);
```

to copy the value that is now in the string **musician[16]** into the string **name[16]**.

Note also that strings that are constants, such as **"Sam"** and **"Amadeus"**, are surrounded by double quotation marks, unlike individual **chars**, such as **'S'**, **'a'**, and **'m'**, which are surrounded by single quotation marks. Of course, a character can be surrounded by double quotes if that character happens to be a one-letter string. For example, the statement

```
strcpy(name,"I");
```

would be equivalent to the following:

```
name[0] = 'I';
name[1] = '\0';
```

The string "I" is made up of the **char 'I'** plus the **char '\0'**.

Finally, note the one tricky thing about the names of the strings that are variables within the **strcpy()** function: the arrays **name[16]** and **musician[16]** are referred to simply as **name** and **musician**, without any brackets after them. The name of an array, without the brackets, refers to the address of the beginning of that array. When you learned the **scanf()** function, you looked briefly at the symbol **&**, which means "the address of." In this example, **name** means **&name[0]**; it is the address of the beginning of the array. You will learn more about addresses in Chapter 6; here, you must simply note that because you generally do not know the exact length of a string, the functions that work with strings must be given the address of each string's first character, so the functions can act on all the characters — from this beginning character's address to the null terminator. Because you need the beginning address of the string so often, being able to refer to the string's name without entering the brackets and the ampersand is a handy shortcut.

Of course, you can still access the letters as individual elements of the string. If you expanded the last example as follows,

```
/* CHAPTER 5, EXAMPLE 1 */
#include <stdio.h>

main()                       /* sample program */
{                            /* initializing a string */
char name[16];

strcpy(name,"Amadeus");
printf("%c%c%c",name[3],name[4],name[5]);
}
```

the program would print **deu**. Here, you can begin to see the convenience of treating words as arrays. Treating words as arrays makes it easy to manipulate them letter by letter.

Another easy way of handling strings is to use the **printf()** and **scanf()** functions, both of which can use the special character **%s** to work with strings, just as they use **%d**, **%f**, and **%c** to work with integers, floats, and characters. For instance, you can make the previous example more meaningful as follows:

```
/* CHAPTER 5, EXAMPLE 2 */
#include <stdio.h>

main()                              /* sample program */
{                                   /* string handling */
char name[16];

strcpy(name,"Amadeus");
printf("The second letter of %s is %c.",name,name[1]);
}
```

This example will print **"The second letter of Amadeus is m."**

If you want to get fancier, you can combine this technique with a loop, as follows:

```
/* CHAPTER 5, EXAMPLE 3 */
#include <stdio.h>

main()                              /* sample program */
{                                   /* using a counter */
char name[16];                      /* with a string */
int cntr;

cntr = 0;
strcpy(name,"Amadeus");
while(name[cntr] != '\0')
    {
    printf("\nLetter %d of %s is %c.",cntr+1,name,name[cntr]);
    cntr = cntr + 1;
    }
}
```

As usual, you must add 1 to the counter when you are talking to the user, who starts counting at 1 rather than at 0. Thus, the first time through the loop, the program will print **"Letter 1 of Amadeus is A."** The program will print a similar message for each letter in the name until it reaches the null terminator. After the program reaches the null terminator, the condition at the top of the loop, **while(name[cntr]** != '\0'), is no longer true, so the program stops executing. You will need to use similar methods of loop control in most functions you write that work with strings.

You can use both **printf()** and **scanf()** with strings to personalize the **"Hello, world"** program you wrote in Chapter 1 so it greets the individual user:

```
/* CHAPTER 5, EXAMPLE 4 */
#include <stdio.h>

main()                           /* sample program */
{                                /* talking with the user */
char name[21];

printf("\nWhat is your name? ");
scanf("%s",name);
printf("\nHello, %s.\n",name);
}
```

Note that when it is used with strings, the **scanf()** function does not need the ampersand (**&**) before the name of the variable. Remember, **scanf()** needs the **&** operator before the names of most variables because **scanf()** expects an address; however, when the name of an array is not followed by brackets, that name already represents an address, so the ampersand is not needed.

If the user entered "John," this program would print out "Hello, John" on the screen, but if John happened to have his Caps Lock key on and entered "JOHN," the program would print out the rather unprofessional looking message: "Hello, JOHN." Here, the problem is just a matter of appearance, but there are many programs in which a name that is entered must be matched up with a name on a list (e.g., so the program can look up the person's address or telephone number). Remember that a computer considers the upper- and lowercase versions of the same letter to be two totally different symbols, each with its own ASCII code, and would not find a match between "h" and "H," for example.

There are two C functions to deal with the problem of capitalization. The function **toupper**() will return the uppercase version of a letter but will not affect character symbols that are not letters. For example, **ltr = toupper('c');** will make the variable **ltr** equal 'C', and **ltr = toupper('$');** will make **ltr** equal '$'. Likewise, the function **tolower**() will make letters lowercase but will not affect ASCII characters other than letters. When you are manipulating a piece of text, it is useful to be able to make certain letters upper- or lowercase without having to worry about mutilating the rest of the text.

To change the program so it does not print "Hello, JOHN," add a loop to adjust the case of whatever letters are entered:

```
/* CHAPTER 5, EXAMPLE 5 */
#include <stdio.h>

main()                                  /* sample program */
{                                       /* talking with the user */
char name[21];                          /* a better way */
int counter;
printf("\nWhat is your name? ");
scanf("%s",name);
name[0] = toupper(name[0]);
counter = 1;
while(name[counter] != '\0')
    {
    name[counter] = tolower(name[counter]);
    counter = counter + 1;
    }
printf("\nHello, %s.\n",name);
}
```

First, the program makes the first letter of the name uppercase; then, the loop makes each of the following letters lowercase, until it comes to the **null** terminator and stops. (If statements such as **name[0] = toupper(name[0]);** make you uncomfortable, just remember that these statements are also assignment statements, similar to **counter = counter + 1**. The statement **name[0] = toupper(name[0]);** can be read as "make the first letter of name equal to the uppercase version of the current first letter of name.")

The function **toupper()** is particularly useful in menus. By now you are probably tired of statements such as the following:

```
choice = ' ';
while(choice!='n' && choice!='N' && choice!='y' && choice!='Y')
    {
    printf("\nWhat is your choice? ");
    scanf("\n%c",&choice);
    }
```

This technique could really become tiresome if you were writing a program with a menu that included numerous letter choices and you had to write a prolonged **if-else-if** ladder and include both the lower- and uppercase letters in each condition. Fortunately, this approach is not necessary; the program can just make the choice uppercase as soon as the user enters the letter. The previous example could be converted to the following:

```
choice = ' ';
while(choice!='N' && choice!='Y')
    {
    printf("\nWhat is your choice? ");
    scanf("\n%c",&choice);
    choice = toupper(choice);
    }
```

Of course, you save even more work in the code that follows because you can see what the program should do next by using the condition **if(choice= =’Y’)** rather than **if(choice= =’Y’ || choice= =’y’)**.

The use of another important string-handling function will become apparent if you notice that Program Example 5, shown previously, capitalizes only the first name; it contains no commands to capitalize the first letter of the last name. When you test this program, you will see that it only gets the first name because **scanf()** used with **%s** reads only up to the first blank of the string.

More precisely, when **scanf()** is used with any formatting character except **%c**, it will not read blank space characters, which include tabs, newline characters, or blank spaces, all of which create blank space on the screen. Of course, this feature of **scanf()** is often useful, but it does mean that **scanf()** cannot be used to read a string that contains blank spaces. Though **printf()** is quite adequate for printing string output, it is better to use a different I/O function to get string input from the user.

So far, you have used only the formatted I/O functions **printf()** and **scanf()** with the special characters **%c**, **%f**, **%i**, and **%s** to print and to access different data types. There is also a set of unformatted I/O functions with a different function for each data type; each type uses **put** or **get** plus some abbreviation of the data type handles. The most standard unformatted I/O functions are **putchar()** and **getchar()**, used to print and read characters, and **puts()** and **gets()**, used to print and read strings.

One reason these functions are sometimes used is that because they are less powerful than **printf()** and **scanf()**, they use less memory; the compiled program can be smaller if its code does not need the formatted I/O functions and can substitute one of the unformatted functions for the I/O it does use. Additionally, **putchar(7);** is simply a far more common way of creating a beep than **printf("%c",7);** — so much so that is seems more natural — and it will be used in the rest of this book.

One reason that **gets()** is one of the most useful functions in the C language is that it reads strings that include blank space characters. Using **scanf("%s",name);**, you can only get the user's first name. To read the user's entire name into the string, you can use the statement **gets(name);**. You can rewrite the example to get an entire name and capitalize it properly, as follows:

```
/* CHAPTER 5, EXAMPLE 6 */
#include <stdio.h>

main()                              /* sample program */
{                                   /* talking with the user */
char name[21];                      /* an even better way */
int counter;
printf("\nWhat is your name? ");
gets(name);
name[0] = toupper(name[0]);
counter = 1;
while(name[counter] != '\0')
    {
    if(name[counter-1]==' ')
        {
        name[counter] = toupper(name[counter]);
        }
    else
        {
        name[counter] = tolower(name[counter]);
        }
    counter = counter + 1;
    }
printf("\nHello, %s.\n",name);
}
```

This program gets an entire name, capitalizes the first letter, and then goes through the rest of the name letter by letter and makes any letter that follows a blank uppercase and any other letter lowercase. If you enter "james a. smith," for example, it will capitalize the "J" and then go through the name and capitalize the "A" and the "S." (Unfortunately, it will not handle names that have capital letters in the middle, such as "Ponce DeLeon," which are the bane of a computer programmer's existence.)

The function **gets**() is also useful for getting menu choices and other forms of single-character input from the user. Up to this point, you have been using **scanf("\n%c")** to avoid having **scanf("%c")** read two characters for each input. Remember that if a loop uses **scanf("%c")** without the **\n**, there will be an echo; the first time through the loop, the program will read the character that the user entered, and the second time through, the program will read the newline character, which is still in the buffer. One problem this approach creates is that the programs do not react if the user simply presses the Enter key. The function **gets**() does not have this problem. If the user presses Enter, **gets**() will simply make '**\0**' the first **char** of the array. If the user presses a letter key first, **gets**() will make that letter the first **char** of the array. You must declare the variable that accepts the menu choice as a string, and after accepting the input you must check for just the first **char**, element **[0]** of the array. Now that you have learned how to use strings, you can make user input work more smoothly.

There are two additional string-handling functions that are very common and that you should know. The function **strcmp**() (short for "string compare") checks to see if two strings are identical. If the strings differ, what this function does differs in various versions of C. Some compilers return the position of the first letter that is different, and some return a negative number if the character that differs is lower or a positive number if the character is higher in the ASCII chart than the character in the string it is being checked against. Because the function is generally used to see whether two strings are identical, the important point to remember is simply that all compilers return a 0 if the strings are the same.

A program that uses a password to keep out unauthorized users is a typical example. The following version of a password module makes input easier for the user by accepting the password in either upper- or lowercase.

```
/* CHAPTER 5, EXAMPLE 7 */
#include <stdio.h>

main()                          /* sample password program */
{
password();
printf("Correct password. You may begin the program");

/* MORE CODE FOR MAIN PROGRAM */
}


password()                      /* get and check password */
{
int ltrCntr, tryCntr;
char userWord[11];

tryCntr= 0;                     /* loop to give user three */
while(1==1)                     /* tries to enter password */
    {
    printf("What is the password? ");
    scanf("%s",userWord);
                                /* capitalize user's entry */
    ltrCntr = 0;
    while(userWord[ltrCntr] != '\0')
        {
        userWord[ltrCntr]  = toupper(userWord[ltrCntr]);
        ltrCntr = ltrCntr + 1;
        }
    if(strcmp(userWord,"OPENSESAME")==0)
        {
        break;                  /* if entry is right */
        }                       /* continue with main program */
    else
        {
        tryCntr = tryCntr + 1;
        if(tryCntr==3)
            {                   /* if three tries are wrong */
            exit();             /* do not let user in program */
            }
        }
    }
}
```

First, the password module gets the password from the user. Then, it goes through the entry one letter at a time, capitalizing each letter until it reaches the final **null**. Then the module compares the entry with **"OPENSESAME,"** which this program uses as the password.

Note how one set of parentheses is nested inside another in this condition: **if(strcmp(userWord,"OPENSESAME")= =0)**. This nesting becomes clear when you remember that, first, the program evaluates the inner function **strcmp(userWord,"OPENSESAME")**. If the two strings are the same, the program returns a 0 so that the condition then is equivalent to **if(0= =0)** and is true. As mentioned in Chapter 4, a beginner might find it easier to perform this task in two steps by declaring an integer variable called, say, **compRslt** to hold the result of the comparison and making the comparison and the condition into two separate lines:

```
compRslt = strcmp(theWord,"OPENSESAME");
if(compRslt==0)
```

Once you become used to the fact that a function such as **strcmp()** returns a value, however, you will find it easy to perform this type of task in a single statement.

If the word entered is **"OPENSESAME"**, the program **break;**s out of the loop and returns to the **main()** module so the user can go on with the rest of the program. If the wrong word is entered, though, the program increments the **tryCntr** and loops up to the top of the **password()** module again to give the user a second try. Before looping, however, the program checks to see how many tries the user has already had. If there have already been three attempts, it **exit()**s so users cannot just keep trying passwords until they find the right one. This example is an excellent illustration of the difference between **break;** and **exit();**.

One final string-handling function you should understand is **strlen()**, which returns the length of a string. This function is useful for error checking because it screens out data that does not fit into the space a program allocates for it. In the program that says "Hello" to the user, which you wrote earlier in this chapter, an array of 21 characters is used to hold the user's name, so it can hold a name that is a maximum of 20 characters long (plus the null character). If a name longer than this is entered, some operating systems would simply lose the data at the end, but most (including MS-DOS) would save this data in the keyboard buffer — the memory reserved to hold input from the keyboard — and would pass it to the next **scanf()** (or any other keyboard input function).

Of course, passing this excess data to the next keyboard input function could create serious problems, so programs often check to make sure that strings entered are of a valid length. You can check string length by first creating your own buffer — a longer array that you read the string into first — then using **strlen**() to check whether the string is longer than the array that will finally hold it, and finally putting the string in that array only if it is not too long. You can modify the program that says "Hello" to the user to incorporate this type of error trapping as follows:

```
/* CHAPTER 5, EXAMPLE 8 */
#include <stdio.h>

main()                                  /* sample program */
{                                       /* talking with the user */
char name[21];                          /* the best way */
char buffer[80];
int counter;
printf("\nWhat is your name? ");
gets(buffer);
if(strlen(buffer)>20)
     {
     printf("Sorry.  That name is too long.");
     }
else
     {
     strcpy(name,buffer);
     name[0] = toupper(name[0]);
     counter = 1;
     while(name[counter] != '\0')
          {
          if(name[counter-1]==' ')
               {
               name[counter] = toupper(name[counter]);
               }
          else
               {
               name[counter] = tolower(name[counter]);
               }
          counter = counter + 1;
          }
     printf("\nHello, %s.\n",name);
     }
}
```

It really does not make sense, however, to have this type of error checking in this program; instead of adding a second array to use as a buffer, you can make the name array itself longer. There are cases, though, in which this error checking would be appropriate. For example, if you are dealing with long lists of words and storing them on disk, as you will learn to do in Chapter 6, you must limit the space each word is allowed so the total list does not waste too much space on the disk. In such a case, you would have good reason to make sure that none of the words entered is longer than the space allocated for it.

THE STRUCT: A PACKAGE OF DATA

Because one word is an array, a list of words is a two-dimensional array. If you wanted your program to say "Hello" to ten users, for example, instead of just one, you could declare the array that holds the users names as follows: **char name[21][10];**. Think of this example as an array of ten names, each of which can hold a maximum of 20 characters (plus the **null** terminator) as did the single name that the last program worked with. If you wanted to list both the first and last name for each user, you might try a three-dimensional array; to add the address, you could use a four-dimensional array.

It is easy for the computer to follow this sort of list, in which the elements are distinguished by changes in one out of three or four index numbers. But for the programmer, following this type of list is even more confusing than following a program with variables that have names such as **x**, **y**, and **z** rather than descriptive names. Also, it is impossible to combine data types by using higher dimensional arrays. Such arrays won't allow you to keep track of employees' names, addresses, and salaries (at least, not if you want the salaries in number form so that you can perform calculations on them).

Fortunately, in C you can create a package of data called a **structure** or **struct** that lets you combine different data types in a way that is easier to follow. To declare the structure, you simply declare each of the structure's elements after the structure's name:

```
struct employee
    {
    char fname[21];
    char lname[31];
    char address[31];
    char city[21];
    char state[3];
    char zip[6];
    char sex;
    int age;
    float salary;
    };
```

This declaration essentially creates a new data type, **employee**, by packaging together a list of existing data types. It includes strings of varying lengths to hold the employee's name and address, a character for the sex code ('M' or 'F'), an integer for the age, and a float for the salary.

Note that the **struct** declaration must end with a semicolon as must any other statement. The other slightly tricky point to remember about the declaration of a **struct** is that the declaration does not create an actual variable. The previous definition of **struct employee**, for example, did not create a variable named **employee**. It essentially created a new data type named **struct employee** that can be used in declarations of variables such as **struct employee smith;** or **struct employee jones;**. Once the type **struct employee** has been declared, these declarations create new variables named **smith** and **jones**, each of which contains slots for name, address, sex code, age, and salary, as outlined in the declaration of the **struct**.

The declaration of the **struct** and of the variables can also be combined, as follows:

```
struct employee
    {
    char fname[21];
    char lname[31];
    char address[31];
    char city[21];
    char state[3];
    char zip[6];
    char sex;
    int age;
    float salary;
    } smith, jones;
```

This declares the **struct employee** and also declares two variables of that type, **smith** and **jones**.

To refer to any of the elements (name, address, sex code, etc.) of one of these variables (**smith** or **jones**), simply use the name of the variable, a period (.), and the element name. For example, to refer to Smith's age or Jones's address, you could use **smith.age** or **jones.address**. These elements can be manipulated in the same way as any other variables of the same data type. To find the total salary of the two workers, for example, you can add the following lines at the appropriate places in the program:

```
float totSal;
totSal = smith.salary + jones.salary;
```

To make sure all the letters in Jones's last name are capitalized, you can add the following lines, just as if you were working with any other string:

```
int counter;
counter = 0;
while(jones.lname[counter] != '\0')
    {
    jones.lname[counter] = toupper(jones.lname[counter]);
    counter = counter + 1;
    }
```

Note that the words **struct employee** are left out of all these statements. Only the names, such as **smith** and **jones**, that you gave to particular variables of this type are used to refer to their elements.

It is not exactly convenient, however, to create a separate variable to store the data for each employee in your company; as you saw when you first learned about arrays, creating a separate variable for each employee means that you must write code for each employee whenever you do anything to the data. You can also create arrays of structs that let you manipulate the data in structs as easily as you manipulate the data in any array. For example, if you had to keep track of the 100 employees in the Acme Company, you could declare an array with the following statement,

```
struct employee acmeEmp[100];
```

which will create 100 variables, with names from **acmeEmpl[0]** to **acmeEmpl[99]**, each of the type **struct employee** (assuming, of course, that you declared **struct employee** earlier in the program).

You can work with this array in much the same way as with any array. For example, you can add up the total salaries of all the workers with the following module.

```
totsal()
{
int counter;
float sumOfSal;

sumOfSal = 0;
counter = 0;
while(counter < 100)
    {
    sumOfSal = sumOfSal + acmeEmp[counter].salary;
    counter = counter + 1;
    }
printf("\ntotal salary is %f",sumOfSal);
}
```

You refer to each employee's salary just as you would with any array, using a variable name, a period, and the name of the element — **salary**. The only difference here is that the variable name includes a counter because it is part of an array of structs. (Note that this module assumes that the array was declared earlier in the program as a global variable and that values for the salaries have been entered in another module.)

Likewise, it is quite easy to look up the name of a particular employee and capitalize it properly. Even though you are working with two arrays — the array that holds the name of a particular employee and the array of structs that holds data on all of the employees — there is none of the potential confusion that would arise if you were working with a two-dimensional array. For example, you can capitalize the last names of all the employees as follows:

```
capitliz()
{
int empCtr, ltrCtr;

empCtr = 0;
while(empCtr<100)
      {
      ltrCtr = 0;
      while(acmeEmp[empCtr].lname[ltrCtr] != '\0')
            {
            acmeEmp[empCtr].lname[ltrCtr] =
                      toupper(acmeEmp[empCtr].lname[ltrCtr];
            ltrCtr = ltrCtr + 1;
            }
      empCtr = empCtr + 1;
      }
}
```

The first time through the outer loop, **empCtr** is equal to 0 so that the program looks at **acmeEmp[0]**. The inner loop capitalizes all the letters of the last name, starting with **acmeEmp[0].lname[0]** and adding 1 to **ltrCtr** until it reaches the final **null** of the last name. Then the outer loop increments **empCtr** and the same is done for **acmeEmp[1]** and all of the other employees up to **acmeEmp[99]**. This program would obviously be more confusing if it simply used a two-dimensional array to keep the records and didn't include the index numbers connected with the words **acmeEmp** and **lname** to remind you of what they are referring to.

LANGUAGE FLASHCARDS

To give you experience working with strings, structs, and arrays of structs, in this section you will develop a language flashcard program to test students in French vocabulary. This program will be similar to the arithmetic quiz in Chapter 3 but will have some major differences.

First, because the program cannot "calculate" the English meaning of a French word as it calculates the answer to an arithmetic problem, it will store the French and English words together in an array of structs. In the first version of this program, these structs will simply be initialized by a function of the program. In Chapter 6, however, you will learn to store these words in files on disk and create a more generalized version of the program that lets the user expand the vocabulary list available on disk.

Second, the arithmetic quiz had separate functions for addition, subtraction, multiplication, and division. It is generally easier for beginners to understand a program if it duplicates code to perform similar functions in separate modules, as did the ASCCHRT program and the arithmetic quiz, in which you used your editor to copy one function and modify it to create the others. This approach gives you a program with an easy-to-understand block structure in which the **main**() menu function simply branches to one of the other functions, depending on the user's choice, but it also gives you a program that is difficult to modify and maintain; if any change is needed in the screen display, for example, all functions must be changed accordingly. It is easy to create four copies of the original, but it is much more difficult to modify and test all four functions than to modify and test one.

Normally, programs are modified considerably as they are developed and tested by potential users because it takes quite a while for programmers to figure out what users really want. And even when a program is complete, it continues to be modified in later versions. In general, then, even though doing so creates a block structure that is easy to understand, it is not good programming style to create similar functions with slight variations. By now, you have reached the point where you can use more sophisticated techniques that let a single function replace several slightly varied functions. What you learned in Chapter 4 about passing parameters — along with a few new points that you need to learn now about using strings as parameters — will let you use a single function to display all of the different types of flashcards in this program.

All language flashcards — computerized or not — give people the choice of translating from their native language (in this case, English) to the foreign language (in this case, French) or from the foreign language to their native language. In addition, you should allow users to retest the words they got wrong the last time through and to test only nouns, only verbs, or only other parts of speech (such as adjectives or prepositions). To do this, you must store the vocabulary in a **struct** that includes the English word, the French word, the part of speech (noun, verb, or other) and some sort of flag to show whether or not there was an error on this word the last time through the cards. The struct can be declared as follows:

```
struct flshcard
    {
    char English[16];
    char French[16];
    char spchPart;
    int errorFlg;
    };
```

This declaration allows words of up to 15 letters (plus the final **null**). The part of speech can be represented by a single letter, 'N' for noun, 'V' for verb, or 'O' for other. The retest flag could be a **char** that is set to 'Y' or 'N', depending on whether or not retesting is needed, but (as you learned earlier) it is more common to use **int**s as flags in C. In this chapter, you will learn how to refer to an **int** as if it were a logical variable.

The pseudocode for the **main**() module is simple and is similar to many menu modules that you have written previously. There is only one additional refinement: you should give users the option of retesting the words that they got wrong the last time only if there are words to be retested (i.e., only if they actually got one or more words wrong). Some flashcard programs always give users this option, even when they first start the program, and simply tell them that there are no errors to retest if they choose the retest option at the wrong time, but you can improve on that sloppy technique by creating a global variable that is a flag to tell you if there are any errors to retest, setting the flag equal to 0 at the beginning of the program, and setting it to 1 when an error is made. The program will only display the retest option if the flag is equal to 1, and it will set the flag to 0 again if another menu option is chosen so that the next time the menu appears, the program again would only display the retest option if there had been an error the last time through the stack of cards.

Bearing the retest option in mind, you can write the pseudocode for the main module as follows:

INITIALIZE THE ARRAY WITH FRENCH, ENGLISH WORDS, ETC.
INITIALIZE THE GLOBAL RETEST FLAG WITH ZERO.
REPEAT AS LONG AS THE USER WANTS TO CONTINUE:
    PRINT A HEADING ON THE SCREEN.
    PRINT THESE OPTIONS FOR TESTING ON THE SCREEN:
    - FRENCH TO ENGLISH FOR ALL WORDS,
    - FRENCH TO ENGLISH FOR NOUNS,
    - FRENCH TO ENGLISH FOR VERBS,
    - FRENCH TO ENGLISH FOR OTHERS,
    - ENGLISH TO FRENCH FOR ALL WORDS,
    - ENGLISH TO FRENCH FOR NOUNS,
    - ENGLISH TO FRENCH FOR VERBS,
    - ENGLISH TO FRENCH FOR OTHERS.
    IF THE GLOBAL RETEST FLAG EQUALS ONE
        PRINT THE OPTION OF RETESTING ERRORS
    PRINT THE OPTION OF QUITTING
    GET THE USER'S CHOICE
    IF THE USER DID NOT CHOOSE RETESTING ERRORS
        MAKE THE RETEST FLAG EQUAL ZERO
    PERFORM THE OPTION THE USER CHOSE.

It may seem odd that this function repeatedly sets the global retest flag to 0 and never gives it any other value, but remember that the function that actually displays the flashcards will set the flag to 1 as soon as the user makes an error.

The final line of the pseudocode, *PERFORM THE OPTION THE USER CHOSE*, is a bit enigmatic. The programs you have written in the past would branch to different functions, depending on the user's choice, but how can you make a single function perform a variety of options? The answer is that you can pass the user's choice to the function as a parameter.

The more obvious way to make this function perform different options is by including **if-else** statements that depend on the parameter passed to the function. **main**() will use this method to pass the option about what part of speech will be used. Name the function that displays the flashcards **testword**(), and give it the parameter **pos** (short for "part of speech"). The function would have the following general form:

```
testword(pos)
char pos;
{
MORE CODE
}
```

Then, depending on whether the user chooses to test nouns, verbs, other words, or all words, **main()** can call the function as **testword('N');** or **testword('V');** or **testword('O');** or **testword('A');**. When **main()** calls the function, the value 'N', 'V', 'O', or 'A' is copied into the variable **pos** in the **testword()** module to bypass a word if that word's part of speech is not the same as **pos**.

At this point, the pseudocode for **testword()** looks like the following:

REPEAT WHILE THERE ARE STILL MORE WORDS IN THE LIST:
    IF THE PART OF SPEECH CALLED FOR IS NOT "ALL"
    AND THE PART OF SPEECH CALLED FOR IS NOT THE
    SAME AS THE PART OF SPEECH OF THE WORD,
        GO TO THE NEXT WORD IN THE LIST.
    OTHERWISE,
        DISPLAY THE HEADING.
        DISPLAY THE (ENGLISH OR FRENCH) WORD.
        GET THE USER'S (FRENCH OR ENGLISH) MEANING.
        IF THE MEANING IS CORRECT,
            CONGRATULATE THE USER.
        OTHERWISE,
            TELL THE USER THE CORRECT MEANING.
            MARK THE WORD FOR RETESTING.
        GO TO THE NEXT WORD.
TELL THE USER THERE ARE NO MORE WORDS IN THE LIST.

Note how economical it is to pass the part of speech to this function as a parameter and use one **if-else** statement in this function to handle the choice of parts of speech, instead of creating four separate functions for the four choices.

Is there any equally economical way to handle the choice of French-English or English-French translation? Your first impulse might be to handle it in a similar way by using a parameter that has eight values to represent each of the four possibilities you have already looked at in either English-French or French-English. This approach would lead to a very complex series of **if-else** statements, however.

There is a simpler way to accomplish the same task—you can use three parameters. One represents which part of speech is being used, as you have already seen, and the other two represent the names of the two languages. The **testword**() function, then, would have the following general form:

```
testword(lang1,lang2,pos)
char pos;
char lang1[];
char lang2[];
{
MORE CODE
}
```

The **testword**() module could, for example, use the following line as the heading of its screen display:

```
printf("\t\t\tTranslating from %s to %s",lang1,lang2);
```

When **main**() calls **testword**(), it uses a command such as the following:

```
testword("English","French",'n')
```

Then **testword**() would give **lang1** the value "**English**" and **lang2** the value "**French**" so that it would print the heading as "**Translating from English to French.**"

Note the declaration of a string as a parameter. Earlier in this chapter, you used string variables as arguments of functions such as **strlen**() and **strcmp**() by simply using the name without any brackets. But this is the first time that you are actually writing a function that takes a string as its argument, so you should examine the function again:

```
testword(lang1,lang2,pos)
char pos;
char lang1[];
char lang2[];
{
MORE CODE
}
```

Note also that, within the parentheses of the function, the names of the string variables **lang1** and **lang2** are simply used without any brackets following them, like string variables within the parentheses of the string-handling functions discussed earlier in this chapter. The declaration of the variables, however, has empty brackets following the variable name. Chapter 6, which includes a discussion of pointers to addresses, will explain the meaning of these uses of string names.

This flashcard program will use the function **gets**() to read the user's input. As you saw previously, **scanf**("%s") will only read a string up to a blank space character. Because many vocabulary words must contain blanks (for example, French nouns must include the article), **gets**() is the only way to accept these words. This program will also take advantage of **gets**() to accept menu choices from the user. Later in this chapter, after you have compiled the program, try pressing the Enter key when the menu screen is displayed, and you will see the advantage of **gets**() over **scanf**() in menus. This program uses the character array **choice[2]** to hold the menu choice so that if the user enters a long string as a menu choice, the program will loop until it has read all the characters. This is common even in commercial programs, but if you want to bulletproof this menu completely and avoid this problem, you can declare the array that gets the menu choice as **char choice[128];** instead.

Look carefully at the relationship between the **main**() and the **testword**() module in the following incomplete version of the program:

```
struct flshcard
    {
    char English[16];
    char French[16];
    char spchPart;
    int errorFlg;
    } enFr[10];
int retstFlg;


main()
{
char choice[2];

initlze();
while(1==1)
    {
    printf("\n\t\t\tLanguage Flashcards\n\n");
    printf("\n\n\t\t1 - English to French, nouns");
    printf("\n\n\t\t2 - English to French, verbs");
    printf("\n\n\t\t3 - English to French, others");
    printf("\n\n\t\t4 - English to French, all");
    printf("\n\n\t\t5 - French to English, nouns");
    printf("\n\n\t\t6 - French to English, verbs");
    printf("\n\n\t\t7 - French to English, others");
    printf("\n\n\t\t8 - French to English, all");
    if(retstFlg==1)
        {
        printf("\n\n\t\t9 - Errors from last test");
        }
    printf("\n\n\t\t0 - Quit");
    if(retstFlg!=1)
        {
        printf("\n\n");
        }
    printf("\n\n\t\t\tWhat is your choice > ")
    gets(choice)
```

continued...

...from previous page

```
if(choice[0]=='1')
    {
    testword("English","French",'N');
    }
else if(choice[0]=='2')
    {
    testword("English","French",'V');
    }
else if(choice[0]=='3')
    {
    testword("English","French",'O');
    }
else if(choice[0]=='4')
    {
    testword("English","French",'A');
    }
else if(choice[0]=='5')
    {
    testword("French","English",'N');
    }
else if(choice[0]=='6')
    {
    testword("French","English",'V');
    }
else if(choice[0]=='7')
    {
    testword("French","English",'O');
    }
else if(choice[0]=='8')
    {
    testword("French","English",'A');
    }

/* ELSE IF CHOICE == 9 */
    /* NOT YET IMPLEMENTED */

else if(choice[0]=='0')
    {
    break;
    }
```

continued...

...from previous page

```
    else
        {
        putchar(7);
        }
    }
}


testword(lang1,lang2,pos)
char pos;
char lang1[];
char lang2[];
{
int wrdCntr, ltrCntr;
char answer[16];
char yorn[2];

wrdCntr = 0;
while(wrdCntr<10)
    {
    if(pos!='A' && pos!=enFr[wrdCntr].spchPart)
        {
        wrdCntr = wrdCntr + 1;
        continue;
        }
    printf("\n\n\n\n");
    printf("\t\t\tTranslation from %s to %s", lang1,lang2);
    printf("\n\n\n\t\t\t\ttest of ");
    if(pos=='N')
        {
        printf("nouns");
        }
    else if(pos=='V')
        {
        printf("verbs");
        }
    else if(pos=='O')
        {
        printf("other words");
        }
```

continued...

...from previous page

```
    else if(pos=='A')
        {
        printf("all words");
        }

    if(lang1[0]=='F')
        {
        printf("\n\n\n\n\n\n\n\n\n");
        printf("\t\t\t\t%s", enFr[wrdCntr].French);
        printf("\n\n\n\n\n\n\n\n);
        printf("What is the English translation > ");

        gets(answer);


        ltrCntr = 0;
        while(answer[ltrCntr] != '\0')
            {
            answer[ltrCntr] = toupper(answer[ltrCntr]);
            ltrCntr = ltrCntr + 1;
            }
         if(strcmp(answer,enFr[wrdCntr].English)==0)
            {
            printf("\n\nCongratulations.  That is right.");
            printf("\nDo you want to try another (Y/N) > ");
            gets(yorn);
            if(toupper(yorn[0])=='N')
            {
            return;
            }
        }
    else
        {
        enFr[wrdCntr].errorFlg = 1;
        retstFlg = 1;
        printf("\n\nThe correct answer is %s.",
                            enFr[wrdCntr].English);
```

continued...

...from previous page

```
        printf("\nDo you want to try another (Y/N) > ");
        gets(yorn);
        if(toupper(yorn[0])=='N')
            {
            return;
            }
        }
    wrdCntr =wrdCntr + 1;
    }


else
    {
    printf("\n\n\n\n\n\n\n\n\n");
    printf("\t\t\t\t%s", enFr[wrdCntr].English);
    printf("\n\n\n\n\n\n\n\n");
    printf("What is the French translation > ");

    gets(answer);

    ltrCntr = 0;
    while(answer[ltrCntr] != '\0')
        {
        answer[ltrCntr] = toupper(answer[ltrCntr]);
        ltrCntr = ltrCntr + 1;
        }
     if(strcmp(answer,enFr[wrdCntr].French)==0)
        {
        printf("\n\nCongratulations.  That is right.");
        printf("\nDo you want to try another (Y/N) > ");
        gets(yorn);
        if(toupper(yorn[0])=='N')
            {
            return;
            }
        }
```

continued...

...from previous page

```
else
    {
    enFr[wrdCntr].errorFlg = 1;
    retstFlg = 1;
    printf("\n\nThe correct answer is %s.",
                            enFr[wrdCntr].French);
    printf("\nDo you want to try another (Y/N) > ");
    gets(yorn);
    if(toupper(yorn[0])=='N')
        {
        return;
        }
    }
    wrdCntr =wrdCntr + 1;
    }
}
}
```

Note that the program begins by declaring the struct named **flshcard**, which contains the elements already discussed, and simultaneously declaring an array of variables of that type named **enFr[10]** (short for English-French Word List). This array only has 10 elements (which means that there will only be 10 vocabulary words to test) because, in this chapter, you will simply initialize it by using a series of **strcpy()** commands within the program. In Chapter 6, when you learn to work with disk files, you will create a much longer word list.

C includes a feature that makes it easy to modify programs in this way. It is generally good programming style in any computer language to list values that might be changed when the program is modified as variables at the beginning of the program; then, when you modify the program, you will only need to change one statement at the beginning rather than look through the entire program for every occurrence of a particular value. C performs this task even more efficiently with the precompiler command **#define**, which lets you define a word (or any string of characters) as representing a value. The next version of this program, for example, will contain the statement **#define MAXWORDS 10**. (Note that like other precompiler commands, this command does not end with a semicolon.) Throughout the program, wherever the counter must be less than 10, you will test whether it is less than **MAXWORDS** instead.

As the **#** sign indicates, this command is processed by the precompiler, as is the command **#include**. Before actual compilation begins, the value **10** will be substituted for the word **MAXWORDS** wherever **MAXWORDS** appears in the program. Because this program uses this constant, it runs more efficiently than programs in languages that use variables that may eventually be changed for values, such as this one. The program does not require extra memory to store a variable or extra time to retrieve it, yet it is as easy for the programmer to change the value of this constant as it would be to change the value of a single variable at the beginning of the program. It is conventional to give this type of defined constant a name that is in all uppercase letters to distinguish it from a variable.

After the initial definitions and declaration of global variables, **main**() displays a menu with nine choices, accepts the user's choice, and then begins a prolonged **if-else-if** ladder to call the **testword**() module with parameters that depend on the user's choice. Toward the beginning of **testword**(), there is also an **if-else-if** ladder to display the heading on the screen as "test of nouns," "test of verbs," etc., depending on whether **pos** is 'N', 'V', etc.

Before displaying the screen, **testword**() checks to make sure the part of speech of the word **wrdCntr** is currently pointing to is the same as **pos**. If it is not the same as **pos** *and* if **pos** is not equal to 'A' (indicating that all words should be tested), then **testword**() adds 1 to **wrdCntr** and loops back to the beginning with the statement **continue;** to try again with the next word in the list and see if it is the right part of speech. If the word is the right part of speech or if all words are being tested, the program displays the English or French word, gets the user's answer, uses a **while** loop to capitalize the user's response (so the user can enter it in either upper- or lowercase letters), compares the user's translation with the French or English word in the database, and tells the user if it is right or wrong. Then the user can enter an 'N' to stop the quiz and **return;** to the main menu. If any other letter is entered, the program loops back to the beginning and goes through the steps again, after checking the condition in the **while**() to make sure that the **wrdCntr** is not equal to 10, which would mean that you have reached the end of the list.

Choice nine on the menu, the option of retesting words that were missed the last time through, has not been discussed yet in order to simplify the development of the program up to this point. To implement this option, you must add another conditional **if()** statement toward the beginning of **testword()**. Just after the **if()** that checks for part of speech (and, if it is not right, adds one to the counter and loops back to the beginning to try again), you would need another **if()** that checks to see if the **errorFlg** for that word is equal to 1 and, if it is not, loops back in just the same way to try the next word. You would also need to add a line of code far-ther down in the program (where it prints an error message if the user gets the word wrong) to set **errorFlg** to 1 in case of error. If the user does not choose retesting from the menu, you would have to make all the **errorFlg**s equal to 0 again, in order to keep a record of the errors on the next round, as in the pseu-docode.

One intriguing thing about the retest option is that the program must record which languages were used the last time through in order to implement that option. The program must know whether to use the **wordtest("English","French",'R');** state-ment or the **wordtest("French","English",'R');** statement. The words that need to be retested are marked, because the **errorFlg** has been made equal to 1, but the program has no way of knowing whether to retest by asking the user these words in English and getting a French translation, or vice versa.

The obvious way to solve this problem is to create two new string variables, which you could call **toAsk** and **toAnswer**. When the user chooses any option, the program stores the word **"English"** in **toAsk** and **"French"** in **toAnswer** if the user is translating from English to French, and the program stores **"French"** in **toAsk** and **"English"** in **toAnswer** if the user is translating from French to English. Then, if the user chooses the option of retesting, you can simply use the command **wordtest(toAsk,toAnswer,'R');**, and the program will interpret that command to mean **wordtest("English","French",'R')** or **wordtest("French","English",'R')**, depending on which of type of test was taken the last time.

You should now begin to have a larger idea about how to simplify that prolonged **if-else-if** ladder in the **main()** module of the program. Why not use the same vari-ables, **toAsk** and **toAnswer**, for all the options? You can give them their values in just one brief **if-else** statement rather than in a prolonged **if-else-if** ladder. This strategy will be easier to understand if you look at the listing that follows. You must also create a new variable for the final parameter, which represents the part of speech or retest option. This variable can be called **whchWrds**.

Now that you have seen the longer version of this choice, you should not have much trouble understanding the shorter but slightly more complex version that follows.

```
/* CHAPTER 5, EXAMPLE 9 */

#include <stdio.h>
#define MAXWORDS 10        /* English-French Flashcard program */

struct flshcard
    {
    char English[16];
    char French[16];      /* struct to hold flashcard data */
    char spchPart;
    int errorFlg;
    } enFr[MAXWORDS];

int retstFlg;

main()                                   /* main menu */
{
char ch[2];
char toAsk[8], toAnswer[8], whchWrds;

initlze();
retstFlg = 0;
while(1==1)                              /* display the menu */
   {
   printf("\n\t\t\tLanguage Flashcards\n\n");
   printf("\n\n\t\t1 - English to French, nouns");
   printf("\n\n\t\t2 - English to French, verbs");
   printf("\n\n\t\t3 - English to French, others");
   printf("\n\n\t\t4 - English to French, all");
   printf("\n\n\t\t5 - French to English, nouns");
   printf("\n\n\t\t6 - French to English, verbs");
   printf("\n\n\t\t7 - French to English, others");
   printf("\n\n\t\t8 - French to English, all");
   if(retstFlg==1)
       {
       printf("\n\n\t\t9 - Errors from last test");
       }
```

continued...

...from previous page

```
printf("\n\n\t\t0 - Quit");
if(retstFlg!=1)
    {
printf("\n\n");
    }
printf("\n\n\t\t\tWhat is your choice > ");
gets(ch);
                            /* get user's choice and */
                            /* set parameters accordingly */

if(ch[0]=='1' || ch[0]=='2' || ch[0]=='3' || ch[0]=='4')
    {
    strcpy(toAsk,"English");
    strcpy(toAnswer,"French");
    }
if(ch[0]=='5' || ch[0]=='6' || ch[0]=='7' || ch[0]=='8')
    {
    strcpy(toAsk,"French");
    strcpy(toAnswer,"English");
    }
if(ch[0]=='1' || ch[0]=='5')
    {
    whchWrds = 'N';
    }

else if(ch[0]=='2' || ch[0]=='6')
    {
    whchWrds = 'V';
    }
else if(ch[0]=='3' || ch[0]=='7')
    {
    whchWrds = 'O';
    }
else if(ch[0]=='4' || ch[0]=='8')
    {
    whchWrds = 'A';
    }
else if(ch[0]=='9' && retstFlg == 1)
    {
    whchWrds = 'R';
    }
```

continued...

...from previous page

```
      else if(ch[0]=='0')
            {
            break;
            }
      else
            {
            putchar(7);
            continue;
            }
      testword(toAsk,toAnswer,whchWrds);
      }
}



initlze()                         /* create list of English */
{                                 /* and French words: to be */
int counter;                      /* improved in Chapter 6 */

counter = 0;
while(counter<MAXWORDS)
      {
      enFr[counter].errorFlg = 0;
      counter = counter + 1;
      }
strcpy(enFr[0].English,"TO SPEAK");
strcpy(enFr[0].French,"PARLER");
enFr[0].spchPart = 'V';
strcpy(enFr[1].English,"TO SELL");
strcpy(enFr[1].French,"VENDRE");
enFr[1].spchPart = 'V';
strcpy(enFr[2].English,"TO GO");
strcpy(enFr[2].French,"ALLER");
enFr[2].spchPart = 'V';
strcpy(enFr[3].English,"THE BOY");
strcpy(enFr[3].French,"LE GARCON");
enFr[3].spchPart = 'N';
```

continued...

...from previous page

```
strcpy(enFr[4].English,"THE PEN");
strcpy(enFr[4].French,"LA PLUME");
enFr[4].spchPart = 'N';
strcpy(enFr[5].English,"THE GIRL");
strcpy(enFr[5].French,"LA FILLE");
enFr[5].spchPart = 'N';
strcpy(enFr[6].English,"IN");
strcpy(enFr[6].French,"DANS");
enFr[6].spchPart = 'O';
strcpy(enFr[7].English,"ON");
strcpy(enFr[7].French,"SUR");
enFr[7].spchPart = 'O';
strcpy(enFr[8].English,"DURING");
strcpy(enFr[8].French,"PENDANT");
enFr[9].spchPart = 'O';
strcpy(enFr[9].English,"BEFORE");
strcpy(enFr[9].French,"AVANT");
enFr[9].spchPart = 'O';
}


testword(lang1,lang2,pos)          /* test user */
char pos;
char lang1[];                      /* using parameters */
char lang2[];                      /* set in main() */
{
int wrdCntr, ltrCntr;
char answer[16];
char yorn[2];
int retestFlg;

wrdCntr = 0;
if(pos!='R')                       /* if not a retest, make */
    {                              /* error flags 0 so they */
    while(wrdCntr<MAXWORDS)        /* can record new errors */
        {
        enFr[wrdCntr].errorFlg = 0;
        wrdCntr = wrdCntr + 1;
        }
    }
```

continued...

...from previous page

```
wrdCntr = 0;                          /* skip those that are */
while(wrdCntr<MAXWORDS)               /* wrong part of speech */
    {
    if(pos!='A' && pos!= 'R' && pos!=enFr[wrdCntr].spchPart)
        {
        wrdCntr = wrdCntr + 1;
        continue;
        }
    if(pos=='R' && enFr[wrdCntr].errorFlg!=1)
        {
        wrdCntr = wrdCntr + 1;
        continue;
        }

    printf("\n\n\n\n\n\n\n");
    printf("\t\t   Translation from %s to %s", lang1,lang2);
    printf("\n\n\t\t\t   test of ");
    if(pos=='N')
        {                                    /* display screen */
        printf("nouns");
        }
    else if(pos=='V')
        {
        printf("verbs");
        }
    else if(pos=='O')
        {
        printf("other words");
        }
    else if(pos=='A')
        {
        printf("all words");
        }

    if(lang1[0]=='F')                    /* French-English */
        {
        printf("\n\n\n\n\n\n\n\n\n");
        printf("\t\t\t\t%s", enFr[wrdCntr].French);
        printf("\n\n\n\n\n\n\n\n");
        printf("What is the English translation > ");
```

continued...

...from previous page

```
    gets(answer);                          /* get user's answer */
                                           /* and capitalize it */
    ltrCntr = 0;
    while(answer[ltrCntr] != '\0')
            {
            answer[ltrCntr] = toupper(answer[ltrCntr]);
            ltrCntr = ltrCntr + 1;
            }

      if(strcmp(answer,enFr[wrdCntr].English)==0)
            {
            printf("\n\nCongratulations.  That is right.");
            printf("\nDo you want to try another (Y/N) > ");
            gets(yorn);
            if(toupper(yorn[0])=='N')
                    {
                    return;
                    }
            }                              /* message for right */
    else                                   /* or wrong answer */
            {
            enFr[wrdCntr].errorFlg = 1;
            retstFlg = 1;
            printf("\n\nThe correct answer is %s.",
                                    enFr[wrdCntr].English);
            printf("\nDo you want to try another (Y/N) > ");
            gets(yorn);
            if(toupper(yorn[0])=='N')
                    {
                    return;
                    }
            }
    wrdCntr =wrdCntr + 1;
    }
    else                                       /* English-French */
            {
```

continued...

...from previous page

```
printf("\n\n\n\n\n\n\n\n\n");
printf("\t\t\t\t%s", enFr[wrdCntr].English);
printf("\n\n\n\n\n\n\n\n\n");
printf("What is the French translation > ");

gets(answer);                        /* get user's answer */
                                     /* and capitalize it */
ltrCntr = 0;
while(answer[ltrCntr] != '\0')
    {
    answer[ltrCntr] = toupper(answer[ltrCntr]);
    ltrCntr = ltrCntr + 1;
    }

 if(strcmp(answer,enFr[wrdCntr].French)==0)
    {
    printf("\n\nCongratulations.  That is right.");
    printf("\nDo you want to try another (Y/N) > ");
    gets(yorn);
    if(toupper(yorn[0])=='N')
        {
        return;
        }
    }                                /* message for right */
else                                 /* or wrong answer */
    {
    enFr[wrdCntr].errorFlg = 1;
    retstFlg = 1;
    printf("\n\nNo, the correct answer is %s.",
                        enFr[wrdCntr].French);
    printf("Do you want to try another (Y/N) ");
    gets(yorn);
    if(toupper(yorn[0])=='N')
        {
        return;
        }
    }
wrdCntr =wrdCntr + 1;
}
}
}
```

Compare this final version of the code in the second half of the **main**() module, which assigns values to the variables used as parameters of the command **testword**();, with the first version of the program, which includes the prolonged **if-else-if** ladder that uses **testword**() with eight different constants as parameters. This may seem like more thinking than you want to do to save just a few lines of code, but it is an excellent exercise in making programs more compact, and, at the same time, it solves the problem of retesting that could not be handled in the first version of the program. If the user chooses option nine, to retest the errors he or she missed last time, the program does not assign any values at all to the variables that represent the names of the languages; it simply leaves them as they were the last time around.

When you start writing programs on your own, it is a good exercise to go over your code and see if it can be made more compact in this way. It will take you more time to write the code at first; as a result, there is always a temptation to do things the quick-and-dirty way by using your editor to create one version after another of the same command or of the same module, each to do something slightly different from the last. But analyzing the program carefully and finding ways to eliminate duplication and make the code more compact — if more complex — will make you a much better and much faster programmer in the long run.

SUMMARY

A **string**, which is used to manipulate words or text in C, is an array of characters terminated by the **null** character, '\0'. It is declared as an array of **chars** and must contain one element more than the maximum number of characters in the word that it will hold to leave a space for the null terminator. For example, the array declared as **char word[21];** would hold a word of up to 20 letters.

It is possible to assign a value to a string by initializing each **char** of the string individually and adding the null terminator, but it is easier to use the function **strcpy**(), which can copy a constant to a variable as follows:

```
char name[16];
strcpy(name,"Amadeus");
```

String constants are enclosed in double quotation marks, unlike **chars**, which are enclosed in single quotation marks.

As with most string-handling functions, the first argument of **strcpy**() is the target that is changed. This function can also be used to copy one variable to another. For example, the statement **strcpy(name,musician);** would copy the string already stored in the variable **musician**[] into the variable **name**[].

The formatted I/O functions **printf**() and **scanf**() can be used with the special character **%s** to handle strings, but **scanf**() will only read a string up to the first blank space character (space, newline, tab, or carriage return).

The unformatted I/O function **gets**() can be used to read a string containing blank spaces. **gets**() is one of a family of unformatted I/O functions that begin with **get** or **put**, including the functions **gets**() and **puts**() for strings and **getchar**() and **putchar**() for characters.

Other functions that are commonly used with strings include the following:

- **toupper**() and **tolower**(), both of which take one **char** as their argument and which make an alphabetic **char** uppercase or lowercase but have no effect on nonalphabetic characters.

- **strcmp**(), which takes two strings as its arguments and returns a 0 if the two are identical.

- **strlen**(), which takes one string as its argument and returns the length of that string.

The **structure** or **struct** can be thought of as a package of data that lets you combine different data types. The declaration of a structure includes each of its elements after its name, as follows:

```
struct employee
    {
    char fname[21];
    char lname[31];
    char address[31];
    char city[21];
    char state[3];
    char zip[6];
    char sex;
    int age;
    float salary;
    };
```

This declaration essentially creates a new data type, named **employee,** by packaging together a list of existing data types. It does not create an actual variable. To create variables of this type, you can use a declaration such as **struct employee smith;.** You can also create arrays of structs, with a declaration such as **struct employee acmeEmp[100];.**

You can also combine the declaration of the struct and of the variables as follows:

```
struct employee
    {
    char fname[21];
    char lname[31];
    char address[31];
    char city[21];
    char state[3];
    char zip[6];
    char sex;
    int age;
    float salary;
    }smith, jones, acmeEmp[100];
```

To refer to individual elements of a variable that is a struct, you must use the name of the variable, plus a period, plus the name of the element, for example, **jones.salary** or **acmeEmp[10].salary** or **acmeEmp[10].lname[0]**.

The precompiler command **#define** makes it easy to modify programs by letting you define a word (or any string of characters) as representing a constant value. For example, the statement **#define MAXWORDS 10** will make the precompiler substitute the value 10 whenever MAXWORDS appears. Note that, like other precompiler commands, this statement does not end with a semicolon. It is conventional to use all uppercase letters for the names of defined constants.

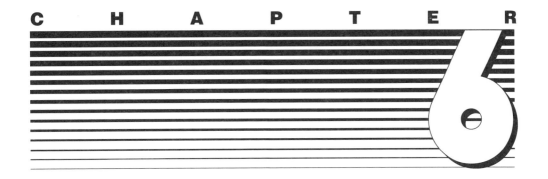

ADDRESSES AND DISK FILES

A WARNING

The main topic of this chapter is saving data in files on disk and reading them back into memory. Because this requires you to use what are called **pointers** — that is, variables that "point" to addresses in memory — this chapter will begin with a brief general overview of pointers. This is a fairly advanced topic, and you should not necessarily try to master it before going on to the rest of the chapter. Virtually every advanced seminar on C programming covers pointers because they can be one of the most difficult features of the language. A few simple uses of pointers are included in this beginning book on C for two reasons: 1) to help you understand the two different ways that one function of a structured program can manipulate variables in another function and 2) to give you some general background on the way computers use addresses, which will fill out your introduction to the concepts of computer programming.

One important warning is needed before you start compiling programs that use pointers. Remember that C is a "robust" language. As you learned in Chapter 1, C will do what you tell it to do, whether your instructions make sense or not, and this potential danger is the source of much of its power. As you saw in Chapter 1, if you tell C to print an integer as a character, it will do so rather than warn you, as most languages would, that you are using an incorrect data type. This characteristic of C made it easy to write the ASCCHRT program, but it adds to your responsibility as a programmer. For example, you can mix up a calculation horribly if you mistakenly define one of the numbers as a **char** and the program, without any error message, simply uses the ASCII value of that number rather than the number itself.

C is equally "robust" when it is working with addresses, which can cause even more problems. Say, for example, that you declare an integer variable named **x** and give it some initial value. Later in the program, if you want to change the variable's value and mistakenly tell C to write a value in *address number* **x**, rather than in the address of the *variable* **x,** your program will place that value in that memory slot instead of in the variable's address, just as you told it to.

When a program is running, the operating system, e.g., MS-DOS, remains in RAM and its services are available for use by the program. If, for example, the addresses in which your program places variables happen to be located in the area of RAM that holds the operating system, your program will simply write over MS-DOS and cause the system to fail. This will not happen if you write data into the addresses of the variables, but it can happen if you just leave out just one little **&** and by mistake write data into the address whose number is the same as the value of the variable.

If you write over your operating system, you must simply turn the computer off and back on. When the computer reboots, MS-DOS will be comfortably installed in RAM again. The real danger when you use pointers is that you might mistakenly write over data that is stored on your disk and lose it permanently. You could overwrite parts of an expensive program that you just installed on your hard disk. In fact, there is a part of your disk that is called the File Allocation Table (or FAT), which is a chart showing where data is stored. The operating system cannot access any data from the disk without this table, and, unfortunately, you can overwrite this table and lose all the data on your hard disk.

The most common way for beginners to lose all their data is by thinking the current drive is drive A (in which they have placed a new floppy disk) when they are in actually in drive C (the hard disk drive). Depending the version of DOS you are using, entering the FORMAT command can cause DOS to format the entire hard disk and wipe out everything on it without even giving you an error message. The most common way for more advanced users to lose the data on their hard disk is by making an apparently minor error in a C program that uses pointers. The obvious lesson is to always keep your hard disk backed up. Get into the habit of performing a routine backup at the end of every week or even every day.

Most important, *be sure your hard disk is completely backed up before you compile and run any C programs that use pointers*.

POINTERS: THE BASICS

You have already learned about one operator that you need in order to work with pointers — the ampersand (&), which means "the address of." The other operator that goes along with it is the asterisk (*), sometimes called the "indirection" operator, which means "the contents of address." Look, for example, at the following program fragment:

```
pSamplVar = &samplVar;
*pSamplVar = 12;
```

The first line means "make **pSamplVar** equal to the address of **samplVar**," and the second line means "make the contents of address **pSamplVar** equal to 12." The contents of address **pSamplVar** is the variable **samplVar**, so this program makes **samplVar** equal to12.

Note that the first line, which assigns the value of some variable's address to the pointer, must precede the second line. If you wrote a program that declared a pointer and placed, for example, 12 in that address without first assigning a value to that pointer, the program would simply interpret whatever random value that pointer happened to have as an address and put the value 12 there, possibly in some key memory location, which is another example of how you can cause your system to crash.

The asterisk is also used in the declaration of a pointer. For example, the previous code fragment would need to be preceded by the declaration **int *pSamplVar;** because **pSamplVar** points to an integer. You use the same kind of declaration to declare pointers to any data type so that a pointer to a character would be declared as **char *pSamplVar;**. The fact that the asterisk is used as an operator in the code and is also used in the declaration is a bit confusing. Remember that in the code the asterisk means "the contents of address" and in the declaration it just means that the variable is a pointer — it holds the number that is the address of some memory slot.

Also remember that the declaration **char *pSamplVar;** or **int *pSamplVar;** does not mean that the pointer variable is a **char** or an **int**. It means that the pointer points to a **char** or an **int**. The compiler needs to know what data type the pointer is the address of to know how many bytes to get to read the contents of that address. If the pointer points to a **char**, then the contents of that address is only one byte long; if the pointer points to an **int**, the contents of the address is two bytes long, and so on.

With this basic background, you can write your first program using pointers, which expands only slightly on the previous program fragment:

```
/* CHAPTER 6, EXAMPLE 1 */
#include <stdio.h>

main()                           /* sample program */
{                                /* using pointers */
int samplVar;
int *pSamplVar;

samplVar = 10;
printf("\nThe sample variable is %d.",samplVar);
pSamplVar = &samplVar;
*pSamplVar = 2;
printf("\nThe sample variable is now %d.",samplVar);
}
```

First, this program makes **samplVar** equal to 10 and prints a message telling you its value. Then it uses pointers to make **samplVar** equal to 2 and prints a message telling you its new value. The important part of the program is the way it changes the value of the variable by using pointers. First it makes **pSamplVar** equal to the address of **samplVar**, and then it makes the contents of the address **pSamplVar** equal to 2. This example is meant to make the use of pointers more real to you by letting you use them to actually change the value of a variable, so *make sure your hard disk is backed up*, and then compile and run this program.

The use of pointers in the previous example was just an illustration. The program could obviously accomplish the same task much more easily by saying **samplVar = 2;**. But there is one very important case in which you will need to change the value of a variable in this roundabout way by using pointers, that is, when the variable is a local variable declared in another function of the program.

Local variables in different functions are, as you have seen, strictly segregated from each other. Up to this point, you have written functions that can be passed variables from other functions, can perform operations on them, and then can return values to the functions that called them. But these functions cannot create any permanent changes in the parameters passed to them.

Consider a slight variation in the program that uses **addint()**, which was used as an example of parameters in Chapter 4. Imagine that you wanted a function that not only added the values of two integers but that incremented each of the integers by 1 first and then added them. You might try writing the program in the following manner:

```
/* CHAPTER 6, EXAMPLE 2 */
#include <stdio.h>

main()                          /* sample program: the wrong way */
{                               /* to change parameters' values */
int numbr1, numbr2, total;

numbr1 = 5;
numbr2 = 3;
total = incadd(numbr1,numbr2);
printf("\n%d plus %d equals %d",numbr1,numbr2,total);
}


incadd(x,y)
int x,y;
{
x = x + 1;
y = y + 1;
return x + y;
}
```

When **main()** calls **incadd()**, the values of the variables **numbr1** and **numbr2** in **main()** are merely copied into the variables **x** and **y** in **incadd()**. Any operations performed by the function that is called affect only the copies of the variables that are passed to the called function and do not affect the original variables in the calling function. In this example, **incadd()** would add 1 to the 5 and 1 to the 3 passed to it, would then add the results, and would finally return a value of 10. But unfortunately, **main()** would print "5 + 3 = 10," rather than "6 + 4 = 10," as the programmer intended. **incadd()** would not affect the values of the variables in **main()**.

This way of passing parameters to a module is known as a "call by value" because only the *values* of the variables in the calling function are known to the function that is called — the called function cannot get at the variables themselves. For the called function to be able to change the variables themselves, you must use what is known as a "call by reference," which actually gives the called function the addresses of the variables so it can affect the variables directly, as in the following program:

```
/* CHAPTER 6, EXAMPLE 3 */
#include <stdio.h>

main()                      /* sample program: the right way */
{                           /* to change parameters' values */
int numbr1, numbr2, total;

numbr1 = 5;
numbr2 = 3;
total = incadd(&numbr1,&numbr2);
printf("\n%d plus %d equals %d",numbr1,numbr2,total);
}


incadd(x,y)
int *x,*y;
{
*x = *x + 1;
*y = *y + 1;
return *x + *y;
}
```

This program does make sense when you translate the asterisks and ampersands into English. First, the calling function, **main()**, must pass the addresses of the variables it wants changed to the function it calls. **main()** assigns values to **numbr1** and **numbr2**, and then it gives a command that can be translated as "let **total** equal the value that is returned when you perform **incadd()** on the address of **numbr1** and the address of **numbr2**." The module **incadd()** then receives two parameters that are addresses. Because these parameters are addresses, they must be declared as pointers at the beginning of **incadd()**, in the statement **int *x,*y;**. Then, **incadd()** says "let the contents of address x equal the contents of address x plus 1; let the contents of address y equal the contents of address y plus 1; and return a value that is equal to the sum of the contents of address x plus the contents of address y."

Because **incadd**() actually made a direct reference to the addresses of the variables in **main**(), the value of these variables is changed, and the program prints "6 + 4 = 10," which is greatly preferable to the "5 + 3 = 10" result you received from the last version.

Now you can understand why the function **scanf**() must take an address as its argument. **scanf**() changes the value of a variable in the calling function. For example, if **main**() uses the command **scanf("%d",&smplNmbr);**, it is calling the function **scanf**() and asking **scanf**() to give some value to the variable **smplNmbr**, which was declared in **main**(). To change the value of a variable in the calling function, you must use a call by reference, which passes the address of the variable to **scanf**().

At this point, you might be ready to object and say that you have already worked with other functions that altered the variables passed to them as parameters — the string-handling functions. For example, if you use the command **strcpy(name,"Amadeus");** the function **strcpy**() will change the value of the variable **name** in the function that calls **strcpy**(). Why didn't you need to use the ampersand to pass the address of **name** to **strcpy**()?

This function works because the name of a string (or of any array) without the brackets following it actually represents the address of the first element of that array. In the example just mentioned, **name** is equivalent to **&name[0]**. In the string-handling function itself, you can declare the parameter either this way,

```
strcpy(str)
str[]
{
CODE
}
```

or this way, which is equivalent:

```
strcpy(str)
*str
{
CODE
}
```

Declaring the parameter with the empty brackets following it seems to indicate that the parameter is an array, and declaring it with an asterisk seems to suggest that it is a pointer, but actually the two declarations mean the same thing to the compiler. C deals with an array by using the address of the array's first element. When you are working with a string or an array as a whole (rather than element by element), it is important to remember that the distinction between a call by value and a call by reference disappears. The function that is called can always change the value of the variable because the name of the string or the array is itself an address.

Advanced C programmers often use pointers to access the elements of an array rather than refer to those elements by their index numbers. The use of index numbers to refer to the elements of an array is a relatively high-level feature of C. Using pointers accomplishes the same task on a lower level, which is closer to the way the computer itself does it. Pointers are used because, like many programs written at a lower level, programs using pointers generally run faster than the higher-level equivalent, although they are more difficult to follow.

Briefly examining this advanced use of pointers will give you more insight into the way the computer actually works with arrays. You can actually see how the program reserves an area of its memory for the elements of the array.

One feature of pointers makes it easy to use them to refer to arrays. The pointer itself is a sort of integer because the locations in memory are numbered in sequence, and the pointer is the address number of one of these locations. But the pointer is an integer of a very peculiar sort. If you add 1 to it, it will give you the address of the next location after the variable it points to, no matter how many slots in memory the variable occupies. If it is a pointer to a **char**, adding 1 to the pointer will be just like adding 1 to any integer and will give you the very next memory address. But if it is a pointer to a **float**, then adding 1 to the pointer will give you the memory location four bytes beyond the location of the **float**, which is the location immediately after the four bytes that hold the **float** (assuming, of course, that the system uses a four-byte float).

If you make a pointer equal to the address of one element of an array of **ints** or **floats**, then adding 1 to that pointer will give you the address of the next **int** or **float** in the array. There is no need to think about how many bytes the elements of the array actually take up. **Pointer arithmetic** does that for you.

Consider as a simple illustration the same program written in two different ways. First, the high-level method is as follows:

```
/* CHAPTER 6, EXAMPLE 4 */
#include <stdio.h>

main()                                  /* printing an array */
{                                       /* higher level method */
int counter, smplArry[9];
counter = 0;
while(counter<9)                        /* give values to all */
     {                                  /* elements of the array */
     smplArry[counter] = counter + 1;
     counter = counter + 1;
     }
nineprnt(smplArry);
}

nineprnt(arry)                          /* print the array */
int arry[];
{
int counter;

counter = 0;                            /* print each element */
while(counter<9)                        /* by index number */
     {
     printf("\nElement %d equals %d.",counter,arry[counter]);
     counter = counter + 1;
     }
}
```

After storing the numbers from 1 to 9 in an array, the previous program prints the array by using a counter as the subscript that refers to each element of the array.

The second version of the **main()** module is the same as the first, but the module that prints out the array uses pointers instead of the ordinary indexing of the array elements:

```
/* CHAPTER 6, EXAMPLE 5 */
#include <stdio.h>

main()                          /* printing an array */
{                               /* lower level method */
int counter, smplArry[9];

counter = 0;
while(counter<9)                /* give values to all */
    {                           /* elements of the array */
    smplArry[counter] = counter + 1;
    counter = counter + 1;
    }
nineprnt(smplArry);
}



nineprnt(arry)                  /* print the array */
int *arry;
{
int counter;

counter = 0;                    /* print each element */
while(counter<9)                /* using pointers */
    {
    printf("\nElement %d equals %d.",counter,*arry+counter);
    counter = counter +1;
    }
}
```

In this second version of the program, during the first time through the loop of
nineprnt(), when **counter** is equal to 0, the program is told to go to the address
arry (plus 0) instead of to element **arry[0]**. The second time through, the program
goes to the address **arry** plus 1 instead of to element **arry[1]**. Of course, these
locations are the same (i.e., **arry** plus 1 is the same as **arry[1]**); the locations in
the second version are simply accessed by address rather than by the usual array
index. Pointer arithmetic insures that when you add one to the address, you get
the address of the next **int** in memory.

You can also refer to higher dimensional arrays on a low level by using pointers, but this use of pointers is a more advanced topic that will not be covered in this book. You should note, however, that when you are using a two-dimensional array with index numbers, you can write the program so either number changes more quickly. For example, if you have an array with 10 rows and 20 columns, declared as **float nmbrs[10][20]** within the program, you can refer to the array as **nmbrs[rowCntr][colCntr]** and use two nested **while()** loops to go through the array, varying either **rowCntr** or **colCntr** more quickly, depending on where you place the inner loop.

As you learned earlier, the first subscript is conventionally said to refer to the rows and the second to the columns. Most applications are easier to understand intuitively if you go through an array row by row. First, you would go through all the numbers in row zero, from **nmbrs[0][0]** to **nmbrs[0][1]** to **numbr[0][2]**, and so on until you got to **nmbrs[0][19]**. Then, you would start the second row, beginning with **nmbrs[1][0]** and continuing through **nmbrs[1][19]**, and so on until you got through the tenth row. This is the order used in the tic-tac-toe program, for example, and is known as going through the array in **row-major** order. Note that the number that represents the columns (i.e., the number on the right) must change more quickly than the number on the left in order to read the array in row-major order.

There is one common application, however, in which row-major order is not the easiest method to understand intuitively — that is, when the two-dimensional array represents a list of words. Say, for example, that you have a list of 100 names, each name with a maximum of 20 letters. It is natural to think of this list as **names[21][100]** because **names[21]** is the array to hold one name, and it seems sensible to add the **[100]** at the end to create a list of 100 of these names. Note, however, that when you go through this list, you must vary the number on the left (i.e., **[21]**) more quickly. You start by reading the first letter of the first name, **names[0][0]**; then you read the second and third letters, **names[1][0]** and **names[2][0]**, and you keep going until you get to the final '\0'. Then you start reading the first letter of the second name, **names[0][1]**, and its second and third letters, **names[1][1]** and **names[2][1]**, and so on. In this case, the index number on the left is varying more quickly, which is not row-major, but **column-major**, order.

Because row-major order makes the most sense for most applications, the compiler actually stores the array in memory in this order. To read the array as it is stored in memory, the index number on the right (the column number) must vary more quickly. Working on a higher level, you can use either order. Although column-major order causes the program to jump back and forth in memory to retrieve the elements of the array, the user will not notice this occurrence. It is generally best, particularly for beginners, to use whichever order is easiest to understand, regardless of the way it is actually stored in memory, which is why this book has used a form similar to **names[21][100]** (column-major) to store lists of words. Advanced programmers, however, would be more likely to declare this list of words as **names[100][21]** (row-major) so that the right index number would change more quickly as the program went through each word, and the left number would change more slowly as the program went through the words on the list. By going through the array of names in row-major order, as the compiler does, advanced programmers store the letters in memory in the same order as they are used in the program, which makes it easier to access them on a lower level. The fact that lists of names or words are often indexed in this apparently reverse way is a bit puzzling at first, but it is not too hard to get used to.

READING FROM AND WRITING TO DISK FILES

As indicated in the beginning of this chapter, pointers are an advanced topic that a beginner need not master. The general background about pointers that has been covered here is meant to help you to understand the reasons behind some concepts you learned in earlier chapters and, most important, to help you see why pointers are used with disk files. Like a string, a disk file is not a fixed length, and so it cannot be handled like an ordinary variable, such as a **float** or **char**, which has a fixed location set aside in memory.

A text file is handled in much the same way as a string. The program must refer to the disk file by using a name that is a pointer to the file's first byte (like the name of an array). And the program knows the file has ended when it finds an end-of-file mark (which works like the '\0' at the end of a string).

C includes two different sets of standard functions to handle disk I/O. There is a low-level I/O system that is powerful but does little for the programmer; it requires you to perform all the basic housekeeping chores yourself. This book will use only the higher-level I/O system that does some of the housekeeping for you.

The most noteworthy built-in feature of this high-level system is the fact that it provides a **buffer** for you. This means that if a program reads a disk file one character at a time, the I/O system will actually read a group of characters into RAM and give those characters to the program one at a time as they are needed, without the programmer specifically telling the I/O system to do so. This part of RAM that holds the characters until the program asks for them is the buffer. By contrast, low-level file I/O not does create a buffer automatically. Low-level file I/O accesses the disk to find one new character each time it is supposed to read a character from a file, unless the programmer explicitly creates a buffer. Because accessing the disk requires physical movement, it is much slower than accessing RAM, and the programmer generally would have to do this extra housekeeping work.

The low-level disk I/O functions are useful to write complex routines for specific tasks; the high-level I/O system is actually written by using these functions and is included as part of the standard input-output package to make it easy to perform the common task of buffered I/O of text files. This chapter will use four basic functions of the high-level I/O system:

- **fopen**() opens a file so it can be used and also returns a pointer to the beginning of the file.

- **fclose**() closes a file after you are done using it.

- **getc**() reads a single character from the file.

- **putc**() writes a single character to the file.

Before opening a file, you must declare the variable that will be used as the pointer to the file, as follows:

```
FILE *filePtr;
```

The asterisk before the variable name means that the variable is a pointer. **FILE** is essentially a new data type. It is written in uppercase because it is actually implemented using a **#define** statement (like **MAXWORDS** in Chapter 5), which is included in **stdio.h**. The details of the implementation are not important, though. You can simply think of this declaration as creating a new data type, a pointer to a file. This type of pointer is often called a **stream** pointer because it keeps track of a stream of characters.

The following simple memo program should make C's high-level file I/O functions easier to understand:

```
/* CHAPTER 6, EXAMPLE 6 */
#include <stdio.h>

main()                          /* write the user's input */
{                               /* into a text file */
FILE *filePtr;
char userInpt;

filePtr = fopen("memo.txt","w");
printf("\nEnter memo > ");
while(userInpt != '\n')
     {
     scanf("%c",&userInpt);
     putc(userInpt,filePtr);
     }
fclose(filePtr);
}
```

First, this program declares the variable **filePtr** as a stream pointer and the variable **userInpt** as a **char**. Then, the program opens the file named **memo.txt**. There are two items to notice about the statement **filePtr = fopen("memo.txt","w");** that opens the file. First, the function **fopen()** takes two arguments: the name of the file that is being opened plus a letter that indicates the mode in which the file is being opened. Here, the mode **"w"** indicates that the file is being opened for the program to write to it; other common modes are **"a"** for append and **"r"** for read. Second, note that the function **fopen()** returns the value of a stream pointer and that the program must assign this value to a variable of that type, such as **filePtr**, in order to use the file.

After opening the file, the program uses a **while()** loop to keep reading characters from the keyboard and writing them to the disk file until the user enters a carriage return (making the condition of the **while()** loop untrue). The function **scanf()** reads the characters from the keyboard one at a time. The function **putc()** writes one character to the disk location that **filePtr** indicates and, at the same time, **putc()** automatically increases the value of **filePtr** so it points to the next character in the disk file and is ready for the next character the user inputs.

Compile and run this program (after making sure your hard disk is backed up). Enter a memo and look at the light that indicates if your disk is being used. Note that the program does not actually write each character to the disk when you enter the character, as the code seems to say it does; the program accesses the disk only when you enter the carriage return and leave the loop that gets and writes characters. You are seeing the automatic input buffer at work. Without your having to worry about creating a buffer in the program, the high-level I/O functions have created a buffer in RAM. The high-level I/O functions read into that buffer the characters the user enters until the buffer is full, and then they write those characters to disk. The short memo the user inputs in this program does not fill the buffer, but the **fclose**() function at the end of the program automatically **flushes** the buffer; that is, **fclose**() writes any characters left in the buffer to the file before closing it. The programmer only needs to think about reading characters from the keyboard and writing them to the disk, and all of the housekeeping just discussed is performed automatically.

After you run this program and enter a sample memo into it, you can use DOS's **DIR** command to confirm that the program has created a new file named "memo.txt" on your disk. You can print the contents of this file on your screen by entering the command **TYPE MEMO.TXT** at the DOS prompt to confirm that the file contains the same memo you typed into it. Run the program again, enter a second sample memo, and print the contents of the file on your screen again. You will see that the first memo has disappeared; only the second memo is now in the file "memo.txt." When **fopen**() is used with the mode "**w**," **fopen**() overwrites and destroys anything that is already in the file.

You can rewrite the program to add new memos to what is already in the file "memo.txt," by using the command **fopen**() with the append mode as follows: **filePtr = fopen("memo.txt","a");**. This new version of the program expands on that command by adding a common form of error testing to it. If **fopen**() is not able to open a file, **fopen**() returns the value **NULL**, which is defined in **stdio.h** to be a pointer to address zero, which is not a valid pointer in C. The **fopen**() function will return **NULL** if the program tries to write to a file that is on a floppy disk that has a write-protect tab on it, for example.

```
/* CHAPTER 6, EXAMPLE 7 */
#include <stdio.h>

main()                              /* append the user's input */
{                                   /* to a text file */
FILE *filePtr;
char userInpt;
filePtr = fopen("memo.txt","a");
if(filePtr == NULL)
     {
     printf("That file cannot be opened");
     exit();
     }
printf("\nAdd to memo > ");
while(userInpt != '\n')
     {
     scanf("%c",&userInpt);
     putc(userInpt,filePtr);
     }
fclose(filePtr);
}
```

Try this program a few times, and note that the new memos are appended to the file that contains the old memos.

Finally, rather than using the MS-DOS **TYPE** command, you can write a program in C whose sole function is to read these memo files. The reading program appears similar to the programs that write the memo files, with a few significant variations. First, of course, it opens the file in the read mode, by using "**r**" in **fopen**() instead of "**a**" or "**w**". Second, it reverses the commands within the **while**() loop. Instead of using **scanf**() to get a character from the user followed by **putc**() to write that character in the file, the read program uses **getc**() to read from the file, followed by **printf**() to write the information on the screen. Note the use of **getc**(): it returns a value that is then assigned to the variable **toWrite**.

The one new concept in this program is the use of **EOF**, the **end-of-file marker**. The use of EOF is parallel with string handling. Just as string-handling functions receive a pointer to the beginning address of the string and keep reading until they reach the '\0' character that terminates strings, functions that work with text files receive a strream pointer to the first character of the file and keep reading until they reach an end-of-file (EOF) marker. In MS-DOS, text files are terminated with ASCII character 26. You can enter this character by holding down the Ctrl key and simultaneously pressing the Z key (Ctrl-Z). This ASCII key notation is usually written as ^Z. Some text editors actually allow you to see this character at the end of files. EOF is defined in **stdio.h** to mean ^Z. To make your programs more portable to other systems, it is best to use EOF rather than the actual character that DOS uses.

If you understood the examples of writing to a file, the way the following program works should be apparent:

```
/* CHAPTER 6, EXAMPLE 8 */
#include <stdio.h>

main()                             /* read the memo file */
{
FILE *filePtr;
char toWrite;

filePtr = fopen("memo.txt","r");
if(filePtr== NULL)
     {
     printf("The memo file cannot be opened");
     exit();
     }
while(toWrite != EOF)
     {
     toWrite = getc(filePtr);
     printf("%c",toWrite);
     }
fclose(filePtr);
}
```

Try running this program to print out the contents of the memo files you have already created. Then, delete the memo file (using the DOS command **DEL MEMO.TXT**) and try it again. You will find that if the file is not there, the program will send you an error message saying that it cannot open the file.

These memo programs would begin to be useful if you could use them with what are called "command line arguments" to create files with names that you choose. Instead of just entering commands such as **writmemo** and **readmemo** (or whatever you happened to name the C source-code files for these programs), it would be good if you could enter commands such as **writmemo meeting.txt** or **readmemo monday** to create or read files with those specific names. The **writememo** and **readmemo** programs have served their purpose for now, but Chapter 8 shows you how to use them with command line arguments.

C includes a number of other functions for high-level file I/O that will not be used in this book. There are several functions for unformatted file I/O that are similar to the functions for unformatted console I/O, for example, **fgets()** and **fputs()**, which work like **gets()** and **puts()**. There are also two functions for formatted file I/O that you will use in Chapter 7 and that will look very familiar to you: **fprintf()** and **fscanf()**. These functions use the same special formatting characters as **printf()** and **scanf()**, respectively. One important purpose of **fprintf()** and **fscanf()** is to format numerical information. In MS-DOS systems, all these high-level functions work only with text files, which means that if your program is working with **floats**, for example, it must place those **floats** on disk and read them from the disk in ASCII form. A **float** is actually handled as four bytes of binary numbers, including a mantissa and an exponent, but if you are storing, for example, the float "2.1415" in a text file, it must be stored as six characters — '2' in the first byte, '.' in the second byte, '1' in the third byte, and so on. The functions **fprintf()** and **fscanf()** are a handy way of making this conversion.

In addition to text files, MS-DOS also uses binary files, which can store **ints** or **floats** in their original form rather than converting them to ASCII strings. This capability is useful if you are actually working with mathematical data because the conversion to and from ASCII can involve rounding errors. These binary files, however, are handled in an entirely different way from text files. Instead of using an end-of-file marker, DOS keeps track of the total length of the files.

File I/O is covered in almost every advanced book on C because it is a complex and sometimes difficult topic. In an introductory book such as this, however, it is more appropriate to use only **putc()** and **getc()** with text files, the most basic and most common form of disk I/O.

LANGUAGE FLASHCARDS ON DISK

You have already learned enough about disk I/O for most practical tasks, certainly enough to complete the flashcard program begun in the last chapter. As you remember, the defect of that program was in its **initlze()** function, which assigned values to the array of structs that contained a list of English and French words and their parts of speech. In that early version, the program used a series of **strcpy()** statements to read words into this list, but this was such a tedious process that the program used a list only ten words long.

To make the flashcard system work properly, you need to write two new programs. The **initlze()** function of the existing program must be rewritten to read words from a disk file and assign them to the elements of the struct; but first, you need a separate program to write the words into a disk file.

Entering the words into a disk file is relatively easy. The program that follows declares variables that are equivalent to the elements of the struct of the flashcard program, **char English[16], char French[16]**, and **char spPrt[2]**. There is no need to make these variables part of a struct here, as it is easy enough to keep them in order. The program opens the file **wordlist.txt** with error checking, just as earlier programs opened the file **memo.txt**. If there is no disk error, the program gets the English and French versions of the word from the user by using a routine series of **printf()** and **gets()** statements. The program then asks the user to confirm the fact that he or she wants to save entries on disk, so there is an escape in case the user wants to correct an error.

The only new thing about this program occurs after the user confirms that the entry should be saved; the program uses a counter along with a **putc()** statement to go through each of the 16 characters of the arrays that hold the English and French words and write them on the disk. The program writes only the first letter of **spPrt** to disk. **spPrt** was declared with two letters only so it could be used with **gets()** to get user input. Then the program asks if the user wants to enter another word. If the user does not, the program **break;**s out of the **while()** loop that performs this data entry and closes the file before ending. This logic should be fairly easy to follow in this preliminary version of the program:

```
/* CHAPTER 6, EXAMPLE  9 */
#include <stdio.h>

main()                          /* enter vocabulary words */
{                               /* into a disk file to be */
                                /* read by flashcard program */
FILE *filePtr;                  /* PRELIMINARY VERSION */

char English[16];
char French[16];
char spPrt[2];

char again[2], confirm[2];
int counter;

filePtr = fopen("wordlist.txt","a");
if(filePtr== NULL)
     {
     printf("Disk Error: the word-list file cannot be opened");
     exit();
     }


while(1==1)
     {
     printf("\n\n\n\n\n\n\n\n\n\n\n");
     printf("\t\t\tENTER VOCABULARY WORDS");
     printf("\n\t\t\t---------------------");
     printf("\n\n\n\n\n\n\n\n\n\n\n\n");
     printf("Enter the English Word > ");
     gets(English);

     printf("\nEnter the French Word > ");
     gets(French);
     while(1==1)
          {
          printf("\nEnter the Part of Speech");
          printf("\n\tN-noun, V-verb, O-other > ");
          gets(spPrt);
          spPrt[0] = toupper(spPrt[0]);
```

continued...

...from previous page

```
            if(spPrt[0]=='N' || spPrt[0]=='V' || spPrt[0]=='O')
                {
                break;
                }
            else
                {
                putchar(7);
                }
        }
    printf("\nDo you want to save this entry (Y/N) > ");
    gets(confirm);
    if(toupper(confirm[0])=='Y')
            {
            counter = 0;
            while(counter<16)
                    {
                    putc(English[counter],filePtr);
                    counter = counter + 1;
                    }
            counter = 0;
            while(counter<16)
                    {
                    putc(French[counter],filePtr);
                    counter = counter + 1;
                    }
            putc(spPrt[0],filePtr);
        }
    printf("\nWould you like to enter another (Y/N) > ");
    gets(again);
    if(toupper(again[0]) != 'Y')
            {
            break;
            }

    }

fclose(filePtr);
}
```

When you compile and run this program, watch the light that shows whether your disk is moving. Your disk does not move each time through the loop. Even though the program contains the **putc**() commands that write to disk, the input is actually being held in the buffer.

Note also that this preliminary version of the program does not initialize all the spaces in **English[16]** and **French[16]** with blanks before getting input from the user. The **gets**() function fills up the beginnings of these arrays with the letters the user enters but does not do anything to the leftover spaces. If you have been working on your computer for a while before running this program, your computer may well have used this part of memory for something else and left random garbage in these spaces. If you examine the file on the screen by using the DOS command **TYPE WORDLIST.TXT**, your screen may may resemble the following:

```
THE BOY R        LE GARCON        NTHE FISH        LE POISSON
    NBEFORE H        AVANT SSON        OAFTER  H        APRES SSON
       ONEAR    H        PRES DE ON        OTO GO  H        ALLER E
ON        VTHE HAT        LE CHAPEAU        N
```

The "R" that follows "BOY," the scattered "H"s, and the "SSON"s are all left-over garbage. It looks as if two earlier runs of the program stored POISSON in this general region, and "AVANT" and "APRES" wrote over the beginning of "POISSON" and just left the "SSON." You might also see graphic characters, such as lines used for drawing boxes, and control characters scattered among the words on screen. Note, however, that there is a blank space after every word here. This space is where the '\0' null character that C uses to terminate strings is stored; '/0' is displayed as a blank. On the other hand, there are other no spaces following any of the part-of-speech symbols, "N," "V," and "O" (except the final "N") because these symbols are stored as characters—not as strings—and words are stored right after them.

For a reason that will become clear, the next version of this program will initialize these strings with all blanks before getting words from the user. For the moment, however, the garbage is useful as an illustration of how strings work. You can write a program to read this file, garbage and all, and then it will print out only the strings because the string-handling functions read only up to the null character that terminates the string and ignore the garbage that follows. To read the file into the flashcard program, this short program (which is similar to the new **initlize**() function that you will write shortly for the flashcard program) just reads the file and then prints the words to screen to make sure they are right. Note how the program counts its way through the series of characters in the file and makes those characters meaningful by assigning the right number of characters to the right variable.

This sample program reads these characters into the same struct the flashcard program uses. After opening the file with the **"r"** (read) option, with the usual error checking, it uses **getc**() to read the characters one at a time as long as it does not reach the end-of-file marker. Up to this point, the program is similar to the memo reading program discussed earlier in this chapter, but then it must use a complex **if-else-if** ladder, with three different counters, to assign these characters to the proper location in the struct. The **if-else-if** ladder assigns the first 16 **char**s it reads to **English[16]**; after that counter reaches 16, the **if-else-if** ladder assigns the next sixteen **char**s to **French[16]**; after that counter runs out, it assigns one **char** to **spchPart**. Then the program sets all these counters back to 0 and adds 0 to the entry-counter; it checks to see if the number of entries is greater than the maximum that the array can hold before it starts to read the next entry. After reading all the words, this sample program prints them all on the screen by using **printf("%s")**. When you run the program, note that it omits all the garbage that follows the null terminator of the strings.

```
/* CHAPTER 6, EXAMPLE 10 */
#include <stdio.h>
#define MAXWORDS 100

struct efWrdLst
    {
    char English[16];
    char French[16];
    char spchPart;
    }entry[MAXWORDS];
```

continued...

...from previous page

```
main()                      /* read word list */
{                           /* high-level method */
FILE *filePtr;


char ltr;
int entrCntr, eLtrCntr, fLtrCntr, posCntr, testCntr;

if( (filePtr = fopen("wordlist.txt","r") )== NULL)
    {
    printf("ERROR: The wordlist file cannot be opened");
    exit();
    }


entrCntr = 0;
eLtrCntr = 0;
fLtrCntr = 0;
posCntr = 0;

while(ltr != EOF)
    {
    ltr = getc(filePtr);
    if(eLtrCntr<16)
        {
        entry[entrCntr].English[eLtrCntr] = ltr;
        eLtrCntr = eLtrCntr + 1;
        }
    else if(fLtrCntr<16)
        {
        entry[entrCntr].French[fLtrCntr] = ltr;
        fLtrCntr = fLtrCntr + 1;
        }
    else if(posCntr<1)
        {
        entry[entrCntr].spchPart = ltr;
        posCntr = posCntr + 1;
        }
```

continued...

...from previous page

```
      if(eLtrCntr==16 && fLtrCntr==16 && posCntr==1)
         {
         entrCntr = entrCntr + 1;
         eLtrCntr = 0;
         fLtrCntr = 0;
         posCntr = 0;


         if(entrCntr > MAXWORDS)
             {
             printf("\nERROR: wordlist file is too long.");
             printf("\n\tThe program will work");
             printf("\n\twith %d words but must",MAXWORDS);
             printf("\n\tbe modified to use all the words");
             break;
             }
         }
      }
fclose(filePtr);


testCntr = 0;
while(testCntr < entrCntr)
      {
      printf("\n\n%s",entry[testCntr].English);
      printf("\n%s",entry[testCntr].French);
      printf("\n%c",entry[testCntr].spchPart);
      testCntr = testCntr + 1;
      }
}
```

One odd thing about this program is that it declares the array of structs that holds the words as a global variable, even though the program contains only one function; however, there is a reason to make this variable global rather than local even though there is no other function to use it. C assumes that all local variables will exist only as long as their function is running and will be discarded when the function is over in order to save memory, and so it stores them in a special section of RAM, called the **stack**, that is reserved for temporary storage to make it easier to create and destroy these variables as the program proceeds. Though the **stack** has enough room for all the local variables you would normally expect to be in use at one time, it does not have enough space for a large block of memory that an array of structs might demand. If you try making this array of structs a local variable, you will find that once you **#define MAXWORDS** to be too large a number, the compiler will give you an error message saying that there is a "stack overflow." Because global variables are not temporary, they are not stored in the stack, so this problem does not arise. (In Chapter 8, you will learn another way of making variables permanent and avoiding this problem.)

Note also that the **if** statement used to check whether it is time to set all the counters back to 0 and start a new entry must be separate from the **if-else-if** ladder. It seems natural to make this statement into a final **else** on this ladder because it is true when all the other conditions on the ladder are untrue. But this strategy would cause the program to go through the loop another time and read an extra **char** from the file (which would not be assigned to any variable) just to see if it was finished, thus throwing itself out of sync by one **char** the next time through.

Obviously, this type of problem can be difficult to program and debug. In this case, it might actually be easier to use a lower-level method of reading the file into the struct, so if you would like to delve into more advanced methods again, consider Program Example 11 that follows.

A struct, like an array, is simply a block of memory. Rather than using an **if-else-if** ladder and three counters to refer to each element by its full name, this program reads right through the disk file one **char** at a time by using pointers. The program declares a **char** pointer named **current** and, after opening the file in the usual way, initializes this pointer with the address of the first **char** of the array with the statement **current = &(entry[0].English[0]);**. Then, it simply reads the disk file one **char** at a time (until it reaches **EOF**) and assigns that **char** to its proper place in the **struct** with the statement ***current = ltr;** ("make the contents of **current** equal to **ltr**"). It makes **current** equal to the next address slot in the **struct** by using the statement **current = current + 1;** before going on to read the next **char** from the file and assigning it to its proper place in the **struct**. Note how much simpler this method is than the **if-else-if** ladder and three variables in the higher-level version of the program.

This low-level version also has a **ltrCntr** variable that it increments each time a letter is written to the file. This variable can take the place of the entry-counter in the high-level version. Because you know that each entry has 33 **char**s, you can check if **ltrCntr/33 > MAXWORDS**, and it is just the same as checking if **entrCntr > MAXWORDS** in the earlier version of the program.

```
/* CHAPTER 6, EXAMPLE 11 */
#include <stdio.h>
#define MAXWORDS 100
struct efWrdLst
    {
    char English[16];
    char French[16];
    char spchPart;
    }entry[MAXWORDS];


main()                      /* read word list */
{                           /* low-level method */
FILE *filePtr;

char ltr;
char *current;
int ltrCntr = 0;
int testCntr = 0;
```

continued...

...from previous page

```
if( (filePtr = fopen("wordlist.txt","r") )== NULL)
    {
    printf("ERROR: The wordlist file cannot be opened");
    exit();
    }

current = &(entry[0].English[0]);

while(ltr != EOF)
    {
    ltr = getc(filePtr);

    *current = ltr;
    current = current + 1;
    ltrCntr = ltrCntr + 1;

    if( (ltrCntr/33) > MAXWORDS)
        {
        printf("\nERROR: wordlist file is too long.");
        printf("\n\tThe program will work");
        printf("\n\twith %d words but must",MAXWORDS);
        printf("\n\tbe modified to use all the words");
        break;
        }

    }
fclose(filePtr);

while(testCntr < (ltrCntr/33) )
    {
    printf("\n\n%s",entry[testCntr].English);
    printf("\n%s",entry[testCntr].French);
    printf("\n%c",entry[testCntr].spchPart);
    testCntr = testCntr + 1;
    }
}
```

This low-level version of the program uses exactly the same code to print out the words as the high-level version did. Of course, the results are the same because each **char** from the file has been read into the same address in the memory location that holds the **struct** in both versions. This program is an elegant example of the fact that working on a lower level can sometimes actually make your life easier because the code is not nearly as hard to write and debug as the high-level program it replaces.

Unless you are extremely unlucky, both of these programs will read your garbage-filled file, **wordlist.txt,** and will print out only the strings that you entered into it, illustrating that the null terminator of strings lives up to its name (i.e., the program reads the string until it gets to the '\0' and then stops). If you are very unlucky, though, one of the bits of garbage in the file will be DOS's end-of-file marker, ASCII character 26 or ^Z ([Ctrl/Z]), which is not visible when you **TYPE** the file to screen. Because the programs that print the file keep reading characters only until they reach the end of the file, a stray end-of-file marker will cause the programs to stop reading before they have read all of the words you entered.

The final version of the program to enter words eliminates this problem and makes the test file look a bit neater also. The only addition it makes to the preliminary version is that it simply blanks out the array with the statements

```
strcpy(English,"               ");
strcpy(French,"               ");
```

before it gets input from the user. Both arrays are initialized as a string of 15 blanks (plus a terminal null), so there is no garbage in that part of RAM when it gets its new value from the user.

Now that you have had the experience of working with files with garbage included, add these two lines to the preliminary version of the program to get the final version. If you were unlucky enough to get a stray end-of-file marker in the middle of the file when you used the last version of the program so that the two programs to read the file mysteriously malfunctioned, try them again after creating a new word file with the following program:

```
/* CHAPTER 6, EXAMPLE 12 */
#include <stdio.h>

main()                          /* enter vocabulary words */
{                               /* into a disk file to be */
                                /* read by flashcard program */
FILE *filePtr;                  /* FINAL VERSION */
char English[16];
char French[16];
char spPrt[2];

char again[2], confirm[2];
int counter;

filePtr = fopen("wordlist.txt","a");
if(filePtr== NULL)
    {
    printf("Disk Error: the word-list file cannot be opened");
    exit();
    }


while(1==1)
    {
    strcpy(English,"                    ");      /* blank out */
    strcpy(French,"                    ");       /* garbage */
    printf("\n\n\n\n\n\n\n\n\n\n\n");
    printf("\t\t\tENTER VOCABULARY WORDS");
    printf("\n\t\t\t--------------------");
    printf("\n\n\n\n\n\n\n\n\n\n\n\n");
    printf("Enter the English Word > ");
    gets(English);

    printf("\nEnter the French Word > ");
    gets(French);
    while(1==1)
        {
        printf("\nEnter the Part of Speech");
        printf("\n\tN-noun, V-verb, O-other > ");
        gets(spPrt);
```

continued...

...from previous page

```
        spPrt[0] = toupper(spPrt[0]);
        if(spPrt[0]=='N' || spPrt[0]=='V' || spPrt[0]=='O')
            {
            break;
            }
        else
            {
            putchar(7);
            }
        }
    printf("\nDo you want to save this entry (Y/N) > ");
    gets(confirm);

    if(toupper(confirm[0])=='Y')
        {
        counter = 0;
        while(counter<16)
            {
            putc(English[counter],filePtr);
            counter = counter + 1;
            }
        counter = 0;
        while(counter<16)
            {
            putc(French[counter],filePtr);
            counter = counter + 1;
            }
        putc(spPrt[0],filePtr);
        }
    printf("\nWould you like to enter another (Y/N) > ");
    gets(again);
    if(toupper(again[0]) != 'Y')
        {
        break;
        }

    }

fclose(filePtr);
}
```

Incidentally, if you wanted to make this program foolproof, you could create your own buffer of perhaps 80 characters in the program and have the user enter the words into that buffer; then, you could use **strlen**() to see if the words were more than the maximum 15 letters that this program can handle. You could also have the program automatically capitalize all the letters entered. The flashcard program capitalizes the user's input before comparing it with the word on disk to make sure the user does not have any problems with upper- and lowercase. In the program to enter the words, however, the assumption is that the user knows to enter words that are not too long and are all uppercase letters because this program will actually be used by someone who is setting up a list of words to be distributed with the flashcard program to the final end-user.

Either of the programs you wrote to read the disk file — high-level or low-level — can be substituted with very little change for the **initlze**() module in the flashcard program. In this book, the final code of that program incorporates the harder high-level version, but you can substitute the low-level version if you want.

There is one other change in the final flashcard program. It begins with the statement **#define FOREIGN French** and uses **FOREIGN** wherever the earlier version used **French**. Now, you can modify it into a flashcard program for any language you choose by simply changing that initial definition into **#define FOREIGN German**, **#define FOREIGN Italian**, or whatever language you want, and using the previous word entry program to enter the appropriate set of foreign and English words into the **wordlist.txt** file.

```
/* CHAPTER 6, EXAMPLE 13 */
/* English-French Flashcard program */
#include <stdio.h>
#define MAXWORDS 100
#define FOREIGN French

struct flshcard
    {
    char English[16];
    char FOREIGN[16];    /* struct to hold flashcard data */
    char spchPart;
    int errorFlg;
    } enFr[MAXWORDS];
```

continued...

...from previous page

```
int retstFlg;

main()                                          /* main menu */
{
char ch[2];
char toAsk[8], toAnswer[8], whchWrds;

initlze();
retstFlg = 0;
while(1==1)                              /* display the menu */
     {
     printf("\n\t\t\tLanguage Flashcards\n\n");
     printf("\n\n\t\t1 - English to FOREIGN, nouns");
     printf("\n\n\t\t2 - English to FOREIGN, verbs");
     printf("\n\n\t\t3 - English to FOREIGN, others");
     printf("\n\n\t\t4 - English to FOREIGN, all");
     printf("\n\n\t\t5 - FOREIGN to English, nouns");
     printf("\n\n\t\t6 - FOREIGN to English, verbs");
     printf("\n\n\t\t7 - FOREIGN to English, others");
     printf("\n\n\t\t8 - FOREIGN to English, all");
     if(retstFlg==1)
          {
          printf("\n\n\t\t9 - Errors from last test");
          }
     printf("\n\n\t\t0 - Quit");
     if(retstFlg!=1)
          {
     printf("\n\n");
          }
     printf("\n\n\t\t\tWhat is your choice > ");
     gets(ch);
                              /* get user's choice and */
                              /* set parameters accordingly */

     if(ch[0]=='1' || ch[0]=='2' || ch[0]=='3' || ch[0]=='4')
          {
          strcpy(toAsk,"English");
          strcpy(toAnswer,"FOREIGN");
          }
```

continued...

...from previous page

```
        if(ch[0]=='5' || ch[0]=='6' || ch[0]=='7' || ch[0]=='8')
            {
            strcpy(toAsk,"FOREIGN");
            strcpy(toAnswer,"English");
            }
        if(ch[0]=='1' || ch[0]=='5')
            {
            whchWrds = 'N';
            }

        else if(ch[0]=='2' || ch[0]=='6')
            {
            whchWrds = 'V';
            }
        else if(ch[0]=='3' || ch[0]=='7')
            {
            whchWrds = 'O';
            }
        else if(ch[0]=='4' || ch[0]=='8')
            {
            whchWrds = 'A';
            }
        else if(ch[0]=='9' && retstFlg == 1)
            {
            whchWrds = 'R';
            }
        else if(ch[0]=='0')
            {
            break;
            }
        else
            {
            putchar(7);
            continue;
            }
        testword(toAsk,toAnswer,whchWrds);
        }
    }
```

continued...

...from previous page

```
initlze()                      /* read word list */
{
FILE *filePtr;


char ltr;
int entrCntr, eLtrCntr, fLtrCntr, posCntr, testCntr;

if( (filePtr = fopen("wordlist.txt","r") )== NULL)
     {
     printf("ERROR: The wordlist file cannot be opened");
     exit();
     }
entrCntr = 0;
eLtrCntr = 0;
fLtrCntr = 0;
posCntr = 0;

while(ltr != EOF)
     {
     ltr = getc(filePtr);
     if(eLtrCntr<16)
          {
          enFr[entrCntr].English[eLtrCntr] = ltr;
          eLtrCntr = eLtrCntr + 1;
          }
     else if(fLtrCntr<16)
          {
          enFr[entrCntr].FOREIGN[fLtrCntr] = ltr;
          fLtrCntr = fLtrCntr + 1;
          }
     else if(posCntr<1)
          {
          enFr[entrCntr].spchPart = ltr;
          posCntr = posCntr + 1;
          }
```

continued...

...from previous page

```
    if(eLtrCntr==16 && fLtrCntr==16 && posCntr==1)
        {
        entrCntr = entrCntr + 1;
        eLtrCntr = 0;
        fLtrCntr = 0;
        posCntr = 0;

        if(entrCntr > MAXWORDS)
            {
            printf("\nERROR: wordlist file is too long.");
            printf("\n\tThe program will work");
            printf("\n\twith %d words but must",MAXWORDS);
            printf("\n\tbe modified to use all the words");
            break;
            }

        }
    }
fclose(filePtr);
}




testword(lang1,lang2,pos)                    /* test user */
char pos;
char lang1[];                                /* using parameters */
char lang2[];                                /* set in main() */

{
int wrdCntr, ltrCntr;
char answer[16];
char yorn[2];
int retestFlg;
```

continued...

...from previous page

```
    wrdCntr = 0;
    if(pos!='R')                        /* if not a retest, make */
        {                               /* error flags 0 so they */
        while(wrdCntr<MAXWORDS)         /* can record new errors */
            {
            enFr[wrdCntr].errorFlg = 0;
            wrdCntr = wrdCntr + 1;
            }
        }
    wrdCntr = 0;                        /* skip those that are */
    while(wrdCntr<MAXWORDS)             /* wrong part of speech */
        {
        if(pos!='A' && pos!= 'R' && pos!=enFr[wrdCntr].spchPart)
            {
            wrdCntr = wrdCntr + 1;
            continue;
            }
        if(pos=='R' && enFr[wrdCntr].errorFlg!=1)
            {
            wrdCntr = wrdCntr + 1;
            continue;
            }

        printf("\n\n\n\n\n\n\n");
        printf("\t\t   Translation from %s to %s", lang1,lang2);
        printf("\n\n\t\t\t   test of ");
        if(pos=='N')
            {                                   /* display screen */
            printf("nouns");
            }
        else if(pos=='V')
            {
            printf("verbs");
            }
        else if(pos=='O')
            {
            printf("other words");
            }
```

continued...

...from previous page

```
else if(pos=='A')
    {
    printf("all words");
    }

if(lang1[0]=='F')                          /* French-English */
    {
    printf("\n\n\n\n\n\n\n\n\n\n");
    printf("\t\t\t\t%s", enFr[wrdCntr].FOREIGN);
    printf("\n\n\n\n\n\n\n\n");
    printf("What is the English translation > ");

    gets(answer);                          /* get user's answer */
                                           /* and capitalize it */
    ltrCntr = 0;
    while(answer[ltrCntr] != '\0')
        {
        answer[ltrCntr] = toupper(answer[ltrCntr]);
        ltrCntr = ltrCntr + 1;
        }

     if(strcmp(answer,enFr[wrdCntr].English)==0)
        {
        printf("\n\nCongratulations.  That is right.");
        printf("\nDo you want to try another (Y/N) > ");
        gets(yorn);
        if(toupper(yorn[0])=='N')
            {
            return;
            }
        }                                  /* message for right */
    else                                   /* or wrong answer */
        {
        enFr[wrdCntr].errorFlg = 1;
        retstFlg = 1;
        printf("\n\nThe correct answer is %s.",
                            enFr[wrdCntr].English);
        printf("\nDo you want to try another (Y/N) > ");
        gets(yorn);
```

continued...

227

...from previous page

```
            if(toupper(yorn[0])=='N')
                {
                return;
                }
            }
        wrdCntr =wrdCntr + 1;
        }

    else                                    /* English-French */
        {
        printf("\n\n\n\n\n\n\n\n\n");
        printf("\t\t\t\t%s", enFr[wrdCntr].English);
        printf("\n\n\n\n\n\n\n\n\n");
        printf("What is the FOREIGN translation > ");

        gets(answer);                       /* get user's answer */
                                            /* and capitalize it */
        ltrCntr = 0;
        while(answer[ltrCntr] != '\0')
            {
            answer[ltrCntr] = toupper(answer[ltrCntr]);
            ltrCntr = ltrCntr + 1;
            }

         if(strcmp(answer,enFr[wrdCntr].FOREIGN)==0)
            {
            printf("\n\nCongratulations.  That is right.");
            printf("\nDo you want to try another (Y/N) > ");
            gets(yorn);
            if(toupper(yorn[0])=='N')
                {
                return;
                }
            }                               /* message for right */
        else                                /* or wrong answer */
            {
            enFr[wrdCntr].errorFlg = 1;
            retstFlg = 1;
            printf("\n\nNo, the correct answer is %s.",
                                    enFr[wrdCntr].FOREIGN);
```

continued...

...from previous page

```
            printf("Do you want to try another (Y/N) ");
            gets(yorn);
            if(toupper(yorn[0])=='N')
                {
                return;
                }
            }
        wrdCntr =wrdCntr + 1;
        }
    }
}
```

SUMMARY

A **pointer** is a variable that is the address of another variable. Two operators are used to work with pointers: the ampersand (**&**) means "the address of," and the asterisk (*****), the indirection operator, means "contents of address." A pointer is declared using the data type of the variable it points to plus an asterisk before its name. For example, **float *pSmplVar;** declares a variable that is a pointer to a float.

For one function to change the value of a local variable of another function, it is necessary to pass the address of that variable to the function that is to change the variable's value. This is a "call by reference." By contrast, if you just pass a function the name of the variable, that is a "call by value." The value of the variable is copied into the parameter, and the called function can change only its copy of the variable, not the variable in the calling function itself.

The name of an array, used without any subscript, refers to the address of the first element of that array. For example, **smplArry** is equivalent to **&smplArry[0]**. Functions that work with strings are always given the address of the first element of the array because an array does not have a fixed size, as ordinary variables do. Thus, functions that handle arrays are always called by reference.

Rather than accessing the elements of an array, using their index numbers (for example, as **smplArry[2]**), it is possible to access those elements by using their addresses (for example, as **smplArry+2**). Both forms refer to the same element of the array. Regardless of the data type a pointer points to, adding 1 to a pointer will give you the address that follows the memory needed to hold that data type. Pointer arithmetic lets you access the next element of an array by adding 1 to the address of the current element.

Low-level disk I/O functions are very powerful but difficult to use. High-level disk I/O functions do some of the routine housekeeping tasks for you. The following four high-level functions are commonly used to work with text files:

- **fopen**() opens a file so it can be used and also returns a pointer to the beginning of the file. This function can be used with the mode **"r"** (read), **"w"** (write), and **"a"** (append).

- **fclose**() closes a file after you are done using it.

- **getc**() reads a single character from the file.

- **putc**() writes a single character to the file.

Before opening a file, you must declare the variable that will be used as the pointer to the file, as follows: **FILE *filePtr;**. FILE can be thought of as a new data type, often called a "stream pointer." After this declaration, a value can be assigned to **filePtr** by using the statement **filePtr = fopen("filename","r");** so the file can be read one character at a time by using **variable = getc(filePtr);**, which will assign the character in the disk file to the variable (which should be declared as a **char** earlier in the program). If the mode **"a"** or **"w"** is used, the file can be written to one character at a time by using **putc(variable,filePtr);**, which will write the character stored in the character variable to the disk file. The mode **"w"** will destroy any data already in the disk file. The mode **"a"** will add what is being written at the end of the disk file.

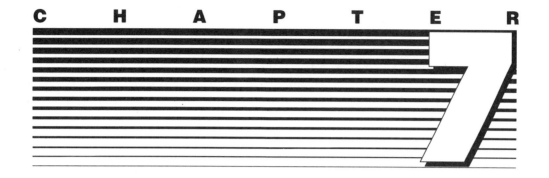

C H A P T E R

7

A PRACTICE PROGRAM:
THE LITTLE BLACK BOOK

A MATTER OF STYLE

In this chapter, to consolidate your knowledge of the ideas you have learned in this book, you will develop an address book and mailing list program. This program will not introduce you to any new concepts that are as basic as arrays, strings, structs, or disk files. It is a sort of "term-project," a fairly ambitious program that begins to approach the complexity of a commercial application. It is intended to bring together most of the concepts you have already learned.

This program is also meant to sharpen your programming style by introducing some of the shortcuts that C programmers habitually use. Up to now, programs in this book have deliberately used a more verbose style than most C programs — an educational style designed to be easier to understand than conventional C programming. By now, though, you are ready to use some of the more compressed ways of writing commands that C programmers routinely use.

One of the most common abbreviations in C is the increment operator, **+ +**, that adds 1 to a variable. For example, the statement **counter + +;** is equivalent to the statement **counter = counter + 1;**.

For beginners, **counter = counter + 1;** is enough to grapple with, and it also has the advantage of being similar to the way you increment the value of a variable in most other languages. Even professional programmers sometimes object to the command **counter + +;** and use it as an example of the fact that C is weird and obscure compared to other programming languages.

Yet this statement is actually one of the most reasonable abbreviations in C. It is based on the fact that most computers' instruction sets include one instruction to add two numbers and (because adding 1 to a counter is so common) a separate instruction to increment a variable by 1. In Assembly Language, these instructions are represented by **ADD** and **INC**. Now, the addition instruction needs to load the two numbers into two registers of the CPU before performing the operation on them. In this case, the instruction would load the variable **counter** into one register and the constant **1** into the other. On the other hand, the increment instruction only needs to load the variable into a register before performing the operation on it.

For this reason, it is faster to increment than to add 1, so the C statement **counter + +;** runs faster than the statement **counter = counter + 1;**. You can test this for yourself with the following two programs:

```
/* CHAPTER 7, EXAMPLE 1 */
#include <stdio.h>

main()
{
long counter;

counter = 0;
printf("start\n");
while(counter<1000000)
     {
     counter = counter + 1;
     }
printf("done\n");
}
```

Compile this program and time how long it takes it to count to 1,000,000, and then compare it with the following program:

```
/* CHAPTER 7, EXAMPLE 2 */
#include <stdio.h>

main()
{
long counter;

counter = 0;
printf("start\n");
while(counter<1000000)
     {
     counter++;
     }
printf("done\n");
}
```

The two programs use **longs** rather than ordinary **ints** as their counters because they would count up to the largest size **int** (just over 32,000) so quickly that they would be hard to time. As they are, they take long enough that you should be able to see if there is any difference using the + + operator. (If you have a fast computer, you might want to change the programs to make them count up to a larger number.) Some compilers now perform extensive optimizing of code and are intelligent enough to use the INC operator to add 1, regardless of the original C source code. With most compilers, however, the program takes somewhere between 2/3 and 4/5 as long to run using the increment operator as it does using ordinary addition.

The + + operator and its slightly less common counterpart, the - - operator, which subtracts 1 from a variable, are among the most frequently used symbols in C programs. These operators can also be used for pointer arithmetic. They are often used in compressed statements, and their usage in these cases is discussed at greater length in Chapter 8.

This program will also take the shortcut of leaving out curly brackets that enclose only one statement. Up to this point, you have used the curly brackets following an **if**, **else**, **if else**, or **while**, even if there was only one statement to be executed following the condition, and this is not necessary. The program menu in this chapter, for example, will use an **if-else-if** ladder that begins as follows,

```
if(choice=='a')
     append();
else if(choice=='m')
     prntmail();
else if(choice=='b')
     prntbook();
else if(choice=='l')
     lookup();
```

instead of using the following form that you used previously:

```
if(choice=='a')
      {
      append();
      }
else if(choice=='m')
      {
      prntmail();
      }
else if(choice=='b')
      {
      prntbook();
      }
else if(choice=='l')
      {
      lookup();
      }
```

The extra brackets set the statements off and make them easier to read, but by now, you should not have trouble understanding the first version, which sets them off using only indentation and saves you a bit of typing in the process.

To be precise, a one-line command terminated by a semicolon is a single simple statement, and all of the commands enclosed within a pair of curly brackets are a single compound statement. A condition must be followed by a single statement that is executed if the condition is true. If there is more than one command to be executed when the condition is true, those commands as a group must be enclosed in curly brackets to make them into a single compound statement. But if there is only one command, it is already a single statement, so the brackets are not needed.

Once you know when brackets can be omitted, you can see that the **if-else-if** ladder is really nothing more than a convenient way of writing a series of **if-else** statements. Using the conventional indentation of **if-else** statements, you could write the previous menu as follows:

```
if(choice=='a')
     append();
else
     if(choice=='m')
          prntmail();
     else
          if(choice=='b')
               prntbook();
          else
               if(choice=='l')
                    lookup();
```

The **if-else-if** ladder is actually just a series of nested **if-else** statements. Any condition lower down on the ladder is not executed if an earlier condition is true because the condition is nested within the **else** of that earlier conditional statement. Because C is a free-form language that lets you use blank spaces, tabs, and carriage returns to make the code more understandable, the **if-else-if** ladder is ordinarily written with all these nested **if-else** statements lined up along the left side of the screen (rather than indented) and with the **if**s put on the same line as the **else**s that they follow, in order to make it easier for the programmer to read. The compiler reads this code just as if it were a series of nested **if-else** statements.

This chapter will use one more common stylistic shortcut, which also will give you more insight into the way that the computer actually works. COBOL generally uses the easy-to-understand symbols "Y" and "N" or "T" and "F" as flags to keep track of whether a condition is true, but C programmers have reasons for using the numbers 1 and 0 instead because the C compiler actually evaluates the number 0 as having the logical value of false and any other number as having the logical value of true.

The tic-tac-toe program in Chapter 4, for example, included a **checkwin()** function to see if either player had won. If this function found a win, it would **return 1;** otherwise, it would **return 0;**. The **main()** function used **checkwin()** to test for a win by using the condition **if(checkwin('O')==1)**. But it could just as well have simply used the condition **if(checkwin('O'))**. If the function **checkwin('O')** returned a 1 (or any other number except 0), it would be evaluated as true and the statements following this condition would be executed; if it returned a 0, it would evaluated as false, and the statements would not be executed.

One handy use of this feature of the compiler is to create infinite loops. Programs in earlier chapters used the condition **while(1= =1)** to create infinite loops (in combination, of course, with the statement **break;** within the loop). But because the number 1 by itself means true, it is more common for C programmers to work at a lower level by using the condition **while(1)** to create an infinite loop instead.

There is one important function that becomes a bit confusing when it is used in this way. Remember that **strcmp()** returns an integer showing where the difference between two strings begins if the strings being compared are different; and if the strings are the same, **strcmp()** returns a 0. The condition **if(!strcmp(str1,str2))** is often used to test if two strings are the same. This condition would normally be read as "if strcmp() of string1 and string2 returns not true," but it actually is true when the strings are identical and **strcmp()** returns a 0. In other words, **strcmp()** works in a way that is just the opposite of what you would expect: **strcmp(str1,str2)** is false if the strings are identical and true if the strings are different. This apparent anomaly makes sense, however, if you remember why **strcmp()** returns an integer (to show where the strings began to differ) or a 0 (to show that they did not begin to differ anywhere), and if you remember that **!strcmp(str1,str2)** is actually not a logical statement in this case; it is simply a shorter way of saying **strcmp(str1,str2)= =0**.

CREATING THE ADDRESS BOOK

Because this program does not introduce new concepts, because its code is relatively easy to understand, and because it is a fairly substantial project to fit into a single chapter, it will be developed rather quickly. Its functions will be explained before they are written but will not be developed using pseudocode, so you will have to study the code itself a bit more closely than in earlier chapters.

The basic functions that an address book program must perform are fairly obvious. To maintain a list of names, addresses, and phone numbers in a disk file, the program must let the user add new entries to the list, look up names in the list, and delete entries that are no longer needed from the list. Most programs of this type also allow the user to edit entries that are already in the list, but this program will not include that feature because it is not possible to write a good editing function unless you have full screen control, which allows you to move the cursor over the existing entry and type over letters you want to change. You might want to try writing an editing function yourself after you get a library package that gives you good screen control capability.

In addition, this address book program should be able to print out a listing of its entries in alphabetical order, providing the user with a handy little pocket phone book. Because it can produce this sort of listing, this program is named **LBB - The Little Black Book**. It also allows the user to print out address labels for mailings.

A bit of basic database terminology will be used in this chapter, terms that are not specific to C but are used whenever databases are being discussed. A **record** is the usual name for one meaningfully connected group of data that is part of a list of similar groups of data, such as name, address, and telephone number or all the data on a single employee. Each individual piece of data within the group—for example, the last name, city, or salary—is called a **field**. The entire list of records is called a **file**. Finally, a collection of related files, which can be connected with each other, is called a **database**, although the term "database" is often used more loosely to refer to a single file of data.

One fact about disk files in C is crucial to this program. Many high-level computer languages let you use two kinds of disk files, called sequential and random files. **Sequential files** can only be read from beginning to end and can only be added to by appending new data onto the end. **Random files** can be read or changed at any point (designated by its offset from the beginning). Naturally, random files are best suited for an address book database application because you might want to search for and read a record located at any point in the file.

C works differently from higher level languages. It offers its low-level file-handling functions, which can be used to manipulate files in most any way you want and are much more powerful (but also more difficult to use) than random files in BASIC. Of course, it is possible to get libraries of C functions for database manipulation that are written using these low-level functions, which makes it extremely easy to use very powerful forms of random file access. There are even packages of functions available that contain a C function that is equivalent to each of the common dBASE commands. These packages allow you to emulate dBASE, the most popular database package available for the IBM-PC. If you are interested in writing database management programs in C, you should get one of these packages after finishing this book—or, if you are more ambitious, you should get a book that teaches you to write this sort of function yourself.

As you have seen, though, the one set of easy-to-use file-handling functions that is included in the standard C Input/Output package is the high-level file I/O system discussed in Chapter 6. These functions allow only for sequential file handling, that is, for reading files from beginning to end and appending new text onto the end of an existing file as you did in Chapter 6.

The address book program in this chapter will use these high-level file I/O functions and will use a fairly simple trick to give the user random access to any record in the file. The file will consist of an array of structs, each with a name, an address, etc. When the program first begins, it will read this entire array into RAM; that is, every name and address will be an active variable in memory, ranging from **entry[0]** up to **entry[99]** (or whatever you define the maximum number of entries to be). Then it is very easy for you to use **entry[10]** or **entry[20]** or any other random point in the file. Finally, before the program ends, it writes the entire file back onto the disk, using **putc()** with the "w" mode, so the version of the file that was on the disk when you started is overwritten and destroyed, and the new version of the file in RAM (with any changes that the user has just made) is saved. This method could not work with a very large database because there is only a limited amount of space in RAM. With a short address book of 100 names or so, however, it is actually better than performing the random access on the disk because accessing the disk requires physical motion, which takes more time than accessing RAM takes.

To use this method, the program needs an option to "initialize" the address book. Whenever it is started, the program must have all 100 entries in a file on the disk so they can be read into the array of structs in RAM — even the first time the program is used — before any data has been put into any of these entries. You will see how this works in more detail when you write the **initliz()** function.

You already have enough background to write the **main()** function, which is really a very simple menu program, similar to what you have written many times before. This **main()** function makes use of a technique called **stub testing**, which is often used in developing complex commercial programs. Because it would be very difficult to compile and test a complex program all at once, after the program is finished, it is common practice to write "stubs" of subordinate functions. A stub might, for example, not do the testing that the function actually needs to see if a condition is true or false but might just return a 0 or a 1 so the main program can be compiled and tested before all the details are completed.

In this case, the program will just contain functions to print "not yet implemented" if any of the menu options is chosen. This strategy allows you to compile **main()** and test it early in the process of development and then to add on each of the menu options and test them when they are written. Note that this program is written using the + + operator and the conditional statement **while(1)** and omitting unnecessary curly brackets.

```
/* CHAPTER 7, EXAMPLE 3A */

/* LBB - Little Black Book */
/* an address book and mailing program */

#include <stdio.h>
#define MAXNAMES 100

struct nmAddrPh
    {                               /* declare an array to hold */
    char fname[21];                 /* a hundred names, addresses */
    char lname[31];                 /* and phone numbers */
    char addr[36];
    char city[21];
    char state[3];
    char zip[6];
    char areaCd[4];
    char phoneNo[9];
    } entry[MAXNAMES];

main()
{
char dummy[2],choice[2];        /* display title screen */
                                /* and wait for key stroke */
clrscrn();
printf("\n\n\n\n\n\t\t\t\tTHE LITTLE BLACK BOOK");
printf("\n\n\n\t\t  copyright 1988 by MyOwn Development
Group");
printf("\n\n\n\n\n\n\n\n\n\n\nPress ENTER to continue ");
gets(dummy);

readbook();             /* read entire book into RAM */

clrscrn();
while(1)                        /* create loop to display choices */
    {
    printf("\n\n\n\n\t\t\t\tMENU\n\n");
    printf("\n\n\t\tA - Add a New Entry");
    printf("\n\n\t\tM - Print Mailing Labels");
    printf("\n\n\t\tB - Print Alphabetical Address Book");
```

continued...

...from previous page

```
    printf("\n\n\t\tL - Look up a Name");
    printf("\n\n\t\tD - Delete an Entry");
    printf("\n\n\t\tI - Initialize a New Address Book");
    printf("\n\n\t\tQ - Quit");
    printf("\n\n\n\n\n\tWHAT IS YOUR CHOICE > ");

    gets(choice);
    choice[0] = tolower(choice[0]);

    if(choice[0]=='a')
        append();
    else if(choice[0]=='l')
        lookup();
    else if(choice[0]=='d')
        delete();
    else if(choice[0]=='m')
        prntmail();
    else if(choice[0]=='b')
        prntbook();
    else if(choice[0]=='i')
        initliz();
    else if(choice[0]=='q')
        {                       /* only way to exit program is */
        savebook();             /* thru menu choice  Q, which */
        break;                  /* automatically saves book */
        }
    else
        putchar(7);             /* if choice is invalid */
    }                           /* beep and loop back to menu */
}


append()
{
printf("not yet implemented");
}
```

continued...

...from previous page

```
clrscrn()
{
printf("not yet implemented");
}


delete()
{
printf("not yet implemented");
}


initliz()
{
printf("not yet implemented");
}


lookup()
{
printf("not yet implemented");
}


prntmail()
{
printf("not yet implemented");
}


prntbook()
{
printf("not yet implemented");
}


readbook()
{
printf("not yet implemented");
}
```

continued...

...from previous page

```
savebook()
{
printf("not yet implemented");
}
```

Even at this early stage, you can test the program. You only need to add the familiar **clrscrn**() function to make the program's output meaningful:

```
/* CHAPTER 7, EXAMPLE 3B */
/* REPLACES THE clrscrn() FUNCTION IN EXAMPLE 3A */

clrscrn()                    /* clear the screen */
{
int counter;

counter = 0;
while(counter < 25)
     {
     printf("\n");
     counter++;
     }
}
```

With this addition, the program will simply display the menu and beep if the user makes an error, but it still is worthwhile to compile and test the program at this point. You can correct any minor typographical errors, redesign the menu screen to your liking, and, if you were developing the program from scratch, you might also find errors to correct in the number or placement of curly brackets. It is easier to find and correct these bugs now than to wait until later and try to find them while you are also struggling with more complex parts of the program.

It is not difficult to initialize the address book, that is, to start a new book filled with blank entries. As a general rule, the program will see if the null terminator that C uses to end strings is in the first letter of a field in order to test whether the field is blank. For example, any functions that read the book will check to see if an entry is blank by seeing if the first letter of **lname** is '\0'.

In essence, all the **initliz()** function does is put these nulls in place, but it also adds a few bells and whistles to make sure **initliz()** is not used by mistake. Such a mistake could be disastrous because **initliz()** would essentially erase any entries that existed in an address book if it were used by mistake. Once **initliz()** puts in a '\0' as the first character of the entry, the function that looks up names considers that entry to be blank. Even worse, if the user did not realize that there was already an address book on the disk or in the subdirectory being used and started a new one using **initliz()**, the new address book would overwrite and destroy the one already on disk when the user selected quit and the program automatically saved the current book.

For this reason, **initliz()** includes two levels of warning. To guard against the possibility of the user entering 'i' by mistake instead of some other menu choice, whenever **initliz()** is used, the program warns the user that it will overwrite any data in RAM and requests confirmation that the user wants to do this. Even if the user does confirm that he or she wants to initialize a new address book, however, the program uses an **fopen()** statement with the mode **"r"** to see if there is already an address book file on the disk and, if there is, warns the user that it will be written over and destroyed if **initliz()** is used; this warning guards against the possibility that the user might want to initialize a new file without realizing that there is already one in the current subdirectory.

The code of the **initliz()** function should not be hard to follow:

```
/* CHAPTER 7, EXAMPLE 3C */
/* REPLACES THE initliz() FUNCTION IN EXAMPLE 3A */
initliz()
{
int counter;        /* write \0 at the beginning of each */
char name[9];       /* entry, so other functions can see */
char yn[2];         /* which are empty */
FILE *filePtr;

clrscrn();
printf("This command is used to create a new address book.");
printf("\n\nIf it is used when an address book is being
used,");
printf("\nor when one exists in the current directory,");
printf("\nit will overwrite that address book.");
printf("\n\n ALL DATA WILL BE LOST.");
printf("\n\nEnter  Y  to continue or press any key to abort >
");
gets(yn);
if(toupper(yn[0]) != 'Y')
     return;

filePtr = fopen("LBB.txt","r");
if(filePtr != NULL)
     {
     fclose(filePtr);
     clrscrn();
     printf("\n\n\nWARNING");
     printf("\n\nThere is already an ADDRESS BOOK FILE");
     printf("\nin this subdirectory or on this floppy disk!!");
     printf("\n\nALL DATA WILL BE DESTROYED!!!!!!!");
     printf("\n\nThe choice I - INITIALIZE should be
selected");
     printf("\nONLY IN A SUBDIRECTORY OR ON A FLOPPY DISK");
     printf("\nWHERE THERE IS NO ADDRESS BOOK !!!!!!!!!");
     printf("\n\nEnter  !  to create a new address book and");
     printf("\n\tDESTROY the one already on disk");
     printf("\n\tor press any key to abort > ");
     gets(yn);
     if(yn[0] != '!')
          return;
     }
```

continued...

...from previous page

```
fclose(filePtr);

counter = 0;
while(counter<MAXNAMES)
     {                                     /* any entry must */
     entry[counter].lname[0] = '\0';      /* have a last name */
     counter++;
     }

clrscrn();
printf("Would you like to make entries now (Y/N) ?");
gets(yn);
if(toupper(yn[0]) == 'Y')
     append();                            /* otherwise, it returns */
}                                         /* to the menu */
```

This function takes advantage of the fact that **fopen**() with the "**r**" mode returns NULL if it does not find the address book file on disk. This is like the error message in Chapter 6, but in reverse. In this case, there is a problem if **fopen** *can* find a file. All address book files must be named **LBB.TXT** (short for "Little Black Book"), and only one file with the same name can exist in one subdirectory or on one floppy disk—though this program can be used to create many address books in different directories or disks.

At the end of the function, the user is given the option of making entries immediately in the address book that has just been created. If this option is not chosen, the program returns to the menu. Remember, the user can only be allowed to quit the program through the menu so that the address book is saved.

Note that the two levels of warning in this function cannot be combined because users might enter "I" from the menu by mistake the first time they are using the program, after entering data but before saving the address book to disk. Given the dire consequences of such an error, it is probably best to have two levels of warning anyway. You might want to add this function to **main**() and compile it just to correct any typographical errors, even though there is no way to test its performance yet.

Reading the file from disk into the array of structs is somewhat similar to reading the word list file in Chapter 6. This function uses a high-level method of reading the file with nested **while()** loops. The inner loops read through each letter of each of the struct's elements, and the outer loop reads through each element of the array of structs (in other words, through each record of the file).

You might want to try using the easier but more advanced method instead. Declare only one counter and a character pointer named ***char begin;**. Make that pointer equal to the address of the beginning of the array of structs with the statement **begin = &entry[0].fname[0];**. Then go through both the file and the array one byte at a time with the statements **counter = 0;**, ***(begin + counter) = getc();**, and **counter + +;**.

Note that in this case you do not need to worry about the end-of-file marker with the high-level method or the low-level method because the file is a constant length. The high-level method that follows keeps reading until **rcrdCntr** is equal to **MAXNAMES**. To use the low-level method, you would need to count the characters and keep going until the total equals **MAXNAMES** multiplied by the total number of characters per record.

Because the end-of-file marker is not used here, you can leave all the garbage you want in the file. The **initliz()** function was able to just put a null in the first space of each **lname** and not blank everything else out, as the function to initialize the list of English and French words in Chapter 6 did. If you prefer a neater text file, you can rewrite that function, using **strcpy()** to copy blanks to all the elements of each struct in the array and then to make the first space of each **lname** a null. If you were writing a commercial program, this would make your product look better, but it is not necessary in this case, and you will probably find it interesting to TYPE the file to screen and compare what is really there with the strings that the program reads.

```
/* CHAPTER 7, EXAMPLE 3D */
/* REPLACES THE readbook() FUNCTION IN EXAMPLE 3A */

readbook()           /* always used at beginning of program */
{                    /* to read entire address book into RAM */
FILE *fp;
int ltrCntr, rcrdCntr;
char dummy[2];

fp = fopen("lbb.txt","r");          /* if there is none, user */
if(fp == NULL)                      /* should select  I  from */
     {                              /* menu to create one */
     clrscrn();
     printf("\n\nThere is no Address Book in this directory.");
     printf("\n\n\tYou must choose I - INITIALIZE");
     printf("\n\tfrom the menu to create one.");
     printf("\n\nPress any key to continue. . . ");
     gets(dummy);
     }

              /* if there is one, all entries are read */
              /* a char at a time and assigned to variables */
else
     {
     printf("\n\nREADING ADDRESS BOOK.  WAIT A MOMENT
PLEASE.");

     rcrdCntr=0;
     while(rcrdCntr<MAXNAMES)
          {
          ltrCntr=0;
          while(ltrCntr<21)
               {
               entry[rcrdCntr].fname[ltrCntr] = getc(fp);
               ltrCntr++;
               }
          ltrCntr=0;
          while(ltrCntr<31)
               {
               entry[rcrdCntr].lname[ltrCntr] = getc(fp);
               ltrCntr++;
               }
```

continued...

...from previous page

```
            ltrCntr=0;
            while(ltrCntr<36)
                    {
                    entry[rcrdCntr].addr[ltrCntr] = getc(fp);
                    ltrCntr++;
                    }
            ltrCntr=0;
            while(ltrCntr<21)
                    {
                    entry[rcrdCntr].city[ltrCntr] = getc(fp);
                    ltrCntr++;
                    }
            ltrCntr=0;
            while(ltrCntr<3)
                    {
                    entry[rcrdCntr].state[ltrCntr] = getc(fp);
                    ltrCntr++;
                    }
            ltrCntr=0;
            while(ltrCntr<6)
                    {
                    entry[rcrdCntr].zip[ltrCntr] = getc(fp);
                    ltrCntr++;
                    }
            ltrCntr=0;
            while(ltrCntr<4)
                    {
                    entry[rcrdCntr].areaCd[ltrCntr] = getc(fp);
                    ltrCntr++;
                    }
            ltrCntr=0;
            while(ltrCntr<9)
                    {
                    entry[rcrdCntr].phoneNo[ltrCntr]=getc(fp);
                    ltrCntr++;
                    }
            rcrdCntr++;
            }
    fclose(fp);
    }
}
```

The **savebook()** function uses much of the same type of nested **while()** loops as **readbook()**, but in reverse, going through the address book in RAM character by character and writing it to disk. **savebook()** does add a fairly urgent warning if it cannot open the file for writing, and it puts this warning in a **while()** loop so the warning is repeated until the user deliberately decides to sacrifice the session's work because of disk failure. Like **readbook()**, **savebook()** prints a message to the screen, telling the user to wait a moment while it is accessing the disk. In general, you will want to give users messages such as this when there is a delay in the program so they do not think the program has stopped working properly.

```
/* CHAPTER 7, EXAMPLE 3E */
/* REPLACES THE savebook() FUNCTION IN EXAMPLE 3A */

savebook()        /* automatically runs when user chooses Q */
{                 /* from menu, writes book in RAM back to disk */
FILE *fp;
int ltrCntr, rcrdCntr;
char yn[2];

fp = fopen("lbb.txt","w");          /* error mesage if */
while( fp==NULL )                   /* file cannot be opened */
    {
    printf("ERROR: can not write to disk.\n");
    printf("If you cannot correct the error,\n");
    printf("\tthis sessions work will be lost.\n\n");
    printf("if you are using a floppy disk\n");
    printf("make sure it does not have a write protect tab\n");
    printf("SHOULD I TRY TO WRITE TO DISK AGAIN (Y/N) > ");
    gets(yn);
    if(toupper(yn[0])=='N')
        exit();
    else
        fp = fopen("lbb.txt","w");
    }
```

continued...

...from previous page

```
printf("SAVING ADDRESS BOOK.  WAIT A MOMENT PLEASE.");
rcrdCntr=0;
while(rcrdCntr<MAXNAMES)                      /* save all records */
     {
     ltrCntr=0;
     while(ltrCntr<21)
          {
          putc(entry[rcrdCntr].fname[ltrCntr],fp);
          ltrCntr++;
          }
     ltrCntr=0;
     while(ltrCntr<31)
          {
          putc(entry[rcrdCntr].lname[ltrCntr],fp);
          ltrCntr++;
          }
     ltrCntr=0;
     while(ltrCntr<36)
          {
          putc(entry[rcrdCntr].addr[ltrCntr],fp);
          ltrCntr++;
          }
     ltrCntr=0;
     while(ltrCntr<21)
          {
          putc(entry[rcrdCntr].city[ltrCntr],fp);
          ltrCntr++;
          }
     ltrCntr=0;
     while(ltrCntr<3)
          {
          putc(entry[rcrdCntr].state[ltrCntr],fp);
          ltrCntr++;
          }
```
continued...

...from previous page

```
    ltrCntr=0;
    while(ltrCntr<6)
            {
            putc(entry[rcrdCntr].zip[ltrCntr],fp);
            ltrCntr++;
            }
    ltrCntr=0;
    while(ltrCntr<4)
            {
            putc(entry[rcrdCntr].areaCd[ltrCntr],fp);
            ltrCntr++;
            }
    ltrCntr=0;
    while(ltrCntr<9)
            {
            putc(entry[rcrdCntr].phoneNo[ltrCntr],fp);
            ltrCntr++;
            }
    rcrdCntr++;
    }
fclose(fp);
}
```

With these functions added, another meaningful test of the program is possible. Add these functions to the **main**() function and — after making sure that your hard disk is well backed up — compile and run the program. Test to see if it gives you the proper message telling you to initialize the book the first time you run it, when there is no address book file. See if it creates a new file named **LBB.TXT** on disk. Also, make sure that it does not give you the message telling you to initialize the address book the second time you run it, when the file already exists.

USING THE ADDRESS BOOK

Now you need to enter some data in the blank file that you have created. The **append**() function, which lets the user enter new names, addresses, and telephone numbers, is not at all difficult to understand, though it is a bit lengthy. It begins with a loop that increments a counter from 0 up to **MAXNAMES**, the total number of names allowed, and checks to see if any of the entries is empty. Remember that an entry is empty if it has '\0' as the first letter of the last name. If the counter equals **MAXNAMES** at the end of the loop, then the program has not found an empty slot, and it tells the user there is no more room in the address book.

Otherwise, the program breaks out of the loop when it finds an empty slot, leaving the value of the counter equal to that entry number. Then the program gets the name, address, and other data from the user and puts that information into the entry with that index number. It checks to make sure the entry will fit into the field by reading the entry into a buffer first. If the string the user entered is too long, the program prints an error message and forces the user to enter data that is the proper length. In a professional program, there would be more error checking than this; for example, the program would also make sure that the zip code was all numbers. Here, for the sake of brevity, the program only checks for the length of the data.

After all the fields are entered, the program asks the user to confirm that the data should be entered in the address book. Many database programs of this type read each of the fields into a temporary variable first and then copy them into the actual variables in the database only if the user confirms that they should be entered. Because of the way the database is being handled here, however, it is possible to enter the data into the actual variables; then, if the user does not confirm that the information should be in the database, the program simply replaces the first letter of the **lname** field with the '\0' that indicates to other functions of the program that this record is empty.

Finally, notice that all of this is nested in a **while**() loop, to allow for multiple entries. At the end of an entry, the program asks if the user wants to enter another piece of information. If so, the 'Y' that the user enters makes the condition of the **while**() loop true, so it is executed again. Note that this **yn[2]** variable serves a number of different purposes in the function, saving the computer a tiny bit of memory, and saving the programmer the trouble of typing multiple declarations.

7 A Practice Program

```
/* CHAPTER 7, EXAMPLE 3F */
/* REPLACES THE append() FUNCTION IN EXAMPLE 3A */

append()
{
int ctr;
char yn[2];
char buffer[80];

yn[0] = 'Y';                          /* create loop to */
while(toupper(yn[0])=='Y')            /* allow multiple entries */
     {
     clrscrn();
     ctr = 0;
     while(ctr<MAXNAMES)              /* find an empty entry */
          {
          if(entry[ctr].lname[0] == '\0')
          break;
          ctr++;
          }

     if(ctr==MAXNAMES)          /* if not found, error message */
          {
          printf("This address book is full.");
          printf("\nNo new entries may be made.");
          printf("\n\nPress Enter to continue ");
          gets(yn);
          break;
          }
                         /* if found, get data and put in */
                                      /* address book */
     printf("ADD A NEW NAME AND ADDRESS\n");
     printf("-------------------------\n");
     while(1)
          {
          printf("\nEnter the First Name > ");
          gets(buffer);
          if( strlen(buffer) < 21 )
               {
               strcpy(entry[ctr].fname,buffer);
               break;
               }
```

continued...

...from previous page

```
        else
            printf("The first name cannot be more than");
            printf("\n\t20 letters long.");
        }

   while(1)
        {
        printf("\nEnter the Last Name > ");
        gets(buffer);
        if( strlen(buffer) < 31 )
            {
            strcpy(entry[ctr].lname,buffer);
            break;
            }
        else
            printf("\nThe last name cannot be more than");
            printf("\n\t30 letters long.");
        }
   while(1)
        {
        printf("\nEnter the address > ");
        gets(buffer);
        if( strlen(buffer) < 36 )
            {
            strcpy(entry[ctr].addr,buffer);
            break;
            }
        else
            printf("\nThe address cannot be more than");
            printf("\n\t35 letters long.");
        }

   while(1)
        {
        printf("\nEnter the city > ");
        gets(buffer);
        if( strlen(buffer) < 21 )
            {
            strcpy(entry[ctr].city,buffer);
            break;
            }
```
continued...

...from previous page

```
        else
            printf("\nThe city name cannot be more than");
            printf("\n\t20 letters long.");
        }

    while(1)
        {
        printf("\nEnter the state - two letters > ");
        gets(buffer);
        if( strlen(buffer) == 2 )
            {
            strcpy(entry[ctr].state,buffer);
            break;
            }
        else
            printf("\nThe state name must be");
            printf("\n\t2 letters long.");
        }

    while(1)
        {
        printf("\nEnter the zip code - five digits > ");
        gets(buffer);
        if( strlen(buffer) == 5 )
            {
            strcpy(entry[ctr].zip,buffer);
            break;
            }
        else
            printf("\nThe the zip code must be");
            printf("\n\t5 digits long.");
        }

    while(1)
        {
        printf("\nenter the area code > ");
        gets(buffer);
        if( strlen(buffer) == 3 )
```

continued...

...from previous page

```
                {
                strcpy(entry[ctr].areaCd,buffer);
                break;
                }
        else
                printf("\nThe the area code must be");
                printf("\n\t3 digits long.");
        }

    while(1)
        {
        printf("\nenter the telephone number > ");
        gets(buffer);
        if( strlen(buffer) == 8 )
                {
                strcpy(entry[ctr].phoneNo,buffer);
                break;
                }
        else
                printf("\nThe the telephone number must");
                printf("\n\thave 7 digits and a hyphen.");
        }

    while(1)
        {
        printf("\n\nDo you want to save this entry (Y/N)> ");
        gets(yn);
        yn[0] = toupper(yn[0]);
        if(yn[0] != 'Y' && yn[0] != 'N')
                putchar(7);
        else            /* force user to enter Y or N */
                break;  /* to escape from while loop */
        }

    if(yn[0] == 'N')            /* if user does not confirm */
                                /* enter the \0 in lname */
        entry[ctr].lname[0]= '\0';   /* to show an */
                                     /* empty entry */

    printf("Do you want to enter another (Y/N)> ");
    gets(yn);
    }
}
```

Once you have this function running, you should enter a few names and then return to the DOS prompt and use the command **TYPE LBB.TXT** to look at the file that holds the names so you can make sure they are at least roughly what they should be. If each entry has two last names and no first name, for example, then it is likely that you made a minor typographical error in **savebook()** and had the program save **lname** twice for each record, rather than first saving **fname** and then **lname**. This is a good time to find and correct this sort of gross error. You can look for more detailed errors after you have written the program to look up a record.

There is one basic problem to grapple with before writing the program to look up a record: differences of upper- and lowercase letters. If a user makes an entry for "Smith," for example, and tries to look up "SMITH" an hour later, it would be pretty baffling (and would probably lead to errors) if the program said that there was no such name in the address book. One way around this problem would be to use the **toupper()** function to enter names in all uppercase letters, but then the program would print out an address book and mailing labels that were all upper-case.

Instead, you can write a special function for the **lookup()** function to use that is similar to **strcmp()** but that compares two strings without regard to case. Then the program will print out names just as the user entered them, but there will be no problems if someone wants to look up a name and does not type it in with this precise capitalization. The function is as follows:

```
/* CHAPTER 7, EXAMPLE 3G */
/* TO BE ADDED TO EXAMPLE 3A */

upstrcmp(str1,str2)
char str1[], str2[];
{
int cntr;

cntr = 0;
while(1)
      {
      if( toupper(str1[cntr]) != toupper(str2[cntr]) )
           return 1;

      if( str1[cntr] == '\0' && str2[cntr] == '\0' )
           return 0;

      cntr++;
      }
}
```

The **upstrcmp**() function simply uses a counter to go through the two strings and compare the uppercase versions of each of their characters. If the function finds characters that are different, then it returns 1, and if it gets to the null terminators of both at the same time (without having found a difference and returned earlier), then it returns 0. The function is called **upstrcmp**() because it compares uppercase versions of strings. It uses the 0 and 1 return values in the same way that **strcmp**() does, so **!upstrcmp(name1,name2)** would be true if the two names were the same.

Now it is easy to look up a record. Simply get the last name to be searched for from the user, and then to go through all the records in the array, using **upstrcmp**() to see if the last name in any record matches the name being looked up. The only minor problem is that two or more people in the list might have the same last name. To get around this problem, when the program finds a name that matches, it displays all the data on that person and asks the user if it is the right entry. If it is the correct entry, the program breaks out of the loop that does the searching, but if it is not the correct entry, the program keeps searching for another entry with the same last name.

This type of search must also be performed by the function that deletes a record. To delete a record, the program will also need to look through all the records for the last name requested and confirm that the record it found is correct before deleting that record, so this search procedure is written in a separate function, called **find()**, that can be used by both **lookup()** and **delete()**.

With this search procedure removed, **lookup()** is extremely simple. **lookup()** prints a heading and calls **find()** for as long as the user wants to keep looking up names. **find()** is also fairly simple. **find()** just keeps looking through the list until the user confirms that it has found the right record. It has one other bit of error-trapping as well. If the user just presses the Enter key, **find()** returns to **lookup()** without going through the list, so it does not find that each of the empty entries is a match for the empty string the user just entered. The connection between these two functions is a bit tricky. **find()** returns the number of the record the user confirms as correct so that **lookup()** knows that the record has not been found if the number returned is equal to **MAXNAMES**.

```
/* CHAPTER 7, EXAMPLE 3H */
/* REPLACES THE lookup() FUNCTION IN EXAMPLE 3A */


lookup()        /* used with find() to search for a record */
{
int recnum;
char yn[2];

while(1)
    {
    clrscrn();
    printf("LOOKUP A RECORD\n");
    printf("---------------\n");
    recnum = find();
    if(recnum == MAXNAMES)
    printf("\n\nNOT FOUND!");
    printf("\n\nWould you like to look up another (Y/N) ");
    gets(yn);
    if( toupper(yn[0]) != 'Y' )
        break;
    }
}
```

continued...

...from previous page

```
find()                      /* locate a record a user wants */
{                           /* called from delete() & lookup() */
int ctr;
char lookName[31];              /* let him search by lname */
char yn[2];

printf("\n\n\nEnter the last name > ");
gets(lookName);
ctr=0;
while(ctr<MAXNAMES)                  /* search */
    {                               /* for lname */

    if(lookName[0] == '\0')         /* if user just presses */
        return MAXNAMES;            /* ENTER, no find */

    if( !strcmp(entry[ctr].lname,lookName) )
        {
        printf("\n\nFirst Name: %s",entry[ctr].fname);
        printf("\n\nLast Name: %s",entry[ctr].lname);
        printf("\n\nAddress: %s",entry[ctr].addr);
        printf("\n\nCSZ: %s, %s %s",
           entry[ctr].city,entry[ctr].state,entry[ctr].zip);
        printf("\n\n\nIs this the correct entry (Y/N) ");
        gets(yn);
        if(toupper(yn[0])=='Y')  /* if it is the one */
             break;              /* that is wanted */
        }                        /* break and use record */
    ctr++;
    }
                                /* if counter equals MAXNAMES */
return(ctr);                     /* record is not found */
}
```

The function to delete a function is very similar to **lookup**(), and it is very easy to write now that **find**() is already written. Like **lookup**(), this function tells the user the record is not found if **find**() returns a value equal to **MAXNAMES**. Otherwise, it deletes the record whose number **find**() returned — after double checking that the user wants it deleted.

```
/* CHAPTER 7, EXAMPLE 3I */
/* REPLACES THE delete() FUNCTION IN EXAMPLE 3A */

delete()                                /* delete a record */
{
int recnum;
char yn[2];

while(1)
     {
     clrscrn();
     printf("DELETE A RECORD\n");
     printf("---------------\n");
     recnum = find();                    /* if find() reaches */
     if(recnum == MAXNAMES)              /* MAXNAMES name was */
          printf("\n\nNOT FOUND!");      /* not found. */
     else
          {
          printf("\n\nDelete this record? (Y/N) > ");
          gets(yn);                       /* otherwise, delete */
          if( toupper(yn[0]) == 'Y' )    /* the record number */
               {                          /* that it returned */
               entry[recnum].lname[0] = '\0';
               entry[recnum].zip[0] = '\0';
               printf("\n\nThe record has been deleted");
               }
          else
               {
               printf("\n\nThe record has NOT been deleted");
               }
          }
          printf("\n\nFind another record to delete? (Y/N)> ");
          gets(yn);
          if( toupper(yn[0]) != 'Y')
               break;
     }
}
```

Now you have a substantial portion of the program ready to be tested. Make several entries, some of which have the same last name. Look up names that are and are not in the database. Delete names and then add some more. Try entering more than **MAXNAMES** entries, in order to make sure you are receiving the right error message. To do this, you will probably want do redefine **MAXNAMES** as 5 or 10. Note how much easier **#define** makes your life.

As you test the program, you might notice a few extra features that you would like to add to it. For example, it is not easy to cancel an entry while you are making it. You must enter all of the fields before the system gives you the option of cancelling. You can get through some fields easily by pressing Enter, but some fields require you to enter the right number of digits, making the task much more difficult. As an exercise, you might want to modify the program so it will accept either entering the right number of digits or just pressing Enter for these fields. Such a modification will also allow the user leave these fields empty.

After deleting entries and making new ones, you should return to the DOS prompt and try using the command **TYPE LBB.TXT** to see what the file looks like. Some deleted entries should be there with only the first letter missing, and others will be overwritten in part by new entries with the ends of some fields showing. Note that if entries were very long, it would be useful to have an undelete command that could search through the database, looking for an **lname** that began with a '\0' and matched all the letters except for the first letter of a name that the user entered; if the user confirmed that the command found the entry, the undelete command would replace the first letter, making the entire entry usable again. In fact, there are well-known MS-DOS utilities to let you recover a file that you deleted by mistake, which work something like this imaginary utility for **LBB**. You must, however, recover the file before a new file is written over it.

PRINTING REPORTS

The remaining functions you must write for the address book program are reminiscent of what many computer programmers spent their time doing in the 1960s. Before there were many packaged programs to manage databases, businesses had teams of programmers dedicated to producing printed reports in various formats and writing custom programs to sort and manipulate the data. You will use one of the most famous of the early algorithms, the "bubble sort," at the end of this chapter.

You should start, however, with the function to print the most simple "report" that this program creates, the mailing labels. Assuming that the printer is loaded with a single-column roll of mailing labels, this function simply needs to print out the first and last name on a single line, the address on the next line, the city, a comma, the state and the zip code on the next line, and then a few newline characters to get down to the next label before printing the next entry.

This is the first time you have written a program that uses the printer, but you actually know how to use the printer already because MS-DOS treats the printer as a file.

If you enter the command **ECHO HELLO WORLD** at the DOS prompt, for example, the computer will print "HELLO WORLD" on the screen. The screen is the standard output — the place where output automatically goes — but it is also possible to redirect output to a file by using the > sign. If you enter the command **ECHO HELLO WORLD > SMPLFILE.TXT**, nothing will appear on the screen. Instead, the system will create a new file named SMPLFILE.TXT, which contains the characters "HELLO WORLD." Finally, you can send output to the printer by entering the command **ECHO HELLO WORLD > PRN**. This command works because DOS treats the printer as a file with the name PRN.

The functions that write reports take advantage of the way that MS-DOS treats the printer by using the statement **prPtr = fopen("prn","w");**. In just the same way that **fopen()** opens any file so the program can write to it, this statement opens the printer so the program can write to the printer.

It would be difficult to use **putc**() to write to the printer in this case because you do not want any extra garbage in the **LBB.TXT** file to be printed. Instead, this function uses **fprintf**() to print just the strings — and also to print needed newline characters. **fprintf**() works like **printf**() except that it must include the name of the file pointer as its first argument, before the usual control string and variable names that you are very familiar with from using **printf**(). The use of **fprintf**() should be clear when you read the code:

```
/* CHAPTER 7, EXAMPLE 3J */
/* REPLACES THE prntmail() FUNCTION IN EXAMPLE 3A */

prntmail()                      /* print mailing labels */
{
char yn[2];
FILE *prPtr;
int cntr;

clrscrn();
printf("\nPRINT MAILING LABELS");
printf("\n--------------------");
printf("\n\n\nMake sure your printer is ready");
printf("\n\tand press ENTER to continue ");
gets(yn);

prPtr = fopen("prn","w");
while(prPtr == NULL)
    {
    putchar(7);
    printf("\n\nPrinter is not working.");
    printf("\n Do you want to try again (Y/N) > ");
    gets(yn);
    if(toupper(yn)=='N')
        return;
    prPtr = fopen("prn","w");
    }

cntr=0;
```

continued...

...from previous page

```
while(cntr<MAXNAMES)
    {
    if(entry[cntr].lname[0] != '\0')
        {
        fprintf(prPtr,"\n%s %s",
                    entry[cntr].fname,entry[cntr].lname);
        fprintf(prPtr,"\n%s",entry[cntr].addr);
        fprintf(prPtr,"\n%s, %s %s",
        entry[cntr].city,entry[cntr].state,entry[cntr].zip);
        fprintf(prPtr,"\n\n\n");
        }
    cntr++;
    }
fclose(prPtr);
}
```

Note that **fprintf()** is identical to **printf()** except for the addition of the stream pointer name.

After creatng a simple report such as the previous one that just prints out raw data, you should not find it difficult to create a formatted report for the address book itself. The formatting in this report involves using two variables. The first is a line counter that sees when the page is ended; at this point, the program needs to skip a few lines and print a new page heading. The second variable counts page numbers, which are printed as part of the heading. (Most business reports would probably have footers in addition to headers and might well use a few more variables to keep subtotals of various numeric fields, such as total wages for the employees in each division, and include routines to print these subtotals at the appropriate place and a running total at the end.)

This function also uses the tab character to indent each line and prints pages that are 5-1/2" high (half as large as ordinary paper) so the user can cut them out and assemble them into a little pocket-sized address book. In a short while, you will add a function to sort the names alphabetically, but for now, you can just use a stub of this function that prints "not yet implemented" until you get the printing working properly.

```
/* CHAPTER 7, EXAMPLE 3K */
/* REPLACES THE prntbook() FUNCTION IN EXAMPLE 3A */

prntbook()                    /* print address book */
{
char yn[2];
FILE *prPtr;
int cntr, lineCntr, pageCntr;

clrscrn();
printf("\nPRINT ADDRESS BOOK");
printf("\n------------------");

printf("\n\nShould the names be alphabetized (Y/N) > ");
gets(yn);
if(toupper(yn[0])=='Y')
    {
    printf("\n\nSORTING: Wait a moment please . . .");
    sort();
    }

printf("\n\n\nMake sure your printer is ready");
printf("\n\tand press ENTER to continue ");
gets(yn);

prPtr = fopen("prn","w");
while(prPtr == NULL)
    {
    putchar(7);
    printf("\n\nPrinter is not working.");
    printf("\n Do you want to try again (Y/N) > ");
    gets(yn);
    if(toupper(yn)=='N')
        return;
    prPtr = fopen("prn","w");
    }
```

continued...

...from previous page

```
cntr=0;
lineCntr = 0;
pageCntr = 1;
while(cntr<MAXNAMES)
     {
     if(lineCntr==0)
          {
          fprintf(prPtr,"\n\n");
          fprintf(prPtr,"\tLITTLE BLACK BOOK: page %d\n",
                                             pageCntr);
          fprintf(prPtr,"\t------------------------\n\n\n");
          lineCntr = 6;
          }

     if(entry[cntr].lname[0] != '\0')
          {
          fprintf(prPtr,"\n\t%s, %s",
                         entry[cntr].lname,entry[cntr].fname);
          fprintf(prPtr,"\n\t%s",entry[cntr].addr);
          fprintf(prPtr,"\n\t%s, %s %s",
          entry[cntr].city,entry[cntr].state,entry[cntr].zip);
          fprintf(prPtr,"\n\t%s  %s",
                    entry[cntr].areaCd,entry[cntr].phoneNo);
          fprintf(prPtr,"\n\n");
          lineCntr = lineCntr + 6;
          }

     if(lineCntr==30)
          {
          fprintf(prPtr,"\n\n\n");
          pageCntr++;
          lineCntr = 0;
          }
     cntr++;
     }
fclose(prPtr);
}

sort()
{
printf("not yet implemented");
}
```

To sort the records, the program will use an algorithm called the **bubble sort**, which was invented in the early days of computer programming. To understand how a bubble sort works, imagine that you have a list of ten names to sort. This algorithm begins by comparing names nine and ten and putting them in proper order: if ten comes before nine alphabetically, it reverses their places. Then it compares names eight and nine and puts them in proper order, and so on until it reaches the top of the list.

Note that, somewhere along the line, the program will get to the name that should be first and then will swap it with every name above that name until it actually is first. After one time through the list, the first name will be in its proper position, but the second name will probably not. Imagine, for example, that before the program begins sorting, "Aaron A. Aardvark" happens to be the tenth name on the list and "Abigail Abacus" happens to be ninth. The program will compare them and swap them. Mr. Aardvark is now number nine, and he will continue to be compared and swapped until he becomes number one. But Ms. Abacus becomes number ten after the swap, and she is not compared again on this pass through the list.

When you begin the second pass through the list, then, you can be sure that the name that should be first already is first. At some point in the second pass, the program will come across the name that should be second and, now that the first name is out of the way, it will keep comparing and swapping that name until it reaches its proper place. After two times through the list, then, you can be sure that the first two names are in their proper places.

Likewise, after going through the list a number of times that is equal to the number of names on the list, you can be sure that all the names are in their proper places. This algorithm is called the "bubble sort" because names rise to the top one at a time, like air bubbling up through water.

The bubble sort could be made more efficient in several ways. It could include a flag to let the program know the sorting is complete if the sort goes through the entire list without changing the place of any record. Instead of comparing all the names each time through, it could omit the first name on the second time through, the first two names the third time through, and so on. In fact, the last time through can be omitted entirely. If all the names except the last one are known to be in the proper order, then obviously all the names are in the proper order. The program will use this final improvement because it is so simple to go through the list a number of times equal to one less than the number of names.

It is not worthwhile to work too hard on improving the efficiency of this algorithm, however, because there are other sorting algorithms that are far more efficient. The bubble sort was popular on mainframe computers that were programmed during the day and were left running all night to process their data, and you will notice that it is slow when you get the program running. Its main virtue is its simplicity.

Start by looking at a slightly abbreviated version of the final bubble-sort function the program will actually use. This function uses three nested **while**() loops. The outermost loop simply repeats the process a number of times equal to **MAXNAMES-1** (remember that you must go through the list comparing and exchanging names a number of times equal to one less than the number of items to be sorted in order to be sure the names are all in place). The middle loop uses the variable **wrdCtr** to go through all of the names in the list, comparing **entry[wrdCtr]** and **entry[wrdCtr-1]**. The innermost loop uses the variable **ltrCtr** to go through the names in these two entries one letter at a time and compare the uppercase versions of each letter in both. As long as the letters in both words are the same, the program keeps looping and comparing the next letter. As soon as it comes to a letter that is different, however, the program knows what order the names should be in. If the letter in the entry that is farther down the list, **entry[wrdCtr]**, is less than the entry that is higher on the list, it changes the order of the two names and then **break**s out of the loop; if the letter in the entry that is higher in the list, **entry[wrdCtr-1]**, is less, then they are already in proper order, and the program simply leaves them by **break**ing out of the loop.

Be sure you understand this version of the function before going on to the next version. The variable **wrdCtr** starts being equal to **MAXNAMES** and is decremented each time through the loop. The program would work just as well if **wrdCtr** started at zero and increased each time through the loop and if names that were higher alphabetically were swapped to the higher numbered entries at the end of the list (having the names bubble upward toward the lower numbered entries is purely for the sake of tradition). The function **swap**(), which changes word orders, will be added on in a moment.

```
sort()
{
int timesCtr, wrdCtr, ltrCtr;

timesCtr = 0;

while(timesCtr < MAXNAMES-1)
      {
      wrdCtr = MAXNAMES-1;
      while(wrdCtr > 0)
            {
            ltrCtr = 0;
            while(1)
                  {

                  if(toupper(entry[wrdCtr].lname[ltrCtr]) <
                          toupper(entry[wrdCtr-1].lname[ltrCtr]) )
                        {
                        swap(wrdCtr);
                        break;
                        }

                  if(toupper(entry[wrdCtr].lname[ltrCtr]) >
                          toupper(entry[wrdCtr-1].lname[ltrCtr]) )
                        break;

                  ltrCtr++;
                  }
            wrdCtr--;
            }
      timesCtr++;
      }
}
```

This preliminary version of the bubble sort includes only two possible results of comparing last names letter by letter. Either one name or the other should come first. But what happens if the program must compare Aaron A. Smith and Xavier X. Smith? If the two last names are the same, the sort must alphabetize on the basis of first name.

The final version of the program deals with this problem by adding a third condition in the inner loop. If the letter of both first names is a '\0', then the program does the same sort on the first name that it just did on the last name. So that time is not wasted on empty entries, it only performs this sort if the '\0' is not the first letter of the last name. Adding this new innermost **while**() loop to sort by first name adds a few new problems. When the program **break**s out of this loop, for example, it is still trapped in the last name sorting loop. There is a definite temptation to use a **goto** to solve this problem, but instead, this program adds a flag called **frstFlg**, which is set ON if the first name must be sorted and used to break the program out of the inner loop. What if the first names are also the same? The program tests for this by seeing if **ltrCtr** is greater than 20, the maximum length of a first name, without any differences. This is a rather complex series of nested loops, but it is not hard to follow if you take the loops one step at a time.

The final version of the program also adds **swap**() to exchange the positions of two entries. Of course, you cannot copy entry two into entry one and then copy entry one into entry two because entry one would be destroyed before it was copied. This is why the program creates a temporary entry to hold the first while the second is being copied into it.

```
/* CHAPTER 7, EXAMPLE 8L */
/* REPLACES THE  sort() FUNCTION IN EXAMPLE 8K */

sort()
{
int timesCtr, wrdCr, lrCr;
int frstFlg = 0;

timesCtr = 0;
```

continued...

...from previous page

```
while(timesCtr < MAXNAMES)
      {
      wrdCr = MAXNAMES-1;
      while(wrdCr > 0)
            {
            lrCr = 0;
            while(1)
                  {

                  if(toupper(entry[wrdCr].lname[lrCr]) <
                        toupper(entry[wrdCr-1].lname[lrCr]) )
                        {
                        swap(wrdCr);
                        break;
                        }

                  if(toupper(entry[wrdCr].lname[lrCr]) >
                        toupper(entry[wrdCr-1].lname[lrCr]) )
                        break;


                  if(entry[wrdCr].lname[lrCr] == '\0' &&
                        entry[wrdCr-1].lname[lrCr] == '\0'&&
                        lrCr != 0)
                        {
                        frstFlg = 1;
                        lrCr = 0;
                        while(1)
                              {
                              if(toupper(entry[wrdCr].fname[lrCr])
                              < toupper(entry[wrdCr-1].fname[lrCr]))
                                    {
                                    swap(wrdCr);
                                    break;
                                    }

                              if(toupper(entry[wrdCr].fname[lrCr])
                              > toupper(entry[wrdCr-1].fname[lrCr]))
                                    break;
```

continued...

...from previous page

```
                           if(lrCr > 20)
                                 break;

                           lrCr++;
                           }
                    }
             if(frstFlg)
                    {
                    frstFlg = 0;
                    break;
                    }
             lrCr++;
             }
        wrdCr--;
        }
    timesCtr++;
    }
}


swap(nmbr)
int nmbr;
{
struct nmAddrPh temp;

strcpy(temp.fname , entry[nmbr].fname);
strcpy(temp.lname , entry[nmbr].lname);
strcpy(temp.addr , entry[nmbr].addr);
strcpy(temp.city , entry[nmbr].city);
strcpy(temp.state , entry[nmbr].state);
strcpy(temp.zip , entry[nmbr].zip);
strcpy(temp.areaCd , entry[nmbr].areaCd);
strcpy(temp.phoneNo , entry[nmbr].phoneNo);
```

continued...

...from previous page

```
strcpy(entry[nmbr].fname , entry[nmbr-1].fname);
strcpy(entry[nmbr].lname , entry[nmbr-1].lname);
strcpy(entry[nmbr].addr , entry[nmbr-1].addr);
strcpy(entry[nmbr].city , entry[nmbr-1].city);
strcpy(entry[nmbr].state , entry[nmbr-1].state);
strcpy(entry[nmbr].zip , entry[nmbr-1].zip);
strcpy(entry[nmbr].areaCd , entry[nmbr-1].areaCd);
strcpy(entry[nmbr].phoneNo , entry[nmbr-1].phoneNo);

strcpy(entry[nmbr-1].fname , temp.fname);
strcpy(entry[nmbr-1].lname , temp.lname);
strcpy(entry[nmbr-1].addr , temp.addr);
strcpy(entry[nmbr-1].city , temp.city);
strcpy(entry[nmbr-1].state , temp.state);
strcpy(entry[nmbr-1].zip , temp.zip);
strcpy(entry[nmbr-1].areaCd , temp.areaCd);
strcpy(entry[nmbr-1].phoneNo , temp.phoneNo);

}
```

Note that there is no problem sorting a pair of names such as "Smith" and "Smithson." When this function compares the '\0' following the "h" in "Smith" and the "s" following the "h" in "Smithson," it will simply consider the null a lower value character — because it is ASCII value zero — and put the shorter name before the longer one, where it should be.

That completes the code needed for a rough-and-ready address book program, but consider how many refinements could be added to it.

Think about adding a field for an organization name as well as a person's name. You would need to add a few **if-else** statements to the sorting function to check if an entry's **lname** is blank and alphabetize the entry in combination with those that have names; for example, AAA Acme Co. would come even before Mr. Aardvark. When you were printing the address book, you would have some entries that had only a name or an organization and some that had both. There would be cases where you would want to have a page break if a longer entry followed but not if a shorter entry followed.

Think about also adding a page break whenever a new letter occurs in the address book, by checking to see if an entry's first letter is the same as the first letter of the previous entry and, if it is not, adding enough new lines to fill out that page and printing a heading for the next.

Or think about making the mailing program more useful. It could sort the entries by zip code to print out labels for bulk rate mailings. It could print labels for only certain states or certain zip codes or add other fields that would let users add criteria of their own for mailings. It could give the user an entire menu of different label forms, such as two or three columns as well as one column, with tab and newline characters used to get the spacing needed by all the popular sizes of commercial labels.

Finally, think about making the program more complex by rewriting it to record contributions that are sent in response to mailings. The best way to do this is to use what is called **database normalization**: to have two files, one with names and addresses and a code number for each person, the other with just the code number and the amount and date of the contribution. Then you could write functions to sort both files on the code number, to read both files simultaneously, to skip through the name file until you found a record that had the same code number as the first code number in the contribution file, to print out that name and address and to continue to print out the contributions until the code number in the contribution file changed, to print out the total of that person's contributions, and to continue this process (with occasional interruptions for page breaks) until you printed out a report with the names and addresses of everyone who contributed.

The features just discussed are ones that a programmer in the management information systems division of any large business might often be working on. Adding these features to the program would make it more powerful than some commercial mailing list programs, and you now know enough about the C programming language to add them in if you want.

SUMMARY

The + + operator increments (adds 1 to) a variable, and the -- operator decrements (subtracts 1 from) a variable. With most compilers, the statements **variable + +;** and **variable--;** will run faster than **variable = variable + 1;** and **variable = variable - 1;**.

A one-line command terminated by a semicolon is a single simple statement. All of the commands enclosed within a pair of curly brackets make up a single compound statement. A condition must be followed by a single statement, either simple or compound. Thus, if there is more than one instruction to be executed if the condition is true, the instructions must be enclosed in curly brackets to make them into a single compound statement. If there is only one instruction, it is already a single statement, and the brackets can be omitted.

The C compiler evaluates the number 0 as having the logical value of false and any other number as having the logical value of true. Thus, instead of **if(checkwin('O') = = 1)**, you can simply say **if(checkwin('O'))**. If the function has a value of 1, it will be evaluated as true by itself. Likewise, instead of **if(checkwin('O') = = 0)**, you can simply say **if(!checkwin('0'))**. Instead of using the condition **while(1 = = 1)** to create an infinite loop, you can use **while(1)**.

A **record** is a connected group of data that is part of a repetitive list, for example, a name, address, and telephone number, or all the data on a single employee. A **field** is an individual piece of data within the group, for example, the last name, the city, or the salary. A **file** is the entire list of related records. A **database** is a group of related files that can be connected with each other, though the term "database" is often used more loosely to refer to a single file of data. These terms are all used generally to refer to databases and are not specific to C.

Most high-level computer languages let you use two kinds of disk files: **sequential** files, which can only be read from beginning to end and can only be added to by appending new data onto the end; and **random** files, which can be read or changed at any point (designated by its offset from the beginning). The high-level file-handling functions that are built into C's standard input/output package can only access files sequentially. C's low-level file-handling functions can be used to write libraries of functions for special uses, such as database programming.

MS-DOS treats the printer as a file with the name **prn**. You can print text by using the high-level file-handling functions to open the printer and write to it just as if it were a file. The statement **prPtr = fopen("prn","w");** opens the printer so the program can write to it, just as **fopen()** opens any file so the program can write to it.

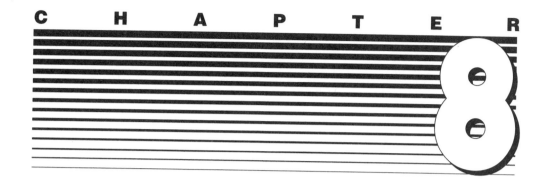

CONTINUING YOUR STUDY OF C

The best way learn a computer language — to get a real feeling for the language that will make you fluent in it — is to study actual programs. Once you know the basics, reading programs can eventually enable you to write code for simple applications, such as menus, almost as easily as you speak your native language. Reading actual programs is also the best way to learn what computer programming can accomplish. You learn what you *can* accomplish by looking at what *is* being accomplished.

Of course, you also need a manual on the language to use as a reference book when you have to figure out difficult code; but the manual should be your secondary source, and the actual programs should be your primary source. Fortunately, there are many excellent books available for intermediate programmers, with useful examples of C code — ranging from screen control to database management to graphics to artificial intelligence.

Before you can go on to study these examples, however, you must fill some of the gaps that this book has left in your knowledge. As stated in the Introduction, the intention of this book is to introduce you to the basics of computer programming by using a somewhat simplified subset of the C language. While you are learning basic techniques, such as looping or working with variables, it is best to avoid most of the abbreviations and shortcuts that make the language easier to use once you are an experienced programmer. When you are learning to control program flow, for example, it is best to learn one or two methods of selection and iteration — not to be forced to clutter your mind with other instructions that perform the same tasks. Having to memorize all these instructions before starting to program is a major obstacle to learning C.

However, when you go on to study code in intermediate books on C, you will be faced with these other instructions. The purpose of this chapter is to outline briefly the frequently used C functions, operators, and techniques that were left out of the main text. It does not attempt to be comprehensive but just to teach you the statements that are commonly used in C so you can go on to study actual programs. Now that you know what a computer language can be capable of, it should not be difficult for you to pick up these slightly different ways of performing the same tasks.

VARIABLES

C includes a few other data types in addition to the four types of variables used in this book, the **char** (character), **int** (integer), **long** (long integer), and **float** (number with a floating decimal point).

The **double** (double-precision, floating decimal-point number) is just like the **float** except that most compilers reserve eight bytes to hold it instead of the four bytes used for a float. The extra width makes it precise to approximately one-trillionth of a unit, while the ordinary float is precise only to about one-millionth of a unit.

In Chapter 3, Program Example 3 illustrated a rounding error. If you entered a wage of **10.10** per week for four weeks, the program might say the total is **40.400002**. Because it uses binary arithmetic, the computer necessarily creates rounding errors such as this when it is converting numbers to and from decimal form. The **float** in Chapter 3 gave a result that was off by two-millionths of a unit. A **double** would give an error of only a few trillionths. The accuracy of the float is adequate for dealing with money. The double is used for more precise calculations.

C also includes three types of integers: the **int**, the **long**, and the **short**. The size of the **int** generally depends on the size of what is called a "word" of the computer, that is, the amount of data normally used by a register. The IBM-PC's word is two bytes long, and so its **short** is equivalent to its **int**. In systems that have a four-byte **int**, the two-byte **short** is used when you want to save memory.

STORAGE CLASSES

The declaration of a variable can also include a modifier before the data type, which indicates the **storage class** of that variable. Storage classes include **unsigned**, **register**, **extern**, and **static**.

The modifier **unsigned** can be used before any type of integer to declare an unsigned integer of that type; the word **unsigned** can also be used alone to declare an **unsigned int**. Ordinarily, the first bit of an integer indicates its sign, so an **int** can have a value ranging from less than -32,000 to greater than 32,000. An **unsigned int** can have a value ranging from 0 to over 64,000. On the IBM-PC (though not on all systems), pointers to addresses are unsigned integers, and you will see how to print one out shortly.

Declaring a variable with the modifier **register** simply gives it priority to be stored in a register rather than in RAM so that it can be processed more quickly. As you learned in the Introduction, variables that are stored in RAM must be moved to the registers of the Central Processing Unit (CPU) before they can be manipulated. It is possible to store a frequently used variable in a register rather than in RAM to speed up the program. Most compilers try to optimize the performance of their code by storing some variables in registers automatically, but they are not always good at guessing which variables it is best to store there. By using the modifier **register**, you determine which variables have priority to be stored in registers.

It is best to use this modifier sparingly. Because the computer has a limited number of registers, there is no guarantee that the variable can be kept in a register. If you declare several variables of this type, you make it less likely that the variable that really needs to be processed quickly will actually get in a register. If you are writing a program with six counters, and one of them (cntrF, for example) is used frequently to count up to a high number while the other five are used infrequently to count up to lower numbers, then you should declare these variables as in the following example,

```
int cntrA, cntrB, cntrC, cntrD, cntrE;
register int cntrF;
```

to make it more likely that the counter that gets the most use will be stored in the register and processed most quickly.

The modifier **extern** is used if you want to repeat the declaration of a global variable within a function. Some programmers use this modifier as a general rule for the sake of clarity. It is necessary to use **extern** if you are compiling several files separately and intend to link the object files that are produced after compiling is finished. When you compile a file that uses a global variable declared in another file, the compiler will give you an error message saying that the variable has not been defined unless you declare it within that file as external. If you declare it without the modifier **extern**, the compiler will create a new, local variable. If a program uses the same name for both a local and a global variable, then the local variable overrides the global one; that is, a global variable is not accessible to a function that uses a local variable with the same name. Thus, this modifier is necessary to let you compile one file that uses a global variable declared in another file.

This is a rather advanced concept that you should not worry about, but you will see the modifier **extern** occasionally in code you examine, and you can just remember that it means the variable is actually defined elsewhere.

The modifier **static** will cause a local variable to remain in memory throughout the execution of a program. Most local variables exist only when the function that contains them is executing, but there are times when you need one that remains between calls of the function. If a function is keeping a running total of salaries for an entire company, for example, and is called by several other functions that give it totals for one division or another to add onto the company total, the variable this function uses to accumulate the running total must be declared as **static**. Without this declaration, the total already accumulated would disappear as soon as the function was no longer being used.

The storage type **static** can also solve a problem you encounterd in Chapter 6, Program Example 10. There, the array of structs that held a list of English and French words was declared as a global variable to avoid a stack overflow error, even though the program that used it had only one function. While they are active, most local variables are kept on the stack, an area of RAM used for temporary storage. But the stack in this example did not have enough room for this array, so you had to declare the array as global to make the storage permanent; however, it would work equally well and would make more sense to declare the array within the function as **static**, as follows:

```
/* CHAPTER 8, EXAMPLE 1 */
/* AN IMPROVEMENT ON CHAPTER 6, EXAMPLE 10 */
#include <stdio.h>
#define MAXWORDS 100

main()                      /* read word list */
{                           /* high-level method */

static struct efWrdLst
     {
     char English[16];
     char French[16];
     char spchPart;
     }entry[MAXWORDS];
```

continued...

...from previous page

```
FILE *filePtr;

char ltr;
int entrCntr, eLtrCntr, fLtrCntr, posCntr, testCntr;

filePtr = fopen("wordlist.txt","r");
if(filePtr== NULL)
     {
     printf("ERROR: The wordlist file cannot be opened");
     exit();
     }


entrCntr = 0;
eLtrCntr = 0;
fLtrCntr = 0;
posCntr = 0;

while(ltr != EOF)
     {
     ltr = getc(filePtr);
     if(eLtrCntr<16)
          {
          entry[entrCntr].English[eLtrCntr] = ltr;
          eLtrCntr = eLtrCntr + 1;
          }
     else if(fLtrCntr<16)
          {
          entry[entrCntr].French[fLtrCntr] = ltr;
          fLtrCntr = fLtrCntr + 1;
          }
     else if(posCntr<1)
          {
          entry[entrCntr].spchPart = ltr;
          posCntr = posCntr + 1;
          }
```

continued...

...from previous page

```
        if(eLtrCntr==16 && fLtrCntr==16 && posCntr==1)
            {
            entrCntr = entrCntr + 1;
            eLtrCntr = 0;
            fLtrCntr = 0;
            posCntr = 0;


            if(entrCntr > MAXWORDS)
                {
                printf("\nERROR: wordlist file is too long.");
                printf("\n\tThe program will work");
                printf("\n\twith %d words but must",MAXWORDS);
                printf("\n\tbe modified to use all the words");
                break;
                }
            }
        }
fclose(filePtr);


testCntr = 0;
while(testCntr < entrCntr)
    {
    printf("\n\n%s",entry[testCntr].English);
    printf("\n%s",entry[testCntr].French);
    printf("\n%c",entry[testCntr].spchPart);
    testCntr = testCntr + 1;
    }
}
```

Declaring this **struct** as static lets you use it as a local variable without stack over-flow rather than declare it as a global variable as you did in Chapter 6. Declaring this **struct** as static makes its storage permanent and takes it off the stack, without implying that it is used by more than one function.

By default — that is, if they are not explicitly declared as being in any storage type — local variables are **automatic,** meaning that (as you have seen) they automatically come into existence when their function is used and go out of existence when their function is done. Some programmers declare this fact explicitly by using the storage type **auto** for most local variables.

DECLARING FUNCTIONS AND THE NEW ANSI STANDARD

It is becoming more common stylistically to make all declarations explicit, rather than simply letting the compiler use the default. Most important, it is becoming common to always declare the data type that functions return.

For the sake of simplicity, this book did not declare the data type of functions: it used only functions that returned **int** values, which C functions return by default if there is no declaration.

Chapter 4 included this simple example of a function that adds two **int**s:

```
addint(x,y)
int x,y;
{
return x+y;
}
```

The value it returns is an **int** by default, simply because no other type was declared, but it is now becoming a more common practice to declare the function's data type explicitly even when it is an **int** and the declaration is not necessary. You must declare the type of the function if you want it to return any data type other than an **int**.

A function's data type is declared in two places: along with the variables within the calling function and before the name of the function that is called. For example, if you wanted to write a separate function to add two double-precision floats (no doubt for the same reason that you wanted a special function to add two **int**s), your program might resemble the following:

```
/* CHAPTER 8, EXAMPLE 2 */
#include <stdio.h>

main()                              /* add two doubles - old style */
{
double nmbr1, nmbr2, total, adddbl();

nmbr1 = 2.6;
nmbr2 = 2.7;
total = adddbl(nmbr1,nmbr2);
printf("\n%f + %f = %f",nmbr1,nmbr2,total);
}

double adddbl(x,y)
double x,y;
{
return x + y;
}
```

Note that the type of **adddbl**() is declared along with all of the other variables of **main**(). Its declaration looks just like the declaration of any other variable, except that it includes the final parentheses that indicate it is a function. The type is also declared in the function **adddbl**() itself; it simply precedes the name of that function.

In addition, it is possible to declare a function as void if it does not return any value, and many would consider doing so to be good style. **void** is a new data type that is used only with functions, as follows:

```
void clrscrn()
{
int cntr;
while(cntr<25)
    printf("\n");
}
```

This declaration makes it obvious that the function that clears the screen does not return a value. The **void** function declaration can make it easier to decipher a complex program.

Most code that you see will not include these unnecessary declarations of functions that return **int**s or **void**s. Leaving them out is another one of those shortcuts that C programmers take. In the future, however, declarations of all functions will probably be required because they are part of the new ANSI standard for C.

The American National Standards Institute (ANSI) has defined standard versions of many computer languages. Until very recently, though, the standard version of C was defined in the book *The C Programming Language* by Brian Kernighan and Dennis Ritchie (Prentice-Hall, 1978), who developed the language at Bell Laboratories. After more than five years of study, beginning in 1983, ANSI has just come out with a standard for C; and Kernighan and Ritchie have produced a second edition of their book that brings it into conformity with the ANSI standard.

Currently, the best compilers support both the ANSI and the original K & R versions of C; and some support only the old K & R standard. In the future, however, you can expect compilers to be produced that support only ANSI C. Programmers are beginning to conform to the new standard now.

The most important innovations in ANSI C have to do with the declaration of functions. Within the calling function, ANSI C allows what is called **function prototyping**. You not only declare the type of the function itself but also the type of its variables. For example, **adddbl()** is declared in the old-fashioned way in the **main()** function above. In ANSI C it would be rewritten as follows:

```
/* CHAPTER 8, EXAMPLE 3A /*
/* TO BE USED IN COMBINATION WITH EXAMPLE 3B */
#include <stdio.h>

main()                              /* add two doubles: ANSI style */
{
double nmbr1, nmbr2, total, adddbl(double a,double b);

nmbr1 = 2.6;
nmbr2 = 2.7;
total = adddbl(nmbr1,nmbr2);
printf("\n%f + %f = %f",nmbr1,nmbr2,total);
}
```

Instead of merely declaring the function as **double adddbl();**, ANSI standard C includes a complete prototype of the function in the declaration **double ad-ddbl(double a, double b);**, including the function's parameters and their data types, which lets the compiler do more error checking. In the previous example, if **nmbr1** and **nmbr2** were mistakenly declared as **int**s, the compiler would be able to tell that the statement **total = adddbl(nmbr1,nmbr2);** contained an error, i.e., that the parameters are not the same data type as the function's prototype says they should be. This type of error checking was impossible with the older version of C.

This same sort of prototyping is carried to the declaration of the parameters of the function that is called, as in the following:

```
/* CHAPTER 8, EXAMPLE 3B /*
/* TO BE USED IN COMBINATION WITH EXAMPLE 3A */

double adddbl(double x, double y)
{
return x + y;
}
```

Instead of being declared between the name of the function and its opening bracket, the parameters are declared within the parentheses of the function name itself. All in all, the older style is simpler and easier for beginners to use, but the newer style is more reliable and, at this point, should not be hard for you to learn.

FORMATTED I/O

This book has used **printf()** with the following special characters for formatting variables:

%d	integer in decimal form
%f	float
%c	char
%s	string

printf() can also be used with the following characters:

%o	integer in octal form
%x	integer in hexadecimal form
%e	scientific (exponential) notation
%g	%f or %e, whichever is shorter
%u	unsigned integer

Note that many compilers support even more formatting characters than are listed here. The formatting character **%u** is particularly interesting because it can be used to print out the actual addresses of variables, as in the following program:

```
/* CHAPTER 8, EXAMPLE 4 */
#include <stdio.h>

main()
{
char samplA, samplB, samplC;
static char samplD, samplE, samplF;
char *ptrA, *ptrB, *ptrC, *ptrD, *ptrE, *ptrF;

ptrA = &samplA;
ptrB = &samplB;
ptrC = &samplC;
ptrD = &samplD;
ptrE = &samplE;
ptrF = &samplF;

printf("\nThe automatic variables are stored at addresses:");
printf("\n\t%u  %u  %u",ptrA,ptrB,ptrC);
printf("\n\nThe static variables are stored at addresses:");
printf("\n\t%u  %u  %u",ptrD,ptrE,ptrF);
}
```

This program will print out the addresses of the memory locations that the system reserved for those variables, and you will be able to see that automatic and static variables are stored in separate areas of memory. (The IBM-PC uses a system of offset addressing that requires two 16-bit addresses to represent a full address: the first to represent the beginning of a segment in memory, and the second to represent the location of a particular address within that segment — that is, how far it is offset from the beginning address. This program only gives you the second part of the full address, the offset, which can be represented by a 16-bit **unsigned int**.)

Printing out memory addresses can also give you a very clear sense of how pointer arithmetic works. You will see that adding one to the pointer will move you to the next memory address of that type. For example, this program declares two arrays, one of **int**s and the other of **double**s. Then, the program creates a pointer of each type, makes it equal to the address of the beginning of the array of that type, and prints out the address of all the elements of both arrays by using pointer arithmetic to increment these pointers.

```
/* CHAPTER 8, EXAMPLE 5 */
#include <stdio.h>

main()
{
int iArry[5];              /* sample program: print */
double dArry[5];           /* addresses using pointer */
int *iPtr;                 /* arithmetic */
double *dPtr;
int counter;

iPtr = &iArry[0];
counter = 0;               /* print address of each */
while(counter < 5)         /* element of array of ints */
     {
     printf("\nThe address of int %d is %u",counter,iPtr);
     counter++;
     iPtr++;
     }

dPtr = &dArry[0];
counter = 0;               /* print address of each */
while(counter < 5)         /* element of array of doubles */
     {
     printf("\nThe address of double %d is %u",counter,dPtr);
     counter++;
     dPtr++;
     }
}
```

When you run the program, note that incrementing the pointer adds 2 to the actual number of the address if the pointer points to an **int** but adds 8 to it if it points to a **double**.

A few more features of **printf**() were not previously covered in the text. You can also use **printf**()'s special formatting characters to control the minimum width of the display. Simply put the width that you want after the %, and the variable will print that width with blanks to fill in the extra spaces if necessary. For example, the statement

```
printf("I%10sI","test");
```

will display

```
I         testI
```

The "I"s at the beginning and end are simply used to show that the string is right justified by default, with six spaces before the four letters of "test." You can also left justify it by adding a minus sign before the number that indicates the width, so that the statement

```
printf("I%-10sI","test");
```

will display

```
Itest     I
```

with the six spaces after "test."

You can control the number of decimal points of a float that are displayed in a similar way. The statement

```
printf("I%8.2fI",123.45);
```

will display

```
I    123.45I
```

The formatting character **%8.2f** here will cause the statement to print the value of the float to two decimal places within a character field whose total width is eight characters. You could use **%-8.2f** to left justify the number within that character field. Or you could simply use **%.2f** to print out two decimal places of the float without controlling the size of its character field.

An important use of this feature of **printf()** is to print out amounts of money. The wages program you wrote in Chapter 3 printed out total wages with six decimal places. Now you can format the total wages properly with two decimal places, as in the following:

```
/* CHAPTER 8, EXAMPLE 6 */
#include <stdio.h>

main()                    /* enter wages for each week */
{                         /* and calculate yearly wage */
float wageWk[52];
int cntr, numOfWks;
float yrlyWage;

printf("\nHow many weeks of wages do you want to enter? ");
scanf("%d",&numOfWks);

cntr = 0;                 /* get each week's wages */
while(cntr < numOfWks && cntr < 52)
    {
    printf("Enter the wage for week %d > ",cntr+1);
    scanf("%f",&wageWk[cntr]);
    cntr = cntr + 1;
    }
```

continued...

...from previous page

```
yrlyWage = 0;                    /* add all weekly wages */
cntr = 0;
while(cntr < numOfWks && cntr < 52)
     {
     yrlyWage = yrlyWage + wageWk[cntr];
     cntr = cntr + 1;
     }
printf("The total yearly wage is %.2f.",yrlyWage);
}
```

Note that formatting the variable in this way will also remove rounding errors.

The previous examples are just the most common features of **printf**(). If you really want to learn more, you should read the reference manual for your compiler.

CONTROL FLOW

In Chapter 2, you learned one form of looping, the **while**() loop, which takes the following form:

```
while(condition)
     {
     statemt1;
     statemt2;
     statemt3;
     }
```

This form of the loop requires you to initialize the variable used in the condition before you enter the loop and to include some statement within the body of the loop that can make the condition false. For example, the menu used for the ASCII chart program gave three options: 1) look up the ASCII character for a number, 2) look up the number for a character, or 3) quit. It then got the user's response, using the following loop:

```
menuOpt[0] = ' '
while(menuOpt != '1' && menuOpt != '2' && menuOpt != '3')
    {
    printf("\n\n\nWHAT IS YOUR CHOICE > ");
    gets(menuOpt);
    }
```

Before entering the loop, you must initialize the variable to make sure the condition is true, which is the reason for the statement **menuOpt[0] = ' ';**. If you do not specifically initialize the variable, the computer will simply look at whatever random piece of data happens to be in the memory location it reserved for that variable. In this case, the condition would probably be false, but there is a very small chance that there would already be a 1, 2, or 3 in that memory location. If you did not initialize the variable, it is likely that the program would work correctly for years and then, one day, would inexplicably execute one of the menu choices that happened to be in memory rather than ask the user which option he or she wants.

The **while()** loop, then, checks the condition before executing the statements in the loop. If you want to make sure that the loop performs at least once, as you do with menus and many other applications, you should begin with a statement that makes the condition true. Of course, if you do very much programming, it becomes tedious initializing the variable before each loop, and so C also provides a type of loop that checks the condition after executing the statements, so you can be sure it executes at least once. This sort of loop takes a form that is easy to understand:

```
do    {
      statemt1;
      statemt2;
      statemt3;
      }while(condition);
```

(Remember that C is a free-form language, and that the code you study will often be laid out differently from the examples you see here.) To indicate that the condition is checked after the loop is executed, **while(condition)** is simply placed at the bottom of the loop instead of at the top. If you follow through the logic of the loop, you will see that the only difference this location makes is that the loop is executed at least once, whether or not the condition is true, so you do not need to worry about the preliminary initialization of the variable used in the condition. (Note that there is a semicolon after the condition here, though there is none in the ordinary **while()** loop, because here it is at the end of the statement.) This form of loop is generally used for menus.

Computer programmers usually call the sort of loop that checks the condition before executing a **do while loop** and the sort of loop that executes before checking the condition a **do until loop**, so you should know these terms. Early computer languages had either one or the other, and most COBOL compilers still have only what that language calls **PERFORM UNTIL**. The language automatically executes the statements once, whether the condition is true or false. If you do not want the language to execute the statements unless the condition is true, you must add an extra **IF/ELSE** statement to avoid it. Fortunately, most modern languages, like C, give you the choice of both types of loops.

There is one other major type of loop in C, the **for()** loop, which is typical of the condensed, cryptic statements for which C is famous. It takes the following form:

```
for(initialization; condition; change of condition)
    {
    statemt1;
    statemt2;
    statemt3;
    }
```

The **for()** loop is actually just an abbreviated form of the **while()** loop. Though the **for()** loop is difficult to learn when you first begin programming, it should not be too difficult for you to pick up now.

When you are using the **while()** loop, you must do the following: 1) initialize the variable before the loop begins, 2) check the condition at the top of the loop with **while(condition)**, and 3) have some statement within the body of the loop that can alter the variable to make the condition untrue. The **for()** loop simply squeezes all three of these actions into the parentheses following the loop. For example, look once again at **clrscrn()**, as it was written in this book:

```
clrscrn()                    /* clear the screen */
{                            /* version in text  */
int counter;

counter = 0;
while(counter < 25)
     {
     printf("\n");
     counter++;
     }
}
```

Most C programmers would actually write this function, using the **for()** loop:

```
clrscrn()                    /* clear the screen */
{                            /* more common version */
int counter;

for(counter=0; counter<25 ; counter++)
     {
     printf("\n");
     }
}
```

This loop is identical to the **while()** loop used in this book, except that the initialization of the variable is squeezed into the parentheses before the testing of the condition, and addition of 1 to the variable is squeezed into the parentheses after the condition. Within the parentheses, the initialization, condition, and change of condition are separated by semicolons. This condensed form of loop is very common in C code.

There are other refinements of the **for()** loop that are less common and more obscure, but you should glance at them for a moment so they will not come as a surprise to you if you do run across them in code. You can initialize multiple variables at the beginning of this loop, as in the following example:

```
for(cntr=1, getcntr=1; cntr+getcntr < 100; cntr++)
    {
    statemt1;
    scanf("%d",&getcntr;);
    statemt2;
    }
```

Both **cntr** and **getcntr** are initialized at the beginning of the loop, and the condition involves both, but only **cntr** is incremented at the beginning of the loop, and **getcntr** is input from the user that comes within the loop.

You can also omit one or more of the usual statements at the beginning of the loop, as in the following example:

```
for(cntr=0; cntr < 100;)
    {
    statemt1;
    scanf("%d",&cntr);
    statemt2;
    }
```

This loop will keep executing until the user enters a value for counter that is greater than 100.

In fact, odd as it seems, you can omit all of these statements at the beginning of the loop, as follows:

```
for(;;)
    {
    statemt1;
    scanf("%d",&cntr);
    if(cntr >= 100)
         break;
    statemt2;
    }
```

Because there is no condition at the beginning, the loop is always true. This is another way of using an infinite loop that includes a conditional **break** statement inside it, like the **while(1==1)** and the **while(1)** loops you used in the text.

The forms of selection available in C are not as varied as the forms of looping. Apart from the methods that you already have learned in this book, there is only one other form of selection that you will run into in C programs — the **switch()** statement — which generally is used in just the same way that this book has used the **if-else-if** ladder.

Many languages have what they call a DO CASE statement, which is just like the **if-else-if** ladder but is listed as a series of cases, just to emphasize the parallelism of all the options. The **switch()** includes one other refinement: if more than one of the conditions is true, the function will execute the statements following all the true conditions, unlike the **if-else-if**, which will execute only the statement following the first condition that is true. To make the **switch** execute only the first statement that is true, you must include a **break** after each statement. The **switch()** is usually found in the following form (assuming that the variable **menuOpt[0]** has been declared as a **char**, that a menu has already been displayed with '1', '2', and '3' as its valid choices, and that input has been received from the user):

```
switch(menuOpt[0])
    {
    case '1':
        statemt1;
        break;
    case '2':
        statemt2;
        break;
    case '3':
        statemt3;
        break;
    default:
        statemt4;
    }
```

The word **case** is followed by a constant, and the statements that follow it are executed if the variable following the **switch**() is equal to that constant. In the previous example, then, **case '1':** is equivalent to **if(menuOpt[0] = = '1')**. The final **default** is similar to the final **else** in the **if-then-else** ladder; the statements following it are executed if none of the other conditions is true.

The **switch**() is commonly used in menus in the form just given. It is probably more common than the **if-else-if** ladder, though it is no clearer or easier to use. The **break;** statements are not really needed, as the variable used to get the menu choice cannot have more than one value, but the **break;** statements are generally included.

NUMERIC FUNCTIONS

This book has concentrated on programs that work with text, and you have learned some of the common functions for manipulating characters, such as **toupper**(). Most C libraries also have a rich variety of functions for working with numbers. Some people say that because C is more structured, it is even better for scientific applications than FORTRAN, which was designed to handle mathematical formulas. Even programmers who will never go near a scientific application should know certain basic number-handling functions that are useful for validating numeric input.

You have learned to validate the length of user input by reading string input into a buffer, using a counter to check how many characters there are before the final '\0', and using the **strcpy()** function to copy the input from the buffer into the actual string you are using, but only if the input is not too long.

There is a simple way of validating numeric input that is very similar. First, you get the input as a string. Then you use a counter to go to each character and make sure it is numeric. This requires a new function, **isdigit()**, which is true if the character is one of the numbers from '0' to '9'. Finally, if all the characters are digits, you can use another new function, **atoi()**, to convert the string of characters into an integer. The name **atoi()** is short for "ASCII To Integer."

Following is a simple example of a program that validates numeric input, using the functions just discussed:

```
/* CHAPTER 8, EXAMPLE 7 */
#include <stdio.h>
#include <ctype.h>
#include <stdlib.h>

main()
{
char toChk[80];
int cntr;
int finalNum;

printf("\nEnter an integer > ");
gets(toChk);
cntr = 0;
while(toChk[cntr] != '\0')
    {
    if(isdigit(toChk[cntr]))
        cntr++;
    else
        {
        printf("Non-numeric input: abnormal termination.");
        exit();
        }
    }
finalNum = atoi(toChk);
printf("\n\nThank you for entering the integer %d",finalNum);
}
```

Note that the program **#include**s two new headers. The function **isdigit**() is declared in **ctype.h** along with a number of other similar functions that are useful for testing data, such as **isalpha**(), which tests if a character is a letter of the alphabet; **isspace**(), which tests if it is a white space character; and **isupper**() and **islower**(), which test if it is upper- or lowercase. The function **atoi**() is declared in **stdlib.h**, along with a number of other functions for converting data types, such as **atol**(), which converts a string of ASCII characters to a long **int**.

When you run this program, note that because you declared **finalNum** as an **int**, the program only works properly if the number entered is less than 32K. In an actual program, you would also test the length of the string to make sure that the number is not out of range. In most cases, you would just want a one-digit integer — for example, a menu choice — and you could break out of the loop and display an error message if the counter were more than 0. In the ASCII Chart program in Chapter 2, you would need to read integers up to three digits long.

To handle numbers larger than 32K, you could declare **finalNum** as a **long** and use the function **atol**() to convert the string to numeric data. (Or you could gain more range by declaring **finalNum** as an **unsigned int**, so it can hold up to 64K.) To get floats, you could use the function **atof**() for conversion and alter the program to accept a decimal point as well as digits, as in the following:

```
/* CHAPTER 8, EXAMPLE 8 */

#include <stdio.h>
#include <ctype.h>
#include <stdlib.h>

main()
{
char toChk[80];
int cntr;
double finalNum;

printf("\nEnter an number > ");
gets(toChk);
cntr = 0;
while(toChk[cntr] != '\0')
    {
    if(isdigit(toChk[cntr]))
        cntr++;
```

continued...

...from previous page

```
     else if(toChk[cntr] == '.')
          cntr++;
     else
          {
          printf("Non-numeric input: abnormal termination.");
          exit();
          }
     }
finalNum = atof(toChk);
printf("\n\nThank you for entering the number %f",finalNum);
}
```

Note that **atof()** actually converts the string to a double-precision float, and the variable is declared as a **double**. This function is declared in both **stdlib.h** and **math.h** in most compilers, though in some compilers it might be declared only in **math.h**. This sort of problem is not uncommon, and the moral is that if you get error messages saying that one of the functions you used is an "undefined symbol" or something similar, look up that function in your user's manual to see what header it is declared in.

COMMAND LINE ARGUMENTS

You can start most commercial programs by either entering the command that stands for the name of that program or by entering the program name along with some **command-line argument** that tells the program what to do when it first starts. For example, if you are using WordPerfect for word processing, you can just enter the command **WP** and start with a blank program screen, or you can enter that command with the name of a file you want to edit, for example, **WP MYFILE.DOC**, and the program will start by displaying the file of that name.

More elementary programming languages do not have the ability to create programs that accept command-line arguments. C can accept command-line arguments as parameters to the **main**() module, in the following form:

```
main(argc, argv)
int argc;
char *argv[];
    {
    /* BODY OF main() */
    }
```

The parameter **argc** (short for "argument count") takes as its value the number of arguments entered on the command line — that is, the number of strings separated by spaces. **argc** will always be equal to 1 or more because the name of the program itself counts as one of the arguments. The parameter **argv** (short for "argument vector" or for "argument value") contains all of the arguments entered at the command line: **argv[0]** is the command that starts the program itself, **argv[1]** is the first parameter after the command, and so on.

In Chapter 6, you were told that in this chapter you would learn to rewrite the memo programs created in Chapter 6 (which can only create files named **memo.txt**), using command-line arguments instead. The program to read a file is a bit simpler, and the use of command-line arguments should be easy to understand if you compare the following version of the program with the version in Chapter 6:

```
/* CHAPTER 8, EXAMPLE 7 */
#include <stdio.h>

main(argc,argv)              /* read a text file */
int argc;
char *argv[];
{
FILE *filePtr;
char toWrite;
```

continued...

...from previous page

```
if(argc != 2)
      {
      printf("\nERROR:");
      printf("\nthe command must be used with one file name.");
      exit();
      }

filePtr = fopen(argv[1],"r");
if(filePtr== NULL)
      {
      printf("The file %s cannot be opened",argv[1]);
      exit();
      }
while(toWrite != EOF)
      {
      toWrite = getc(filePtr);
      printf("%c",toWrite);
      }
fclose(filePtr);
}
```

If you enter this program in a file named **readmemo.c** and compile it, you will create a command, **READMEMO**, that you must use with the name of a file. For example, from the DOS prompt, you can enter **READMEMO MYFILE.TXT**.

There are only two significant differences between this program and the program in Chapter 6. First, this program tests to make sure that the right number of arguments have been entered: **if(argc != 2)**; that is, if the user has not entered the command name plus one command line argument, the program gives an error message and terminates. Second, this program refers to the file by using the variable **argv[1]**. Whatever string was entered following the command is the name of the file that the command tries to open.

The program to write the memo file checks for one additional error. After making sure that the right number of arguments was entered, it checks to see if a file of that name already exists. This program uses **fopen**() with the mode "**w**" so that it will overwrite and destroy the contents of a file of that name that already exists. To warn the user before doing this, the program takes advantage of the fact that **fopen**() with the mode "**r**" will return a **NULL** if a file of that name does not exist because there is nothing for it to read. Thus, if **fopen**() does not return a **NULL**, a file of that name already exists, and the user is given a chance to escape from the program rather than overwrite the file.

```
/* CHAPTER 8, EXAMPLE 8 */
#include <stdio.h>

main(argc,argv)            /* write a memo file */
int argc;
char *argv[];
{
FILE *filePtr;
char userInpt, confirm[2];

if(argc != 2)
    {
    printf("\nERROR:");
    printf("\nthe command must be used with one file name.");
    exit();
    }

filePtr = fopen(argv[1],"r");
if(filePtr != NULL)
    {
    fclose(filePtr);
    printf("\nA file named %s already exists.",argv[1]);
    printf("\nDo you want to destroy that file? (Y/N) > ");
    gets(confirm);
    if(toupper(confirm[0]) != 'Y')
        exit();
    }
fclose(filePtr);

filePtr = fopen(argv[1],"w");
if(filePtr== NULL)
```

continued...

...from previous page

```
        {
        fclose(filePtr);
        printf("\nThat file cannot be written to");
        exit();
        }

printf("\nENTER TEXT > ");

do    {
        scanf("%c",&userInpt);
        putc(userInpt,filePtr);
        }while(userInpt != '\n');

fclose(filePtr);
}
```

Note that this program uses a **do-while** loop to get the memo from the user because it must get at least one character.

OPERATORS

Previously in this book, you learned about the following operators:

Arithmetic Operators

+	plus
–	minus
*	times
/	divided by
%	remainder after division

Increment and Decrement Operators

++   increment
– –   decrement

Logical and Relational Operators

&&   and
| | or
==   is equal to
! =   is not equal to
>   is greater than
<   is less than
>=   is greater than or equal to
<=   is less than or equal to

Pointer Operators

&   the address of
*   the contents of address

The other major class of operators in C is the **bitwise operators**, which is an advanced topic that is not covered in any detail in this book. Bitwise operators are mentioned here to give you at least a small notion of what they do and to make sure that you know what you do not know so that you will not confuse them with similar looking operators if you see them in a program. & and | are the "bitwise and" and the "bitwise or." ^ is the "exclusive or" and ~ is the "one's complement." > > is the "shift right," and < < is the "shift left."

The "bitwise or," for example, will make any bit in the result equal to 1 if the corresponding bit in either of the bytes being operated on is 1. If you were using the lowest order bit of a byte as a flag and wanted to make it 1 to show that the condition is true, you could OR it with 1. You can visualize the operation as follows:

```
    10110110
  | 00000001
    --------
    10110111
```

In this example, the programmer wanted to change just one bit of the upper byte. The bitwise OR will make a bit 1 if it is 1 either in the upper byte or in the lower byte. Thus, ORing the upper byte with 00000001 will leave its seven leftmost bits as they were and will make the lowest order bit on the right into a 1. This example gives you a basic idea of the purpose of bitwise operators.

You also need to know a type of shorthand commonly used with arithmetic operators in assignment statements. The statement **x += 2;**, for example, is shorthand for **x = x + 2;**. The same shorthand works with all operators in C. For example, **x *= 2;** is equivalent to **x = x * 2;**.

There is also a pair of operators used to create very compressed statements in C. **?** and **:** are used to squeeze an **if-else** statement onto a single line. For example,

```
positive = numbr > 0 ? 1 : 0;
```

is equivalent to the following:

```
if(numbr > 0)
     positive = 1;
else
     positive = 0;
```

Statements using this pair of operators (**?** and **:**) are useful within a function to cause the function to use one value if the condition is true and another if it is false. When used unnecessarily, however, this method is typical of the programming style that gives C a bad reputation; that is, the programmer saves a few seconds of typing at the expense of later programmers who must decipher and maintain the program.

Another form of shorthand is also used with the increment and decrement operators. Both of these operators can be used either before or after a variable. Within an assignment statement, if they are used before the variable, then the program will perform the increment or decrement operation before the assignment, but if they are used after the variable, then the program will perform the increment or decrement operation after the assignment. For example, after the following assignment,

```
smplNmbr = 10;
othrNmbr = ++smplNmbr;
```

the values of **smplNmbr** and **othrNmbr** will both be 11. The program will increment **smplNmbr** first, making it 11, and then will assign that value to **othrNmbr**. On the other hand, after the following assignment,

```
smplNmbr = 10;
othrNmbr = smplNmbr++;
```

the value of **smplNmbr** will be 11, but the value of **othrNmbr** will still be 10. The program will assign the value of **smplNmbr** to **othrNmbr** first and then increment the value of **smplNmbr**.

CONDENSED STYLE

The previous few uses of operators are examples of the compressed programming style that gives C its reputation as a difficult language. As you saw previously, it is common, for example, to declare more than one variable at a time, with statements such as the following:

```
int cntrA, cntrB, cntrC, cntrD;
```

Also, values are frequently assigned to more than one variable at a time, with statements such as the following:

```
cntrA = cntrB = cntrC = cntrD = 0;
```

Finally, variables are frequently declared and initialized in a single statement, as in the following:

```
int cntrA = 0;
```

All these shortcuts are useful to save time on typing and are not difficult to understand.

C programmers also tend to nest one statement inside another. Programmers often open a file and test for an error in the same statement, for example, instead of the following,

```
filePtr = fopen("memo.txt","a")
if(filePtr == NULL)
    printf("ERROR");
```

C programmers almost always will write

```
if( (filePtr = fopen("memo.txt","a") )== NULL)
    printf("ERROR");
```

Note that the entire statement **filePtr = fopen("memo.txt","a")** must be in parentheses, which are nested within the parentheses of the **if()** statement so that there are three levels of nested parentheses. This single line, which executes the **fopen()** function and also tests to see if it has returned a NULL indicating an error, is an example of C's cryptic style, but in this case, the technique is used so frequently that before long you will use it without thinking.

There are many cases, then, where C's abbreviated style saves time and does not cause any problems. On the other hand, some C programmers seem to take pleasure in figuring out how to write code in compressed ways that are difficult to understand — even if it takes them extra time. C is capable of more compression and terseness than other languages, but using this capability to the point where it makes a program harder to decipher is obviously bad style. C programmers who are guilty of this abuse should be given permanent jobs maintaining COBOL programs that were written when GOTO was most common method of directing the flow of program control.

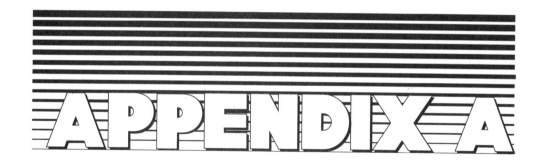

GETTING STARTED WITH TURBO C

Turbo C is so powerful and has so many features that a novice can find the user's manual overwhelming. It is hard enough to learn the C language without having to learn all of the features of this compiler at the same time.

The purpose of this appendix is to teach you — as quickly as possible — enough about Turbo C to compile and run the programs in this book. If there are two or three ways of doing the same thing, this appendix will generally just cover the one that is easiest to learn. It will also omit many advanced features of the compiler. After reading this brief appendix, you will be able to use Turbo C to learn the C language from the programs in this book. When you do more programming, you should skim through the Turbo C user's manual on occasion; at that point, you will be eager to learn features of the compiler that would make you shudder now, but they will ultimately make your programming easier.

The first step is the hardest. The manuals look extremely thick and complicated when you are trying to figure out how to compile your first program. This appendix will get you past that first step.

INSTALLING TURBO C

(If you have already installed Turbo C and set your search path so you can use it from any subdirectory, skip this section and the next two sections. Go straight to the section called "Running Turbo C.")

Before using any program, you should make a backup copy of it, just in case the program becomes damaged when you use it. You must have one blank formatted disk for each of the disks that the program is distributed on.

(You must format disks before you can use them. If you have a two-floppy system, put your DOS disk in drive **A** and a disk from the package of new disks in drive **B** and enter the command **FORMAT B:**. If you have a hard disk, just put a new disk in your floppy-disk drive and enter the command **FORMAT A:**. DOS will count up to 39 and ask you for a volume name; just press **Enter** to give the volume no name. Then DOS will ask if you want to format another disk. Enter **Y**, place another new disk in the drive, and press **Enter** to format it.)

Once you have enough formatted disks, back up the distribution disks. If you have a dual-floppy disk system, place a Turbo C disk in drive **A** and a new disk in drive **B**, and enter the command **DISKCOPY A: B:**. If you have only one floppy-disk drive, put the Turbo C disk in it and enter the command **DISKCOPY A: B:**. DOS will use the single drive to emulate both the **A** and **B** drives and will tell you when to insert the disk for drive **A** and when to insert the disk for drive **B**. Just remember that Turbo C is the disk for drive **A** and the new disk is the disk for drive **B**. After you are done copying the first disk, copy all of the other disks in the same way.

Now that Turbo C is backed up, you are ready to install it on your hard disk (if you have one). If you have a system with no hard disk, you will need at least three blank, formatted floppy disks before you start installation.

Turbo C includes an installation program that walks you through most of the steps of installing the compiler on your computer. Just find the disk in your package that is labeled either "Installation Disk" or "Install/Help." Put that disk in drive **A**. Enter the command **A:** at the DOS prompt; this will make **A** your current drive, and you will notice the light next to your **A** drive go on briefly as the system makes sure there is a disk in that drive. Then enter the command **INSTALL** at the DOS prompt. The program will tell you what to do next. Essentially, it will simply tell you to put one Turbo C disk after another into the drive so the right files can be copied from them. Just follow its directions.

CREATING SUBDIRECTORIES

If you have a hard disk, after you finish with the installation program, you should change your system's search path so you can use Turbo C to compile programs that are in any subdirectory. This section includes a description of MS-DOS subdirectories for readers who are not familiar with them. If you already know about subdirectories, skip to the next section, which tells you how to set your search path.

At the top of the MS-DOS subdirectory system there is always a directory named with simply a backslash (\), which is called the **root directory**. When you first boot up your computer, you are in the root directory.

You can create new directories under the root directory, using a command such as **MD DIRNAME**. **MD** stands for "Make Directory," and this command will create a directory named **DIRNAME**. Of course, you can create directories with any name you like, but it is good to use descriptive names; for example, when you run the installation program, Turbo C automatically creates a directory named **TURBOC** that it copies itself into.

To work on the programs in this book, you might want to create a separate subdirectory for each chapter; you can use the commands **MD CH1**, **MD CH2**, and so on to do this. If you made all of these subdirectories of the root directory, however, the root directory would be too cluttered; files and directories in it could be hard for you to find. It is best to organize them all as subdirectories of a subdirectory of the root directory.

This is not as complicated as it sounds. From within the root directory, enter the command **MD TEACHC** to create a new subdirectory named TEACHC. Enter the command **DIR** to get a listing of the root directory; you will see that, in addition to the files you had in the root directory, TEACHC is also listed, with the specification that it is a directory.

Then enter the command **CD TEACHC**. CD stands for "Change Directory," and this command will make TEACHC your current directory. Enter the command **DIR** again, and you will see that all the files in your root directory are no longer listed. Only the two directories are listed; there is just a dot in place of the name of one and two dots in place of the name of the other. Do not worry about these directories; they are there to help DOS navigate through the subdirectory system, and you will not need to do anything with them.

Now that TEACHC is your current directory, enter the commands **MD CH1**, **MD CH2**, and so on up to **MD CH8**. This will create a separate subdirectory for the sample programs in each chapter of the book. Enter the command **DIR**, and you will see that the directory listing now includes all of the subdirectories you just created.

Change to one of these subdirectories by using the command **CD CH1**. Enter **DIR** again, and you will see that, within this subdirectory, you begin with a clean slate. Nothing is there but the directories named with one and two dots, which you can ignore.

Then go back to the root directory by entering the command **CD **. Enter **DIR** and you will see that TEACHC is a subdirectory under the root directory but that the individual directories for each chapter are nowhere to be seen. Instead of cluttering up your root directory with all eight of them, you have organized them as subdirectories of the TEACHC subdirectory. First enter the command **CD TEACHC** and then the command **DIR**, and you will see that those directories are still there.

Up to this point, you have just been moving to the subdirectory that is immediately below the one you are in. You can move to any subdirectory on the disk by using the full path name of the directory. The path name gives the whole picture of how that directory fits under the root directory. For example, the full path name of **CH1** is **C:\TEACHC\CH1**. This name shows that, on disk C, TEACHC is under the root directory and CH1 is under TEACHC. The first backslash in the path name stands for the root directory; other backslashes simply separate the name of a subdirectory and the parent directory that it is under. You also use a backslash at the end of the path name to refer to a file in that directory. If you have a file in the directory CH1 that is named PROGRAM1.C, for example, its full path name is **C:\TEACHC\CH1\PROGRAM1.C**

If you are already in the C drive, you can omit the **C:** from the beginning of the path name. For example, as long as you are in the **C** drive, you can use the DOS command **TYPE** to display the contents of this file, no matter where you are in the subdirectory system, by entering **TYPE \TEACHC\CH1\PROGRAM1.C**. On the other hand, if you enter the command **TYPE PROGRAM1.C**, DOS will tell you that it cannot find that file unless you are currently in the CH1 subdirectory.

The only other command you need to learn at this point is **RD**, which stands for "Remove directory." First enter the command **CD \TEACHC** to make sure you are in the TEACHC directory. Then enter **RD CH8**. When you use the command **DIR** to list the contents of that directory again, you will find that the subdirectory CH8 has disappeared. You can remove a directory only if it has no files in it and no subdirectories under it, so you will need to do a bit of work when you are done with this book, first erasing all the files in the subdirectories from CH1 to CH8 and then removing each of those directories before you can remove the directory TEACHC. (To erase all the files in a directory at the same time, incidentally, you can use the command **DEL \TEACHC\CH1*.***. Just be sure you really want to remove *all* of the files before you do so.)

SETTING THE SEARCH PATH

After you use Turbo C's **INSTALL** command, the command **TC**, which starts the program, will only work when you are in the **TURBOC** subdirectory. When you enter a command at the DOS prompt, the operating system looks in the current directory for that command and then looks in the directories in its search path. If you are in the TURBOC subdirectory, the system will find the command **TC** when it looks in the current directory. But to be able to use the command **TC** when you are in any subdirectory on your disk, you must change the search path to include the TURBOC subdirectory.

The search path is set automatically when you turn on your computer. One of the first things the operating system does when the power goes on is to look for a file named **AUTOEXEC.BAT** in the root directory; the system automatically executes the commands in this file, which usually include a command to set the search path. To make sure that you have an AUTOEXEC.BAT file, return to the root directory by entering the command **CD ** if you have a hard disk; if you have dual floppies, put the disk that you boot up with in your drive. Then enter the command **TYPE AUTOEXEC.BAT**. If you do not have a file of that name, the system will say "File not found." If you do have that file, the system will display its contents on your screen.

AUTOEXEC.BAT might contain a command to set the search path that resembles the following:

```
PATH C:\;C:\DOS;C:\UTIL;C:\WORDPERF
```

In this example, the system first searches for commands in the root directory, then in a directory named **\DOS** that contains most of the DOS commands, then in a directory named **\UTIL** that contains utility programs, and finally in one named **\WORDPERF** that contains WordPerfect. Note that the command to set the search path simply consists of the word **PATH** plus the full path names of all the directories that you want to be searched; the names of the directories are separated by semicolons.

To add the directory **\TURBOC** to your search path, just use any text editor or word processor to edit the file **AUTOEXEC.BAT**. (First back it up by using the command **COPY AUTOEXEC.BAT AUTOEXEC.BAK**. Then, if anything goes wrong when you are editing the file, you can recover the original with the command **COPY AUTOEXEC.BAK AUTOEXEC.BAT**.) If you are using a word processor, make sure that you save the file in plain ASCII form, not in document form (which, in addition to the text you see on screen, contains formatting codes that DOS will not understand when it reads the file).

Just add the name of the directory **C:\TURBOC** at the end of the search path so that the path command in **AUTOEXEC.BAT** now resembles the following:

```
PATH C:\;C:\DOS;C:\UTIL;C:\WORDPERF;C:\TURBOC
```

If you do not have an AUTOEXEC.BAT file, use your editor to create one, with the command **PATH C\;C\TURBOC** in it.

Because you are editing your **AUTOEXEC.BAT** file, you should probably also add the command **PROMPT $P $G** to it, if this command is not already there; just type it in on a separate line in the file. This command will make your DOS prompt display the path name of the directory you are in. For example, instead of the ordinary DOS prompt **C>**, the system will display the prompt **C:\TEACHC\CH1>** when you are in that subdirectory. Needless to say, having a prompt that tells you where you are makes it much easier to navigate around the subdirectory system.

Though it is a bit of a nuisance to set up your subdirectory system, you will find that it is much more convenient to keep related groups of C programs that you write in separate subdirectories. It makes it easier to find the program you are looking for if you have only 10 or 12 programs in a directory rather than 100 programs scrolling by after you enter the command **DIR**. It also makes it easy to erase your practice programs when you are done with them.

RUNNING TURBO C

Now you are ready to use Turbo C itself. First, change to the subdirectory in which you want to save the programs that you will be working on — or, if you are working on programs that you have begun writing previously, change to the subdirectory in which those programs have been saved. Use a command such as **CD \PROGRAMS\CH1** to change to the correct subdirectory.

Then enter the command **TC** to start Turbo C. When the program begins, there will be a title in the center of the screen — the name Turbo C, the version number, and the copyright notice surrounded by a highlighted square. Press **Enter** to make the title disappear.

At the top of the screen, you will see the program's main menu, a list of words, each of which has its first letter highlighted.

In addition, at this point, when you first start the program, the word **File** is completely highlighted, appearing in reverse video, because you are most likely to want to retrieve a file that you have already worked on when you first start, so the **File** option is the default that you can choose simply by pressing the **Enter** key again. You will use this default choice a little later.

For now, you should press the **Esc** key to eliminate the highlighting of **File**. The cursor will appear at the beginning of the editing window. You are now in the Edit mode, and you can just start typing the first sample program into the computer:

```
/* CHAPTER 1, EXAMPLE 1 */
#include <stdio.h>                /* first program */
main()
{
printf("Hello, world.\n");
}
```

As you enter this program, you will find that Turbo C's editor uses the standard editing keys that you are probably familiar with from using other word processing programs. The arrow keys move the cursor one space at a time in their respective directions. If you hold down the **Ctrl** key and press the left or right arrow key, the cursor will move one word at a time in the specified direction. The **Home** and **End** keys move the cursor to the beginning or end of a line. The **Del** key deletes the character that the cursor is currently on. The **Backspace** key (the key above the **Enter** key — with an arrow pointing to the left) moves the cursor one space to the left and deletes the character in the space where it is moved. The **Enter** key will insert a new line and position the cursor at the beginning of it, and the **Tab** key will indent text.

Once you have typed in this small sample program, you are ready to use some of Turbo C's menu options. The way to use the menu is simply to hold down the **Alt** key and, at the same time, press the highlighted first letter of one of the menu options. Start off by pressing the **Alt-F** key combination (that is, hold down **Alt** and simultaneously press the letter **F**). A menu of options will appear under the word **File**. The first of these options, **Load**, is highlighted by a light bar. Push the up and down arrow keys to move this light bar through the list of choices.

It is always a good idea to save a file before compiling it, so you should move the light bar to the option **Save** and press the **Enter** key. The program will ask you for the name of the file you want to save and, because this file has never been named before, it will suggest the name **NONAME.C**. The cursor is positioned right after this suggested name, so you just need to press the **Backspace** key to erase this name and then type in whatever name you want to use for this file. Note that the program prompts you with the entire path name of the file; it will be something like **C:\PROGRAMS\CH1\NONAME.C**. Backspace just far enough to erase the file name and not the path; add the new name after the backslash. C programs must have the extension **C** following the dot in their name, but you do not need to type in the period and the **C**. Turbo C will automatically add them for you. Just type in a name such as **GREET1** and press **Enter**. After you compile the file, you will be able to run the program you create by entering its name at the DOS prompt.

After the program has been saved, you might want to try out one other useful option from the **File** menu. First press the **Alt-F** key combination to pull the menu down again. The option **OS Shell** will let you use your operating system. Rather than moving the light bar to this option, choose it the easy way: just press the letter **O**. You will seem to leave Turbo C (though it is really still there) and return to DOS. Enter the command **DIR** at the DOS prompt to make sure that the file **GREET1.C** was actually saved when you chose that option. Then, to return to Turbo C, enter the command **EXIT** at the DOS prompt. (Remember the **EXIT** command; it is one of the few commands that is not menu-driven in this program.)

You have already used two ways of entering Turbo C commands. You must press the **Alt** key plus the highlighted first letter of one of the main menu choices that is always at the top of your screen to pull down one of the light-bar menus. And then you can move the light bar to the choice you want and press the **Enter** key, or you can just press the first letter of the choice you want.

Pressing the first letter of the choice seems much easier than highlighting the choice and pressing the **Enter** key, so that technique will be used in the rest of this appendix. You can use whichever method you prefer. Note that some menu choices also have the name of a function key (such as **F6**, **F7**, **F8**, etc.) next to them. These function keys are **hot keys** that can invoke these choices right from the editor without going through the menus at all. These keys are harder to remember than menu-driven choices, but you will eventually find some of them quite useful.

You can compile a program by using either the **Compile** or the **Run** option on the main menu. **Compile** will produce an **OBJ** file (that can be linked with other **OBJ** files to make a larger program) or an **EXE** file that is already compiled and linked and can be executed from the DOS prompt. **Run** will produce these same files, but it will also automatically test-run the program it just created.

Then press the **Alt-R** key combination to pull down the **Run** menu, and (after releasing **Alt**) press the **R** key to choose **Run** from that menu. (The light bar is already on the option **Run**, so you might prefer just pressing **Enter** after pulling down this menu.) A box will appear in the center of the screen that tells you what is being done as the program is being compiled and linked. First, the box will tell you which line is being compiled. (Remember that line numbers will be much higher than the numbers you entered because **stdio.h** has been read into the file.) Then, assuming that there were no errors, the box will tell you that it is linking with library files. Then, again assuming that there are no errors, it will run the program. If you have Turbo C version 1, it will display the message "Hello, world" on the screen until you press **Enter** to return to the Turbo C screen. If you have version 2, it will display "Hello, world" for an instant — not long enough for you to read it — and return to the Turbo C screen. To view its display, press the **Alt-F5** key combination; then press **Enter** to return to Turbo C.

On the other hand, if the program does have errors so that compiling cannot be completed, Turbo C will display a message saying that there are errors and telling you to press any key to continue. (If the program compiled successfully the first time, try deleting its final curly bracket, one of the parentheses after **main**(), and one of the quotation marks within the **printf**() statement; then recompile it so you can learn to correct errors.)

After you press a key, the screen will be divided into two parts: the program will still be at the top of the screen, and a list of (one or more) errors, with their location and a description of what is wrong, will be at the bottom of the screen. The first error on the list will be highlighted by a light bar, and the line in the source code that the error message describes will be highlighted at the top of the screen. (Remember that this is not necessarily the actual error in the code; as Chapter 1 explains, you could just as likely have made an error earlier in the code that is not itself an error in C syntax but that causes the compiler to misinterpret a later statement as a syntax error.)

It is easy to correct errors by pressing the **F6** key to toggle back and forth between the editor at the top of the screen and the list of errors below. First, press **F6** to move out of the error list and into the editor. The light bar will disappear from the error list, and, instead, a small bullet will appear to the left of the error that had been highlighted. At this point, you will be able to use the editor to correct the error by moving your cursor around the editing screen with the arrow keys and by using the other keys just as you did when you were first typing in the program. After you have corrected the first error in the list, press the **F6** key to toggle back to the error list. The light bar will appear down there again, and you can move it to the next error on the list. When you do, the point in the program that the next error message describes will be highlighted in the upper half of the screen. Press **F6** to toggle back to the editor and correct that error.

Because one actual error can cause the compiler to misinterpret later code, some error messages will not make any sense to you later on, when you are working on more complex programs. When this happens, just correct all the errors that you can and then recompile the program by pressing the **Alt-R** key combination followed by **R** again. Perhaps the compilation will succeed; at least the error list will be shorter, and it will be easier for you to correct errors on it before recompiling again.

When you are done, save the final version of your program. Press the **Alt-F** key combination to pull down the **File** menu, and press the **S** key to Save the program in the editor. Then quit Turbo C by pressing the **Alt-F** key combination to pull down the **File** menu again and pressing the **Q** key for Quit. The program will pause for a moment and then return you to the DOS prompt.

You can easily retrieve the file that you just saved when you begin Turbo C again. If the file name is GREET1.C, then you can enter the command **TC GREET1** and that file will be on the screen when the program starts. (Note that the program again assumes the **.C** extension; you just need to tell it the first part of the file name.)

It is even easier simply to enter **TC** to start the program. Again, the **File** option is highlighted when the program starts, so after pressing the **Enter** key to make the title disappear, you can simply press **Enter** again to select this option and pull down the file menu. When the menu is pulled down, the light bar is positioned on the option **Load**, so you simply need to press the **Enter** key again to load a file. The program will prompt you to enter the name of the file you want, but instead of typing in a name, just press **Enter** one more time, and it will display a window with a list of all the C programs in the current directory. Move the light bar among these choices by using the arrow keys to highlight the one you want. Then press **Enter** to load that program.

The easiest way to start Turbo C and load a file into it is as follows: just enter **TC** at the DOS prompt and then keep pressing the **Enter** key until the menu of all the available C programs appears on the screen.

Using your own word processor or editor, you can also create programs and then load them into Turbo C in the manner just discussed. Just make your word processor save them in a file with a .C extension, and be sure to save them as plain ASCII files. If they look strange when you load them into Turbo C, either because they contain characters you did not enter or because what you typed is not in the location in which you originally typed it, then you mistakenly made your word processor save the files as formatted documents rather than as plain text. Check the documentation for your word processor to find out how to save files as plain ASCII text.

Though Turbo C has many other advanced features, this is all you need to know to get started with the compiler and to run all the programs in this book.

THE DEBUGGER

One other feature, which is only available in version 2 of Turbo C, is not essential but can be very instructive: the integrated debugger. The debugger will walk you through the program step by step; each line of code will be highlighted with a light bar as it is executed, which is very useful to show beginners the actual flow of program control. You can watch the light bar go through a **while()** loop until the loop's condition is untrue or watch it select one of the options of an **if-else-if** ladder.

To run the debugger, you must first check two options and make sure they are set to **on**; they probably will be on already when you start the program. First, press the **Alt-D** key combination to select **Debug** from the main menu. One of the options on its light-bar menu will probably say **Source debugging on**; if so, **Debug** is set properly, and you can just press **Esc** to return to the main menu. In general, you can always backtrack one step through the menu system by pressing the **Esc** key.

If, however, the word **on** does not follow **Source debugging**, then press the **S** key to select this option, and another small light-bar menu will appear below it; move the bar to **on**, press **Enter**, and then **Escape** back to the main menu.

To check whether or not the other switch you need is **on**, press the **Alt-O** key combination to select **Options** from the main menu. Then press the **C** key to select **Compiler** from the light-bar menu that appears. Another light-bar menu will appear below that menu; press **C** to select **Code generation** from the bottom menu. Yet another light-bar menu will appear, and one of its options should be **OBJ debug information on**. If this option says **off** instead of **on**, just press **O** to select the **OBJ debug information** option and it will change to **on**. Note that no new menu appears; this option simply toggles **on** and **off** when you select it. Once it is on, you can press the **Esc** key until all of the light-bar menus disappear.

Now that the options are set properly, the file will be compiled in a way that allows the debugger to work with it. You do not want to use **Alt-R** and **R** to compile and run the file, as you usually do, because you do not want it to run in the ordinary way after it is compiled. Instead, press **Alt-C** to select the **Compile** option from the main menu. Then press **B** to select **Build all** from the light-bar menu that appears.

Assuming that the program compiles successfully, you now can step through it in one of two ways. Press the **Alt-R** key combination to select **Run** from the main menu. Two of the options under **Run** are **Trace into F7** and **Step over F8**. **Trace into F7** will take you through the program one line at a time, going into functions that are called and also going through those functions line by line. **Step over F8** will take you through a program line by line but will not go into functions that are called; though it will perform the functions, it will not show you how it is doing them one step at a time.

When you select either of these options, by selecting **T** (for "Trace") or **S** (for "Step") from the **Run** menu, a large light bar will highlight the first line of the program that is being executed; select whichever option you selected again, and the bar will highlight and execute the next line of the program. Obviously, there is a great advantage to using the "hot keys" **F7** and **F8** rather than the menu to select these options because you must select the option you want over and over again as you step through each line of the program; these hot keys are listed at the bottom of the screen as **F7 Trace** and **F8 Step**, so you won't forget them. At first, you should use the **F7** key to step through all the functions of your programs because stepping through them shows you graphically how control flow works.

Eventually, you will get tired of stepping through some functions. The function **clrscrn**() in Chapter 2, for example, loops 25 times, and you must press the **F7** key several times to go through each loop. You then can simply press the **F8** key and step over **clrscrn**() when it comes up in a program. You can press the **F7** key to trace into most functions of a program and press the **F8** key only when you reach reliable functions such as **clrscrn**().

The debugger is generally used because even after a programmer has gotten all the syntax errors out of a program so that it finally compiles and runs, the program usually still has run-time errors. Though the compiler does not detect any errors in syntax, there may still be errors in logic. Perhaps you did not think through what certain statements would cause the program to do, or you carelessly placed a curly bracket incorrectly so statements are not executed in the order you intended. In such cases, it is useful to go through the program step by step to figure out why it is not performing as expected.

For a beginner, however, it is useful to watch the program execute step by step even if it is doing what you want, just to watch the flow of program control.

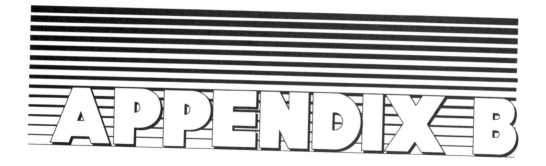

GETTING STARTED WITH QUICKC

QuickC is so powerful and has so many features that a novice can find the user's manual overwhelming. It is hard enough to learn the C language without having to learn all of the features of this compiler at the same time.

The purpose of this appendix is to teach you — as quickly as possible — enough about QuickC to compile and run the programs in this book. If there are two or three ways of performing the same task, this appendix will generally just cover the one that is easiest to learn; it will also omit many advanced features of the compiler. After reading this brief appendix, you will be able to use QuickC to learn the C language from the programs in this book. When you do more programming, you should skim through the QuickC user's manual on occasion. At that point, you will be eager to learn features of the compiler that would make you shudder now, but they will make your programming easier.

The first step is the hardest. The manuals look extremely thick and complicated when you are trying to figure out how to compile your first program. This appendix will get you past that first step.

INSTALLING QUICKC

If you have already installed QuickC, skip this section. Go straight to the section called "Running QuickC."

Before using any program, you should make a backup copy of it, just in case the program is damaged when you use it. You must have one blank formatted disk for each of the disks that the program is distributed on.

Note that you must format blank disks before you can use them. If you have a two-floppy drive system, place your DOS disk in drive **A** and a new disk in drive **B**, and enter the command **FORMAT B:**. If you have a hard disk, just put a new disk in your floppy-disk drive and enter the command **FORMAT A:**. DOS will count up to 39 and ask you for a volume name. Just press the **Enter** key to give the volume no name. Then DOS will ask you if you want to format another disk. Enter **Y**, put another new disk in the drive, and press the **Enter** key to format it.

Once you have enough formatted disks, back up the distribution disks. If you have a dual-floppy drive system, put a QuickC disk in drive **A** and a new disk in drive **B** and enter the command **DISKCOPY A: B:**. If you have only one floppy-disk drive, place the QuickC disk in that drive and enter the command **DISKCOPY A: B:**. DOS will use the single drive to emulate both the **A** and **B** drives and will tell you when to insert the disk for drive **A** and when to insert the disk for drive **B**. Just remember that QuickC is the disk for drive **A** and the new disk is the disk for drive **B**. After you are done copying the first disk, copy all of the other disks in the same way.

Now that QuickC is backed up, you are ready to install it. QuickC includes a setup program that walks you through most of the steps of installing the compiler on your computer.

If you have a hard disk, before running this program you should create a subdirectory for QuickC. Make sure you are in the root directory of your **C** drive. When the DOS prompt says **C>**, enter the command **CD **. Then, to create a new subdirectory, enter the command **MD QUICKC**. (For a more complete explanation of how to work with subdirectories, see "Creating Subdirectories" in Appendix A.)

If you have a dual-floppy system, you must have at least two blank, formatted floppy disks available when you begin to install QuickC.

Now find the disk in your QuickC package that is labeled "Product Disk." Put it in disk drive **A**. Enter the command **A:** at the DOS prompt and press the **Enter** key to make **A** your current drive. The light next to your **A** drive will go on briefly while the system makes sure there is a disk in that drive.

The command you should enter now to install the program depends on whether you have a hard disk or dual floppy disk system.

If you have a hard disk and have already created a subdirectory called **QUICKC**, enter the command **SETUP H C:\QUICKC M EM GR**. The **H** means that you are setting up on a hard disk. **C:\QUICKC** means that the program will be installed in (and under) the subdirectory with that name. **M** means that you are using the medium memory model, which is the default for QuickC's programming environment. **EM** means that your system does not have an 8087 mathematics coprocessor and that your microprocessor must emulate its functions; if you have an 8087 or 80287 chip, replace **EM** in the command with **87**. Finally, **GR** means that you are installing QuickC's graphic functions. These require only about 50K of disk space, so there is really no reason not to install them; but if you do not want the graphic functions, just leave out the **GR** from the command.

If you have dual floppy drives, place a formatted blank disk in drive **B**, and enter the command **SETUP F B: M EM GR**. The **F** means that you are installing the program on a floppy disk. The **B:** means that it will be installed on the B drive. The other arguments are explained in the previous paragraph. Read that explanation to see whether you need to change any of them.

The program will tell you what to do next. Essentially, it will simply tell you to put one QuickC disk after another into the drive so the right files can be copied from those disks. Just follow the program's directions. The program will also ask you if you want sample programs copied onto your disk. Because this book includes all the sample programs you will need, you can enter **N** for no. When the program asks you if you want unnecessary library subcomponents deleted, answer **Y**. The parts of SETUP that build libraries can take time, so be patient.

CONFIGURING YOUR SYSTEM

After running the setup program, you must change your **AUTOEXEC.BAT** and **CONFIG.SYS** files so your system is configured properly to run QuickC.

Almost immediately after the power goes on, the operating system looks for these two files in the root directory of your hard disk or on your boot disk; it automatically executes the commands in the AUTOEXEC.BAT file, and it configures the system in certain ways that are specified in the CONFIG.SYS file.

To make sure that you have an AUTOEXEC.BAT file, change to the root directory by entering the command **CD ** if you have a hard disk; or put your boot disk in the drive if you have dual floppy drives. Then, enter the command **TYPE AUTOEXEC.BAT**. If you do not have a file of that name, the system will say "File not found." If you do have that file, the system will display its contents on your screen.

If you do not already have an AUTOEXEC.BAT file and you are working on a hard disk system, create a file named AUTOEXEC.BAT in your root directory that contains the following commands:

```
PATH=C:\QUICKC\BIN
SET INCLUDE=C:\QUICKC\INCLUDE
SET LIB=C:\QUICKC\LIB
SET TMP=C:\QUICKC\TMP
```

First make sure you are in the root directory by entering the command **CD **. Then use any word processor to type these commands into a file named AUTOEXEC.BAT. Make sure you save the file as plain ASCII text and not in document form (which, in addition to the text you see on screen, contains formatting codes that DOS will not understand when it reads the file).

If you have a dual-floppy system and do not have an AUTOEXEC.BAT file on your boot disk, using any word processor that can create plain ASCII files, you should create an AUTOEXEC.BAT file containing the following commands:

```
SET PATH=A:
SET LIB=A:
SET INCLUDE=A:\INCLUDE
```

After you have finished creating the file, check it by entering the command **TYPE AUTOEXEC.BAT** at the DOS prompt. If the file does not appear as you expected — that is, if it has characters that you did not enter or the characters that you did enter are not where you expected them to be — then you saved the file as a formatted document and not as plain ASCII text. Check your word processor's manual to find out how to create ASCII text files.

Depending on whether you have a hard disk or dual floppy drives, add all the commands that were previously listed as entries for a new **AUTOEXEC.BAT** file to the end of the existing file — *except one*. The command that includes the word **PATH**, which sets the system's search path, should only be added to AUTOEXEC.BAT if that file does not already contain a PATH command. If there is already a PATH command in your **AUTOEXEC.BAT** file, you should simply add QuickC to it.

If you already have an **AUTOEXEC.BAT** file, you should use your word processor to edit it. (First back the file up by using the command **COPY AUTOEXEC.BAT AUTOEXEC.BAK**. Then, if anything goes wrong when you are editing it, you can recover the original with the command **COPY AUTOEXEC.BAK AUTOEXEC.BAT**.)

The search path is where DOS looks for commands. When you enter a command at the DOS prompt, the operating system looks in the current directory for that command and then looks in the directories in its search path. If you are currently in the QUICKC subdirectory, the system will find the command **QC** when it looks in the current directory; however, to be able to use the command **QC** when you are in any subdirectory on your disk, you must add the QUICKC subdirectory to the search path.

Your **AUTOEXEC.BAT** file might already have a command to set the search path that resembles the following:

```
PATH C:\;C:\DOS;C:\UTIL;C:\WORDPERF
```

In this example, the operating system searches for commands first in the root directory, then in a directory named **\DOS** that contains most of the DOS commands, then in a directory named **\UTIL** that contains utility programs, and finally in one named **\WORDPERF** that contains WordPerfect. Note that the command to set the search path simply consists of the word **PATH** plus the full path names of all the directories that you want to be searched; the names of the directories are separated by semicolons.

To add the directory **\QUICKC** to your search path, just use your word processor to add the name of the directory **C:\QUICKC** at the end of the search path so the path command in **AUTOEXEC.BAT** resembles the following:

```
PATH C:\;C:\DOS;C:\UTIL;C:\WORDPERF;C:\QUICKC
```

Because you are editing your **AUTOEXEC.BAT** file, you should probably also add the command **PROMPT $P $G** to it if this command is not already there. Simply type the command in on a separate line in the file. This command will cause your DOS prompt to display the path name of the directory you are in. For example, instead of the ordinary DOS prompt **C>**, the system will display the prompt **C:\QUICKC >** when you are in the \QUICKC subdirectory. Having a prompt that tells you exactly where you are makes it much easier to navigate around the subdirectory system.

After saving AUTOEXEC.BAT and exiting from your word processor, view your AUTOEXEC.BAT file by using the command **TYPE AUTOEXEC.BAT** to make sure you saved it in plain ASCII form.

Your CONFIG.SYS file contains statements that configure your system. If you have installed a RAM disk or the ANSI.SYS screen driver in your system, for example, you must have a CONFIG.SYS file in the root directory of your hard disk or on your boot disk to tell your operating system to use the RAM disk or screen driver.

CONFIG.SYS also can contain a statement telling the operating system the maximum number of files and buffers it can open. When MS-DOS was first written, RAM was expensive and scarce, so the default was set low to save memory. Now that memory is more abundant, many programs require you to add commands to CONFIG.SYS that increase the number of files and buffers it can open.

If you have two floppy-disk drives, your CONFIG.SYS file must contain the following lines:

```
files=15
buffers=10
```

If you have a hard disk, the SETUP program will create a file called NEW-CONF.SYS that will tell you what values you should use for files and buffers. This file is in the directory **C:\QUICKC\BIN\SAMPLE**. Use the command **TYPE C:QUICKC\BIN\SAMPLE\NEW-CONF.SYS** to see the contents of this file. It will probably contain

```
files=20
buffers=10
```

which is the maximum number of files and buffers that can be opened.

If you already have a CONFIG.SYS file, use your editor to add the appropriate statements to it. If you *do not* have a CONFIG.SYS file, you can use your editor to create one, or (if you have a hard disk) you can simply use the file NEW-CONF.SYS itself by entering the command

```
COPY C:QUICKC\BIN\SAMPLE\NEW-CONF.SYS C:\CONFIG.SYS.
```

(Do not use this **COPY** command if you already have a CONFIG.SYS file because this command will destroy it.) If you used your editor to work on CONFIG.SYS, then make sure that you saved the file as plain ASCII text by entering the command **TYPE CONFIG.SYS** and examining the file.

Now that you have configured your system, you must boot up again so the operating system has a chance to read everything you have entered. You can turn the computer off and then on, or you can hold down the **Ctrl**, **Alt**, and **Del** keys (**Ctrl-Alt-Del**) at the same time, which will reboot the computer.

RUNNING QUICKC

Now you are ready to use QuickC itself. First get into the subdirectory in which you want to save the programs you will be working on; or, if you are working on programs that you have begun writing previously, change to the subdirectory in which they have been saved. (For more information on using subdirectories, see the section called "Creating Subdirectories" in Appendix A.)

Then enter the command **QC** to start QuickC. At the top of the screen, you will see the program's main menu, a light bar containing a list of words in reverse video. Below this list of words is the editing window, which includes the title of the current file at the top. Because you have not given this file a title, it will automatically have the name UNTITLED.C. The cursor is at the beginning of the editing window.

You are now in the Edit mode, and you can begin typing the first sample program into the computer:

```
/* CHAPTER 1, EXAMPLE 1 */
#include <stdio.h>                /* first program */
main()
{
printf("Hello, world.\n");
}
```

As you enter the program, you will find that QuickC's editor uses the standard editing keys that you are probably familiar with from using other word processing programs. The arrow keys move the cursor one space at a time in their respective directions. If you hold down the **Ctrl** key and press the left or right arrow key, the cursor moves one word at a time in the specified direction. The **Home** and **End** keys move the cursor to the beginning or end of a line. The **Del** key deletes the character that the cursor is currently positioned on. The **Backspace** key (the key with an arrow pointing left on it, above the **Enter** key) moves the cursor one character to the left, deleting that character in the process. The **Enter** key will insert a new line and place the cursor at the beginning of that line, and the **Tab** key will indent text.

After you have typed in this small sample program, you are ready to use some of QuickC's menu options. The way to use the menu is simply to hold down the **Alt** key and, at the same time, press the first letter of one of the menu options. Start off by pressing the **Alt-F** key combination (that is, hold down the **Alt** key and simultaneously press the letter **F** key). A menu of options will appear under the word **File**. The first of these options, **NEW**, is highlighted by a light bar. Push the up and down arrow keys to move this light bar through the list of choices.

It is always a good idea to save a file before compiling it, so you should move the light bar to the option **Save** and press the **Enter** key. The program will ask you for the name of the file you want to save, and because this file has never been named before, it will suggest the name **UNTITLED.C**. The cursor is positioned right after this suggested name, so you can use the **Backspace** key to erase this name and then type in whatever name you want to use for this file. The names of C programs must have the extension **C** following the period, but you do not need to type in the period and the **C**. QuickC will automatically add them for you. Just type in a name such as **GREET1** and press the **Enter** key. After you compile the file, you will be able to run the program you create by entering its file name at the DOS prompt. (Note that the new name appears at the top of the editing window.)

After the program has been saved, you might want to try out one other useful option from the **File** menu. First press the **Alt-F** key combination to pull the menu down again. The option **DOS Shell** will let you use your operating system. Rather than moving the light bar to this option, choose **DOS Shell** the easy way; just press the letter **D**. You will seem to leave QuickC (though it is really still there) and return to DOS. Enter the command **DIR** at the DOS prompt to make sure that the file **GREET1.C** was actually saved when you chose that option. Then, to return to QuickC, enter the **EXIT** command at the DOS prompt. (Remember the **EXIT** command; it is one of the few commands in this program that is not menu driven.)

You have already used two ways of entering QuickC commands. You must press the **Alt** key plus the first letter of one of the main menu choices that is always at the top of your screen to pull down one of the light bar menus. Then, you can use the cursor keys to move the light bar to the choice you want and press the **Enter** key, or you can just press the highlighted letter of the choice you want. Simply pressing the highlighted letter seems easier, so that technique will be used in the rest of this appendix. You can use whichever method you prefer. As you use the program, you will notice that some of these menu choices also include the name of a function key (**F8**, **F10**, etc.) next to them. These are **hot keys** that can invoke these choices right from the editor, without going through the menus at all. Hot keys are harder to remember than menu-driven choices, but you will ultimately find some of them useful.

You can compile a program by using the **Run** option on the main menu. When you are developing the program, it is easiest just to press the **Alt-R** key combination to pull down the **Run** menu and (after releasing the **Alt** key) press **S** to choose **Start** from that menu. (Because the light bar is already on the option **Start**, you might prefer just pressing the **Enter** key after pulling down this menu.) A full screen display will appear with a box in the center that tells you which line is being compiled. Remember that line numbers will be much higher than the numbers you entered because **stdio.h** has been read into the file. Then, assuming that there were no errors, QuickC will run the program. The program will display the message "Hello, world" on the screen, until you press the **Enter** key to return to the QuickC screen.

This program has been compiled and linked in memory but not on disk, so you have not created an executable EXE file yet. QuickC keeps many of the most common library functions in memory, so it can link the program extremely quickly, which saves you time when you are first developing and testing a program because you might have to change it and recompile it many times.

Once the program is complete and correct and you are ready to create an EXE file, press the **Alt-R** key combination to pull down the **Run** menu, and then select **C** for **Compile**. Rather than running the program immediately, this selection will give you the chance to switch the default option so that the program does not just link in memory. Note that the screen has three lists of different options: one that allows you to choose **Warning** level, one that allows you to choose **Output**, and one labeled **Miscellaneous**. The only option you need to worry about is **Output**. You can use the **Tab** key to move from one list to another and the up and down arrow keys to select an option within a list. Press the **Tab** key once to move the cursor to the **Output** list. Then, press the down arrow key once to choose the EXE option from that list. Note that there is a period to the left of the chosen option. Keep pressing the **Tab** key until you reach the box at the bottom of the screen that contains the option **Build Program**, and then press the **Enter** key. QuickC should create an EXE file on disk.

The previous instructions assumed that the program compiled successfully. If the program has errors that prevent compiling from being completed, QuickC will display a message at the bottom of the screen, telling you how many errors there are and describing the first one. The cursor will also move to the location of the first error in the editing window so you can correct it. (Remember, however, that this is not necessarily the actual error in the code. As explained in Chapter 1, you may have made an error earlier in the code that is not an error in C syntax itself but that causes the compiler to misinterpret a later statement as a syntax error.)

If the program did compile successfully, try creating some errors. You can type in extra lines in a few places in the program, each with a few random letters and a semicolon at the end and delete the final curly bracket of the program. Then try recompiling the program so you can practice correcting errors.

It is easy to edit all the errors in the program. Press the **Shift-F3** key combination to move to the next error on the list and press **Shift-F4** to return to the previous error (keeping an eye on the bottom of the screen, which changes to tell you the number of the error you are currently on and how many total errors there are.

Because one actual error can cause the compiler to misinterpret later code, some error messages will not make any sense to you later on when you are working with more complex programs. When this happens, just correct all the errors you can and then recompile the program by pressing **Alt-R** followed by **S** again. Perhaps the compilation will succeed. At least the error list will be shorter, and it will be easier for you to correct the errors on it before recompiling again.

When you are done, save the final version of your program. Press the **Alt-F** key combination to pull down the **File** menu and then press the **S** key to save the program in the editor. Finally, exit from QuickC by pressing the **Alt-F** key combination to pull down the **File** menu again and then pressing the **X** key for Quit. The program will return you to the DOS prompt.

You can easily retrieve the file that you just saved when you begin QuickC again. If the file name is GREET1.C, then you can enter the command **QC GREET1**, and that file will appear on the screen when the program starts. (Note that the program again assumes the **.C** extension; you only need to tell it the first part of the name.)

Another way to retrieve a file is simply to enter **QC** to start the program. Then press **Alt-F** to pull down the **File** menu and press **O** to select **Open**. The program will prompt you to enter the name of the file you want and will also display a window with a listing of the current directory. If you do not want to enter the name of the file, press the **Tab** key to move the cursor to the window with the directory. Then use the arrow keys to select the file you want and press the **Enter** key to load the file into the editor.

Using your own word processor or editor, you can also create programs and then load them into QuickC in the manner just described. Just make sure your word processor saves the programs in a file with a **.C** extension, and be sure to save the programs as plain ASCII files, as you did when you were creating the AUTOEXEC.BAT and CONFIG.SYS files. If the programs look strange when you load them into QuickC, either because they contain characters you did not enter or because what you typed does not appear in its original location, then you mistakenly made your word processor save the files as formatted documents rather than as plain ASCII text.

QuickC has many other advanced features, but you now know enough to get started with the compiler and to run all the programs in this book.

THE DEBUGGER

One other feature of QuickC is not essential but can be very instructive: the integrated debugger. The debugger will walk you through a program step by step. Each line of code will be highlighted with a light bar as it is executed, which is very useful to show beginners the actual flow of program control. You can watch the light bar go through a **while()** loop until its condition is untrue or watch it select one of the options of an **if-else-if** ladder.

To run the debugger, you must first compile the program with the **Debug** option set on. As you learn to do this, you will also learn an easier way of compiling programs in general.

First press the **Alt-R** key combination to pull down the **Run** menu. Then press **C** to select **Compile** from this menu, and the compile screen will appear. The last time you compiled, you used the **Tab** key to move through this screen. Now, just press **D** to select the **Debug** option. The cursor will immediately move to **Debug**. Then press **D** again and an **X** will appear to the left of the option to indicate that the **Debug** option is on. Note that **Debug** toggles on and off. Press **D** a few times, and you will see the **X** disappear and reappear. Make sure the **X** is there to indicate that the option is on, and then you can simply press **Enter** to compile.

With the **Debug** option set on, the file will be compiled in a way that allows you to use the debugger. Assuming that the program has compiled successfully, you could step through it by using the **Run** menu. Because you would need to select the same menu options again and again to go through each line of the program, however, you will probably want to use the single-keystroke debugging commands instead.

Pressing the **F8** key will take you through the program one line at a time, going into functions that are called and going through them line by line also. Pressing the **F10** key will take you through a program line by line but will not go into functions that are called. Though it will perform the functions, it will not show you how it is doing them one step at a time.

When you select either of these options, the first line of the program that is being executed will be underlined. Select the same option again, and QuickC will underline and execute the next line of the program. At first, you should use the **F8** key to step through all the functions of your programs because this option shows you graphically how control flow works.

Eventually you will get tired of stepping through some functions. The function **clrscrn**() in Chapter 2, for example, loops 25 times, and you must press **F8** several times to get through each loop. In such cases, you can press **F10** and step over **clrscrn**() when you reach that function in a program. You can press **F8** to trace through most functions of a program and press **F10** only when you reach familiar and reliable functions such as **clrscrn**().

The debugger is generally used because, after a programmer has gotten all the syntax errors out of a program so that it finally compiles and runs, the program usually still has run-time errors. Though the compiler does not detect any errors in syntax, there may still be errors in logic. Perhaps you did not think through what certain statements would make the program do, or you carelessly put a curly bracket in the wrong place, so statements are not executed in the order you intended. In such cases, it is very useful to go through the program step by step in order to figure out why it is not doing what you expected.

For a beginner, however, it is useful to watch the program execute step by step even if the program is behaving as expected, just to watch the flow of program control.

A

ADD (COBOL), ix
ADD (ASSEMBLER), xii, 232
addition, 71-74, 77-78, 84-87, 105, 232, 299, ix, *See also* +, arithmetic operators
address (in computer memory), 11, 20, 25, 99, 147, 149, 190-197, 199, 204, 206, 216, 218, 229-230, 247, 281, 290-293, 309, vi
algorithm, 269, 270
American Standard Code for Information Interchange, viii, *See also* ASCII
American National Standards Institute (ANSI), 288
ANSI STANDARD C, 286
argc, 305
argument, 4, 168, 185, 196, 207, 265, 304-306
argv, 305
arithmetic operators, iv, 75, 105, 308, 310
Arithmetic Logic Unit, viii
array, 64-72, 78, 82-84, 90, 98-105, 108, 125, 128, 144-147, 149, 154, 156-158, 161-162, 163, 165, 168, 174, 184, 186, 196-201, 211-212, 215-216, 218, 229-230, 239, 240, 247, 283, 292
ASCII, viii, 10-11, 18-19, 23, 30-32, 34, 35, 37, 39-46, 49-52, 144, 149-150, 206, 207, 218, 275, 303, 321, 333, 335, 336, 340
assembler, ix
assembly language, iv, vi, ix, xi, 58, 232
assembly language instructions
    ADD xii, 232
    BR, xi
    JMP, xi
    SUB, ix, 65
assigning values to variables 9-11, 13, 20, 25, 36, 123, 142, 150, 184, 192, 212, 216, 310, 311
atof(), 303, 304
atoi(), 302, 303
atol(), 303
auto, 285
AUTOEXEC.BAT, 320, 321, 332-335, 340
automatic, 285

B

BASIC, iv, v, vi, x, xi, xii, xiii, 2, 4, 7, 9, 12, 28, 29, 48, 49, 64, 74, 75, 78, 109, 115, 192, 201, 202, 207, 232, 237, 238, 258, 280, 301, 310
BASIC commands
    GOTO, xi
    LOCATE, 48
    PRINT (BASIC), 48
    SYSTEM, 74
beep, 10, 43-44, 50, 152
Bell Laboratories, 288
binary arithmetic, vii, viii, 11-12, 13, 18, 281
binary digit, vi, *See also* bit
bit, vii, 12, 13, 266, 281, 291, 309-310
bitwise and, 309
bitwise or, 309
bitwise operators, iv, 309, 310
Boolean operators, 51
bottom-up program design, 108
BR, xi
break;, 54-56, 58, 61, 118, 124, 156, 237, 300-301
bubble sort, 264, 269-275
buffer, 32, 154, 156-158, 202, 204, 211, 221, 253, 302, 335-336
byte, vi, viii, 11, 18, 192, 197, 201, 207, 247, 281, 309, 310

C

call by value, 194, 197, 229
call by reference, 194, 196, 197, 229
case, 300-301
cathode ray tube, 47
C functions
    atof(), 303, 304
    atoi(), 302, 303
    atol(), 303
    exit(), 56, 61, 156
    fclose(), 202, 204, 230

E

F

fclose(), 202, 204, 230
fgets(), 207
field, 238, 244, 253, 277
fixed-length records, 211
flag, 119, 164, 165, 269, 272, 309
float, 10, 12, 16-17, 21, 25, 75, 76, 186, 197, 207, 229, 281, 293-294, *See also*
    atof()
flow, *See* control flow
fopen(), 202-205, 230, 244, 246, 264, 277, 307, 312
for loop, 297-300
FORMAT, 316, 330
formatting disks, 316, 330
formatting,
    variables, 4, 14, 15, 18, 25, 152, 207, 290, 293, 294, 295
formatting characters
    %e, 290
    %g, 290
    %o, 290
    %u, 290
    %x, 290
FORTRAN, 301
fprintf(), 207, 265, 266
fputs(), 207
free-form language, 3, 236
fscanf(), 207
function prototyping, 288
functions, *See* C functions

G

getc(), 202, 205, 207, 212, 230, 247
getchar(), 152, 185
gets(), 152, 154, 168, 185, 207, 208, 211
global variables, 78-82, 101, 105, 115-118, 122, 128, 141, 164-165, 215, 282-285
GOTO, *See also* goto

general, 28
BASIC, xi
COBOL, 313
goto
    C, 57-58, 61, 272

H

header, x, xii, 6-7, 24, 304
    ctype.h, 302-303
    math.h, 304
    stdlib.h, 302-304
    stdio.h, 5-7, 24
heuristics, 140
high-level disk I/O, 202, 204, 230
high-level language, 48

I

if-else, v, 28, 38, 39, 51, 56-57, 59-61, 87, 138, 139, 165-167, 235-236, 297, 310
if-else-if ladder, 42-43, 55-56, 60, 82, 84, 175, 176, 184, 212, 215, 216, 234-236, 300-301
INC, 232, 234
increment, 232, 234, 292, 309, 311, *See also* + +
infinite loop, 29, 56, 74, 237, 277, 300
input/output, 7, 24, 238, 277
installing QuickC, 330-332
installing Turbo C, 316-317
instruction set, viii, ix
int, 10, 11-12, 13, 14, 17-18, 20-21, 25, 75-77, 192, 281, *See also* atoi()
integer, 10-14, 18, 19, 25, 39, 42, 75-77, 105, 118, 119, 156, 192, 197, 281, 290, 302, 303
interpreter, x, 74
isalpha(), 303
isdigit(), 302, 303
islower() 303

isspace(), 303
isupper(), 303
iteration, 28, 29, 38, 59, 280

J

JMP, xi

K

K & R standard, 288
Kernighan, 288
keyboard buffer, 32, 156

L

label (used with goto), 57, 58, 61
library, 5, 7, 24, 48, 54, 79, 98, 117, 237, 238, 277, 301, 324, 332, 338
link, 7, 282, 334
local variables, 81-82, 105, 115-117, 141, 142, 193, 215, 229, 282, 283, 285
LOCATE, 48
logical variable, 164
logical operators, iv, 32, 33, 50, 51, 60, 78, 105
long, 10, 12, 25, 75, 281, *See also* atol()
long integer, 10, 12, 25, 75, 281
looping, v, 28, 32, 33, 35, 128, 156, 270, 280, 295, 300, *See also* while loop,
    do while loop, for loop.
low-level disk I/O, 201-202
low-level language, ix, 4

M

Macintosh, 47
main(), 2, 4, 8, *See also* command-line argument
mantissa, 12, 207

math.h, 304
MD, 318, 331
microprocessor, vii, 331
modular, v, xi, 24, 28
modulo division, 75, 77, 105, 308, *See also* %, arithmetic operators
MS-DOS, *See* DOS
multiplication, 75, 77, 78, 105, *See also* *, arithmetic operators

N

nested parentheses, 312
nesting, 34, 53, 57, 132, 156
normalization, 276
null ('\0'), 144-147, 149, 150, 156, 158, 162, 164, 184, 211-212, 218, 244, 259, 275
NULL (defined in stdio.h), 204-206, 209, 224, 246, 307, 312
NUMERIC FUNCTIONS, 301

O

offset addressing, 291
one's complement, 309
operators, iv, v, 32, 50, 51, 53, 60, 75, 78, 105, 191, 229, 234, 277, 308-311
   !=, 33, 51, 53, 309
   ?:, 310
   +, 75, 78, 105, 308
   ++, 232-234, 277, 309, 311
   +=, 310
   *, 75, 78, 105, 308
   *=, 310
   ^, 309
   <, 51, 53, 309
   <=, 51, 309
   <<, 309
   =, 9, 32
   ==, 32, 51, 309
   >, 51, 53, 309

> =, 51, 309
> >, 309
%, 75, 77, 105, 308
& (address operator), 20, 25, 149, 190-191, 229, 309
& (bitwise and), 309
&&, 33-35, 51, 60, 78, 105, 309
|, 309
||, 33, 51, 52, 60, 309
~, 309
- -, 234, 277, 309, 311
-, 75, 105, 308
/, 75, 308
OS/2, 47

P

parameter, 115-118, 122, 141-142, 165-168, 193-197, 229, 289-290, 305
Pascal, iv, v, xiii, 49
PATH, 320-321, 333-334
PC-DOS, *See* DOS
PERFORM UNTIL, 297
PL-1, 49
pointer arithmetic, 197-199, 230, 234, 292-293
pointers, 192-193, 195, 197-199, 201-204, 206, 216, 229-230, 234, 247, 265-266,
    292-293, 309
precedence, 77, 78, 105
precompiler, 6, 24, 79, 174, 175, 187
primary storage, vii
PRINT (BASIC), 48
PRINT (DOS), 41
printf(), 4, 7, 12-21, 23, 25, 43, 70, 147-149, 152, 290, 293-295
PRN, 264, 265, 277
PROMPT, 321, 335
pseudocode, 108-112, 114, 115, 118, 119, 125, 129, 130, 237
putc(), 202, 203, 205, 207, 208, 211, 230, 239, 265
putchar(), 152, 185
puts(), 152, 185, 207

Q

QuickC, iv, x, 6, 7, 329-336
    debugger, 340-342
    installing, 330-332
    running 336-340

R

RAM, vii, viii, x, 190, 191, 202, 204, 215, 218, 239, 240, 244, 248, 250, 282, 283, 332
random access memory, vii, *See also* RAM
random files, 238, 277
RD, 319
record, 238, 277
register, viii, ix, 232, 282, 344
register (storage class), 281, 282
relational operators, 51, 309
return, 116-119, 286-289
Ritchie, 288
rounding errors, 53, 69, 207, 281, 295
row-major order, 200, 201
running QuickC, 336-340
running Turbo C, 321-326

S

scanf(), 19-23, 25, 32, 47, 147, 149, 151, 152, 168, 185, 196
scrolling, 36, 47-48, 98, 126, 128
search path, *See* PATH
secondary storage, vii
selection, 28, 38, 59, 280, 300, 334
sequence, 14, 28, 38, 59, 99, 102, 110, 197
sequential files, 238, 277
shareware, 48
shift right, 309

Turbo C, iv, x, 6, 7, 316-328
    debugger, 326-328
    installing, 316-317
    running, 321-326
two-dimensional arrays, 99, 102, 103, 108, 200
TYPE, 204, 205, 211, 218, 247, 258, 263, 319, 332, 333, 335, 336

U

Unix, 7
unsigned int, 281, 290, 291, 303

V

variables, 9-16, 18-23, 25, 78-82, 104-105, 115-117, 141-142, 145, 175, 184,
    190-197, 202, 215, 229, 281-283, 285, 290-291, 296, 311, 312
void, 287, 288

W

while loop, 28-36, 56-57, 59, 60, 61, 295-297

RELATED TITLES FROM MIS:PRESS